# Ethical Visions
# of Education

# Ethical Visions
# of Education

## PHILOSOPHIES IN PRACTICE

**Edited by David T. Hansen**

*DEVELOPED IN ASSOCIATION WITH THE BOSTON
RESEARCH CENTER FOR THE 21ST CENTURY*

Teachers College, Columbia University
New York and London

Published by Teachers College Press, 1234 Amsterdam Avenue, New York, NY
10027

*Library of Congress Cataloging-in-Publication Data*

Ethical visions of education : philosophies in practice / edited by
David T. Hansen.
     p.  cm.
  Includes bibliographical references and index.
  ISBN-13: 978-0-8077-4758-2 (pbk : alk. paper)
  ISBN-13: 978-0-8077-4759-9 (cloth : alk. paper)
  1. Education—Aims and objectives.  2. Education—Philosophy.  3. Moral
education.  I. Hansen, David T., 1952–

  LB41.E777 2007
  370.1—dc22

                    2006032459

978-0-8077-4758-2 (paper)
978-0-8077-4759-9 (cloth)

Printed on acid-free paper
Manufactured in the United States of America

14  13  12  11  10  09  08  07    8  7  6  5  4  3  2  1

# Contents

**PART III**
**Unleashing Human Growth and Potential**

# Foreword

RALPH WALDO EMERSON (1803–1882) wrote that education should be as broad as humanity itself. As one who experienced the harrowing effects of narrow, parochial education, I find myself in full concurrence with the prescient words of the philosopher of the American Renaissance.

When World War II ended some 60 years ago, I was just 17 years old. There is no greater folly than war. By the end of hostilities, Japan had been reduced to a charred wasteland, and people were preoccupied with the basic questions of daily survival. Yet what loomed even larger was a yawning sense of spiritual emptiness, an inner craving for meaning.

At the time, I was suffering from tuberculosis, working days and attending school at night. But even then, like one driven to slake an unquenchable thirst, I used every spare moment to find and read the great works of past and present, East and West. Today this youthful experience of intensive reading stays with me as a fond and treasured memory.

Education in the Japan of my youth was run through with militarism: We Japanese were taught that the noblest possible expression of virtue was to offer ourselves in selfless sacrifice to our "land of the gods." It is clear that education based on this kind of xenophobic nationalism played a key role in propelling Japan on the barbaric course of its inhuman wars of invasion. The resulting horrific suffering experienced by the people of Asia and the Pacific region stands as an unforgettable lesson and admonition. The importance of actions taken in the economic and political spheres cannot be denied; but errors in education can inflict incurable harm on the future.

This reality confronts us today. Despite extraordinary advances in the fields of science and technology, one cannot help but question the degree of actual human progress. Ecological degradation on a global scale continues unabated. The gap between the world's "haves" and "have-nots" expands without ceasing. Violent conflicts continue to plague the planet.

We are compelled to return to our first and original point of departure. And that, in my view, must be human happiness. Not an exclusive happiness limited to oneself only, but the authentic happiness that is shared by self and other. The achievement of such happiness must be the focus of education.

Human beings bear within themselves, in their inner lives, secret stores of infinite possibility, sources of boundless strength that can be unleashed and directed toward the challenge of meeting and overcoming all trials and difficulties. Education holds the key to releasing this power, the immense and primordial potentialities that exist in all people. These are the convictions that have driven my determination to make education the culminating undertaking of my life, to establish the foundation for genuinely humanistic education.

Over the years I have been privileged to hold dialogues with many of the world's leading thinkers and activists. In the course of this effort, I have been consistently impressed by the great importance such people attach to the value of education. Among these was the great historian Arnold J. Toynbee. Surveying the vast scope of human history not merely in centuries but in millennia, he was convinced that the only means by which the tragic cycles of war and violence could be broken was through the power of education—specifically through the persistent and determined effort to foster a sense of global citizenship among all people everywhere.

The speed and momentum of globalization have made encounters between people of diverse cultural, ethnic, religious, and philosophical backgrounds a more frequent inevitability. Thus it is all the more crucial that we foster a consciousness of global citizenship. Only in this way can we ensure that mutual differences will serve to inspire creativity, that hatred will be subsumed in empathy, and that conflict will be resolved and harmonized on a higher plane of common commitment. No age has more urgently required education for global citizenship than our own.

Nine years ago, in June 1996, I had the opportunity to speak at Teachers College, Columbia University. Titling my lecture "Thoughts on Education for Global Citizenship," I stressed the following as essential elements of such citizenship: the wisdom to perceive the dignity of all life, the courage not to fear but to respect difference, and the compassion to maintain empathetic connection with others.

Each of the 10 educators whose ideas and practices are presented in this volume embodies these qualities; as such they stand as models and exemplars of global citizenship. Each was a pioneer who courageously took up the noble challenge of transforming, through committed educational efforts, the culture of violence and war that prevails in our world into a new culture of peace. Throughout the world, from the end of the 19th into the 20th century, these pioneers consecrated their lives to bringing to full flower authentically humane forms of education. Their ideas and actions are a brilliant source of hope lighting the human future.

As founder of the Boston Research Center for the 21st Century, I take great delight in the realization of this publication, which examines the treasures of educational philosophy and practice forged by these remarkable individuals. As Professor David Hansen, the dedicated and inspired editor of this book, has written, a shared feature of these educators lies in the fact that they *responded*, rather than simply *reacted*, to the pressures they encountered. The drama of a transformation from reaction to response suggests a fundamental shift in life orientation: from one of fated destiny to one of chosen mission.

The lives of these 10 philosophers—committed educators who worked to build a human society in which all may savor happiness—are reminiscent of the transcendent arc of Beethoven's Ninth Symphony: piercing the darkness of personal suffering to reach and reveal a shared and universal joy. This book indeed captures the symphonic tones issuing from the depths of these great lives.

Education must never be subservient to the demands of the state or its ideology. Education must be lit by the inner glow of human dignity and happiness. It is my sincere hope that this book will provide the nourishment of courage and hope both to the educators of all lands and to the members of the rising generation, on whom the hopes of the new century rest.

I would like to close by expressing my sincere gratitude to Professor Hansen, to the authors of each chapter, and to all those whose efforts have made this publication possible.

Daisaku Ikeda
*Founder, Boston Research Center for the 21st Century*
*President, Soka Gakkai International*

# Preface

WHENEVER I FEEL overwhelmed, especially when I am discouraged about the state of the world, I have learned that this is exactly the time to pause and shift my focus from the seemingly insurmountable problems right in front of me to larger philosophical questions: Why was I born? What am I here to do? These simple and profound questions walk with me always, though I may be unaware of their presence most of the time. When I turn to them, they never fail to shed new light on what I'm doing right now and give me the courage I need at a crucial moment to live a larger life.

This book tells of extraordinary individuals who reflected profoundly on the meaning of life in the midst of the great challenges of the 20th century and used their lives—courageously and generously—to open educational pathways for us, their successors. They bring practical perspectives from various lands, including the United States, Brazil, France, Italy, Austria, India, China, and Japan.

In the United States, most instructors of undergraduate and graduate courses of educational philosophy are content to focus on the towering figure of John Dewey and the storehouse he left behind. In this volume we expand the inquiry: What can we learn at this crucial time in world history by seeking the wisdom of educational leaders from other cultures and other walks of life? If we put their insights into conversation with Dewey's, can we strengthen our confidence as educational leaders ourselves to expand the focus of an increasingly narrow and stale public discourse about education? Can we move beyond the questions of *what* and *how*, as Parker Palmer advises in *The Courage to Teach,* and grapple with the larger questions of *who* and *why*?

As a developer of books for teachers, we at the Boston Research Center for the 21st Century (BRC) hope that the collective wisdom gathered in this volume will give future educational leaders a broader and firmer foundation for upholding the aims of humanistic education in a multicultural world. At the end of her book *Happiness and Education*, Nel Noddings observes that "basically happy people who retain an uneasy social conscience will contribute to a happier world." I can find no better description of the people in this book than this one sentence, and probably no better description of the students and teachers who will read, enjoy, and use this volume.

After we finished our previous book project, *Educating Citizens for Global Awareness*, in 2004, Nel Noddings, its editor, was kind enough to connect BRC president Masao Yokota and me with educational philosopher David Hansen, author of *Exploring the Moral Heart of Teaching*, one of our favorite books. We discussed with him some nascent ideas we had about helping to expand the multicultural philosophical resources offered in education courses. From these discussions emerged a wonderful partnership between Professor Hansen and our publications manager, Patti Marxsen, on a project that has inspired all of us at the BRC in so many ways at every step in its development. Anyone who knows David can imagine the learning opportunities he created as our vision came into focus, authors were recruited, chapters developed, and manuscripts edited with care and extraordinary respect. We got to see *his* philosophy and practice of education in action, and this was a precious gift.

At a recent meeting of the American Educational Research Association in San Francisco, the BRC sponsored a panel discussion at which four of the chapter authors presented the ideas and historical contexts of their chosen figures—Dewey, Maria Montessori, Rabindranath Tagore, and Tsunesaburo Makiguchi—and engaged fellow educators in exploring the relevance of their insights to the challenges facing teachers today. We can imagine our present volume sparking many more such valuable conversations at universities and elsewhere in the United States and beyond. What a joy it would be if this book were to strengthen the chorus of international voices, past and present, extolling a vision of holistic education.

Virginia Benson
*Executive Director*
*Boston Research Center for the 21st Century*

# Ideas, Action, and Ethical Vision in Education

## David T. Hansen

IDEAS HAVE CONSEQUENCES. This truism holds for educational ideas as much as it does for ideas about government, science, and health. The notion that children should learn to read, write, and numerate; the idea that places named *schools* should be organized for educating; the claim that men and women called *teachers* ought to play leading roles in the process—these ideas and countless others like them have had profound, enduring effects on educational policy and practice the world over.

Ideas do not spring from a vacuum, and they are never inevitable. They are not like the wind, the tide, or the rising and setting of the sun. They do not derive from nature's inexorable course. Rather, ideas take form through the initiative of individual persons who seek to respond to particular concerns, problems, fears, and hopes. Ideas originate with human beings, not impersonal forces. The cliché that ideas have consequences harbors a truth that is all too easy to overlook as people go about their daily affairs: What individual persons think and do can make a genuine difference in the course of events. Mind and imagination can transform the quality of life.

The purpose of this book is to challenge and encourage all who care about education to cultivate mind and imagination in the world. The authors of the chapters ahead pursue this aim by presenting the core ideas of some of the most influential educational thinkers and activists of the 20th century. The authors also examine the consequences of these persons' ideas on educational thought and practice. The figures are Jane Addams, John Dewey, W. E. B. Du Bois, Paulo Friere, Tsunesaburo Makiguchi, Maria Montessori,

Albert Schweitzer, Rudolf Steiner, Rabindranath Tagore, and Tao Xingzhi. Much has been said over the years about these extraordinary persons. But this book is the first to bring their vibrant legacies together in a single "conversation" about the nature and consequences of educational ideas. As readers will see, the power, originality, and profound relevance of the ideas of these theorists stand out when they are brought together in the dialogue this book represents.

Readers will also discern a deep ethical impulse that resides behind the ideas and actions of these thinkers, who believed that human beings matter more than flawed institutions, that education comprises a moral commitment to the betterment of individuals and communities, and that it is possible to educate meaningfully even in the face of difficult challenges and obstacles. They demonstrate what it means to cultivate a sense of self that extends beyond the troublesome, often confusing present, and that grows and deepens in service to others.

The chapter authors take a sympathetic and critical approach toward these luminaries. They do not treat them as canonized role models proffering educational blueprints for others to follow. Quite the contrary. The collective lesson of this volume is that educators ought not to mimic one another but rather should learn from one another how to use their own minds and imagination. In this way, *every* educator can make a unique difference in the world, however modest in scope. Every educator can experience why pedagogical work constitutes one of the world's truly great vocations of hope, possibility, and accomplishment.

In this introductory chapter, I will orient readers to the chapters ahead by responding to a number of questions. First, what are ideas? How do they differ from facts and information? How does a person develop an idea? How do educational ideas relate to educational practice? What do we learn from the educators featured in this book about the dynamic relation between ideas and action? Second, what is an educational philosophy? Why is it important for educators to cultivate a philosophy and to be aware of its origins, substance, and consequences? How does a philosophy of education differ from a theory of education, and why is the difference significant for teachers? Finally, how can there be more than one reasonable, defensible, and inspiring philosophy of education? Why don't all educators, such as those featured in this book, have the same philosophy? Why is it valuable for educators to study different philosophies of education? How and what can educators learn from looking at the similarities and differences among them? My responses to these questions will be suggestive rather than definitive. I hope that after reading this book readers will feel not only disposed to respond, but also excited about answering the questions in their own ways.

In the first section below, I take up questions about the nature and efficacy of ideas in education. In the ensuing section, I examine how a philosophy of education provides educators with an articulate sense of values, a moral compass to guide their work, and a fruitful source of ideas for their day-to-day efforts. The third section provides a brief overview of each of the 10 figures' central educational ideas and actions. In the final section, I discuss the criteria that led to the inclusion of these philosophers in this book while also providing further perspectives on what we can learn from their work.

## IDEAS AND THEIR SIGNIFICANCE

The world abounds in facts and information. From computers, television, radio, cell phones, newspapers, magazines, billboards on the highway, and more, facts and information flood into our lives. Contemporary humanity is indeed drowning in facts and information. Ideas, by contrast, are rarer, and they are more difficult to recognize. They do not arise automatically and instantly, unlike facts and information. Ideas emerge through individual attempts to articulate in a sustained fashion a thought, a feeling, a hunch, an interpretation, a response.

Because ideas are essential for intelligent and humane action, it is worthwhile taking some time to think about what they are. Moreover, it is indispensable for educators to grasp fully why ideas differ from facts and information. If they do not do so, they will have no intellectual basis upon which to criticize curriculum and assessment policies that privilege the mastery of fact over the development of genuine thinking (Boostrom, 2005). My analysis will dramatize how significant and timely for education are the ideas of the individuals featured in this book. Moreover, as readers will see, it is striking how alert they were to the creative power of ideas.

Unlike ideas, facts and information are inert and stable. In metaphorical terms, they exist passively. They are lifeless until persons take them up and employ them in thought and action. In contrast, ideas are always active, in motion, and in transformation. As such, they cannot be scooped up and absorbed as can facts and information. Moreover, ideas remain ideas only if they are dynamic and subject to change. When they harden or become routine, as all too many do, they lose their vitality and take on the passive aspect of facts and information. In such cases they may sidetrack or even suppress the emergence of new ideas.

John Dewey addresses these points in his wide-ranging inquiry *Democracy and Education* (MW9).[1] After examining the nature and place of thinking in education, he offers the following remarks:

> The educational moral I am chiefly concerned to draw is not, however, that teachers would find their own work less of a grind and strain if school conditions

favored learning in the sense of discovery and not in that of storing away what others pour into them; nor that it would be possible to give even children and youth the delights of personal intellectual productiveness—true and important as are these things. It is that no thought, no idea, can possibly be conveyed as an idea from one person to another. When it is told, it is, to the one to whom it is told, another given fact, not an idea. The communication may stimulate the other person to realize the question for himself and to think out a like idea, or it may smother his intellectual interest and suppress his dawning effort at thought. But what he directly gets cannot be an idea. Only by wrestling with the conditions of the problem at first hand, seeking and finding his own way out, does he think. (pp. 159–160)

Dewey stresses how burdensome and unfulfilling schooling becomes when it is dominated by the river of facts and information that saturates the world and when no time and space are provided for cultivating and expressing ideas. What he calls "personal intellectual productivity" results from deploying facts and information *in* the process of thinking rather than trying to swallow them apart from it. Conceiving and expressing ideas is "delightful," to paraphrase Dewey, because the process calls upon the student's intellectual and reflective resources, and because it is an active rather than passive undertaking. Ideas and the thinking that gives rise to them constitute a fundamental aspect of education, regardless of whether one has in mind a child first learning what can be done with numbers or a scientist recognizing the meaning of an experimental outcome.

Dewey emphasizes that nobody, whether an educator or layperson, can "give" an idea to another person. Only facts and information can be handed over, like a ladle of water, from one person to the next. In contrast, ideas emerge from what Dewey calls "wrestling" with conditions, circumstances, and situations and working one's way forward. This process does not necessitate unprecedented originality, creativity, or genius. A young child who grasps the logic of addition has a genuine mathematical idea, even though countless other persons have had it before. The bottom line is that ideas involve thinking, activity, and personal transformation, however modest in scope.

This last point underscores why ideas have consequences, whereas facts and information taken in themselves do not. Depending on the situation, facts and information can either distract people from thinking and cloud their judgment, or they can serve as a useful resource for thinking. But only ideas can lead to explicit, overt, and intentional change. Facts and information, in and of themselves, can have only an implicit or subconscious effect. With regard to human hopes and aspirations, it is what people *do* with facts and information that has consequences. The child who now has a mathematical idea is a transformed being. He or she will never look at mathematics in the same way again, an outcome that can influence any number of subsequent engagements the child has with the curriculum of school and life. For the teacher, the consequences of the child's having an idea include a better understanding of how the child thinks, a chance now to present new challenges to him or her, and the opportunity to attend for the moment to other students perhaps struggling to bring forth ideas in response to the presented facts.

Although the consequences in this example are positive, such an outcome is obviously not always the case with ideas. A child who suddenly has an idea of what matches and fire can do may be a danger to others and to him- or herself, if the child has no corresponding ideas or dispositions about safety and responsibility. Thus the *particular* ideas that experience generates matter enormously. Education constitutes not only the process of conceiving ideas but also the enterprise of seeking to understand their consequences, and therefore to grasp why some ideas are better and more worthy of support than others. All the influential figures featured in the chapters ahead worked persistently to identify what they viewed as better ideas. They sought to bring to life more enlightened, ethical, and intellectually robust ideas that could serve humanity's quest for meaning and fulfillment.

Dewey refers to the "educational moral" of his argument in the quote cited above, and I draw from his remark two meanings. The first is that all ideas are potentially moral in their consequences. All ideas can lead either to a positive or harmful change in individuals and communities. The child with the new mathematical idea is now in a position to generate further ideas. Thus the child learns, however modestly and subtly, what it means to engage the world in more meaningful and expansive ways. On a broader scale, the idea that all people are created equal has not only launched a famous revolution but also has led to countless political and social transformations around the world.

At the same time, some ideas lead to morally harmful and even disastrous consequences. A student whose mathematical ideas contain logical flaws will go on to struggle with the subject, perhaps in worse ways than if he or she had simply not grasped the logic at all. The student may lose academic confidence, and teachers may regard him or her as a problem. The idea that a government's primary responsibility is to support the growth of business has led to many problematic consequences regarding equity, social stability, the environment, and more. In short, no idea is inherently neutral from a moral point of view. Even an apparently laudable idea such as teaching everyone how to read does not automatically result in beneficial consequences if what persons go on to read warps or indoctrinates their minds and outlook (Weaver, 1948, pp. 13–14). The individuals featured in this book illuminate why one aspect of being an educated person is sensitivity to the human consequences of ideas, whether they be large or small in scope.

The second lesson I derive from Dewey's choice of terms is that having the opportunity to conceive and express ideas is itself a moral issue. An educational system can be described as morally deficient if it simply pours material into students and systematically denies them opportunities to engage their minds. Such a system undermines and negates human potential. Because it suppresses rather than fuels positive human development, it renders the world a shallower, less productive, and less fulfilling place than it could otherwise be. The politician, policy maker, or educator who regards education as solely a matter of transferring facts and information (vital as they are) may be unwittingly damaging future prospects for human freedom and creativity.

The individuals featured in this book cherished the freedom to conceive and express ideas. They loved thinking. They worked against the anti-intellectual pressures of conformity. They responded to the expanding tide of facts and information in the world with genuinely educational ideas. Moreover, many of the so-called facts they confronted boiled down to taken-for-granted prejudices and biases. For example, Maria Montessori had to confront the "fact" that in her time and milieu women were not supposed to embark on professional careers. W. E. B. Du Bois had to move beyond the "fact" that Black Americans were not eligible for a place at the table of national political and cultural life. Tsunesaburo Makiguchi rejected the "fact" that education should be conducted purely in the service of the state rather than for the sake of individual development and freedom. Their collective experience alerts us to the possibility that every person on the planet struggles, at one time or another, with environments that work against thinking and the creation of humane and empowering ideas.

The ideas and conduct of the thinkers in this volume illuminate modes of responding to difficult situations. Rather than accepting custom and other people's ideas uncritically, they thought about them, examined them, and in so doing formed their own distinctive ideas and plans of action. I invite readers to study the chapters ahead not solely for the biographical facts and information that they contain, important as these are, but to engage them to form their own ideas about education, society, individuality, and the meanings of life. Moreover, the chapters challenge readers not only to conceive and express their own ideas but also to keep their thinking dynamic and vivid. This notion points to the value of an educational philosophy, the topic of the following section.

## THE PRACTICAL MEANING AND NECESSITY OF A PHILOSOPHY OF EDUCATION

People often describe philosophy as the love of wisdom. This eulogistic definition can be translated into the maxim that since ideas matter for the conduct of life, it is wise to put forward the most ethical and empowering ideas possible.

The figures in this book sought to articulate and disseminate generative educational ideas and did so in an extraordinary variety of ways. They wrote scholarly and popular texts and, in the case of Rabindranath Tagore, also published fiction and poetry. They were active public speakers, addressing audiences of educators, politicians, policy makers, community leaders, parents, students, and more. They organized schools or other institutions supportive of learning. They mobilized people and resources by participating in various social and political movements. Their drive to make a difference in the world also led them to study philosophy, art, history, science, and other subjects. Each brought to bear sustained curiosity about the world and a deep belief in the values of human development.

The fact that these persons were serious students of life suggests that a common denominator in their efforts, however disparate these were, was a commitment to the importance of acting through a mature educational philosophy. An educational philosophy comprises (1) a statement of values, (2) a moral compass, and (3) an abiding engine of ideas. As a statement of values, an educational philosophy reflects what the thinker or community esteems: learning to read and to write critically, to conduct scientific experiments, to produce artistic works, to speak well and courageously, to engage other people respectfully and honestly, and so forth. As a moral compass, an educational philosophy guides the educator or community in making decisions, for example, that a particular approach to teaching is better to adopt than its alternatives because it treats subject matter intellectually rather than as solely a store of facts, which means regarding students as human beings capable of thought rather than merely of absorption. As an engine of ideas, an educational philosophy helps the educator or community respond intelligently to new situations and conditions; for example, it leads the teacher to ask a thoughtful question about the novel at hand when students are restless rather than automatically piling on more information about it. In other words, instead of relying uncritically on custom, convention, or prepackaged scripts, educators can draw upon their educational philosophy to devise creative, fruitful responses to issues and problems that are tailored to their specific circumstances.

Popular opinion often equates philosophy with a more or less pointless recycling of perennial questions, such as, What is the meaning of life? Because philosophers and others have provided so many disparate and incompatible answers to such questions, the popular impression (unsurprisingly) is that philosophy boils down to a fruitless intellectual game far removed from the concrete affairs of life. In a famous passage in Plato's dialogue *Gorgias*, Socrates and the brash young politician he has been questioning, Callicles, find their dialogue breaking down (if, indeed, it can be said to have ever got off the ground). Callicles has mocked and often refused to answer Socrates' questions about what values he believes are worthy in life. He declares that Socrates' pursuit of philosophy is childish and unpractical. At one juncture in the dialogue he sneers, "Always the same old language, Socrates," to which Socrates replies, "Yes, Callicles, and on the same subjects" (490e; quote from Plato, 2004, p. 77). Socrates' point is that anyone who aspires to lead a consciously chosen and deliberate life—and, more specifically, a good and humane life—*does* end up facing "the same subjects," such as whether the ends justify the means (if I want to make a lot of money, is it OK to cheat and lie?) and whether obligations to others sometimes override self-interest (should I go to the movie or attend to my sick child?). For the educator who wants to do the right thing for students, the educational equivalent of such questions includes what approach to take toward teaching, assessment, curriculum, colleagues, parents, and one's own professional development. Every educator the world over faces these "same subjects."

A lesson I draw from Socrates' timeless exchange with Callicles is that while some philosophy is esoteric, other philosophy—such as the educational philosophy articulated by the people in this book—constitutes the most practical thing of all for a human being to pursue. This claim may sound strange because ideas, unlike actions, are not immediately material and observable. However, sound practical action involves more than mere brawn. It also implies thoughtfulness, perspective, imagination, and sometimes even a vision of a better world. Moreover, consider what it would mean if a teacher operated without a philosophy of education. In its absence, the teacher would have no recourse but to rely on unexamined habit; on memories of his or her own teachers as well as experiences as a student; and on resources contrived by other people whose outlook may or may not be compatible, much less more enlightened, than the teacher's own. As I have suggested, an educational philosophy provides the educator with an articulated sense of values, with a moral compass, and with an abiding engine of ideas to employ in his or her work. In the chapters ahead, we will see these functions of educational philosophy play themselves out in concrete practice. We will witness the consequences of educational ideas.

Readers will also encounter the issues of how and why educational philosophies can differ, with correspondingly different consequences for practical affairs in schools and elsewhere. Later in this chapter I will suggest that the genuine differences in these philosophies constitute not a problem to be solved or a mystery to be cleared up, but rather a splendid spur to thinking and educational imagination. However, first let me offer a brief synopsis of each of the figures' philosophies and their impact on practice. In the ensuing and final sections of the chapter, I will explain the criteria of selection that led to including these particular individuals in the book. I will also show how these criteria mirror the values touched on here regarding the vitality of educational philosophy.

## CHAPTER OVERVIEWS: ETHICAL VISIONS

Chapter 1, which I contribute to this volume, focuses on the American John Dewey's (1859–1952) idea that education is a process of enhancing the quality of life. By *quality* Dewey meant a life of meaningful activity, of thoughtful conduct, and of open communication and interaction with other people. Dewey viewed the enhancement of the quality of life for all persons as the primary purpose of a democratic society. He conceived an approach to education that would equip individuals with the skills and the outlook that he believed were necessary for taking on the hardships and possibilities of life and thereby for building a better world. In the chapter I emphasize Dewey's core concepts of growth, experience, and meaning. I show how these ideas emerged from and guided his active life as a founder of a famous school, as a public speaker, as a widely read public intellectual, and as a leader of numerous democratic organizations. Dewey's ideas remain alive and vivid today in the academy, in colleges of education, and in the lives of many teachers and schools.

Stephen Fishman and Lucille McCarthy, in Chapter 2, describe the contours of Paulo Freire's (1921–1997) influential philosophy of education. These derive from a Marxist critique of economic and social inequalities produced by capitalism, a postcolonial critique of imperialism and its human consequences, an existentialist view that humans have a fundamental desire for freedom that is too often thwarted by social arrangements, and a Christian notion of the necessity for individual—rather than solely societal—transformation if the world is to become a just and humane setting for all. Determined to address the socioeconomic inequities in his native Brazil, Freire fused his critique of society with a belief in the values in genuine dialogue. He advanced a conception of educational practice centered directly around dialogue between teachers; students; and, at important moments, members of local communities. Through dialogue, Freire maintained, people can learn to articulate (or "name," as he puts it) their concerns, aspirations, and ideas for how to improve conditions. He advocated a genuinely communicative environment in the educational setting through which people can learn to think and act critically. He contrasted this outlook with what he called the "banking approach," in which facts and information are "deposited" in the minds of students without creating circumstances in which the students feel empowered to raise questions. Fishman and McCarthy show how Freire sought to bring his vision to life through a variety of influential educational roles.

In Chapter 3, Rodino Anderson focuses on W. E. B. Du Bois's (1868–1963) remarkable book *The Souls of Black Folk*. Anderson suggests that the work expresses Du Bois's belief that a liberal education was crucial to the intellectual emancipation of Black Americans, who had been systematically denied education under the brutal regime of slavery and who continued to live under racist conditions after the American Civil War. Du Bois believed that intellectual emancipation would equip Blacks to challenge and undermine racism and thereby both open opportunity to them and help bring the nation closer to its democratic ideals. Such an education would position Black Americans to claim their rightful role as national "creators of culture," a process in which they could infuse society with their distinctive achievements as other individuals and groups within society would do the same. Anderson shows that Du Bois's educational philosophy points not so much to what is today called multiculturalism as toward the centrality of an aesthetic education for all people. Du Bois's unique take on liberal education merges the study of important events and texts (historical, philosophical, scientific) from around the world with a focus on equipping and propelling people to create and express meaning in life. Anderson's inquiry into *The Souls of Black Folk* becomes a springboard for showing how Du Bois's outlook links educational and political aims in a manner that continues to inform educational thought and practice today.

In Chapter 4, Andrew Gebert and Monte Joffee describe Tsunesaburo Makiguchi's (1871–1944) innovative idea of "value creation" as the aim of education. A teacher, school principal, public speaker, activist, and author, Makiguchi sought to humanize education in his native Japan by insisting that it serve individuals and communities rather than the political and economic needs of the state (which was increasingly militaristic and coercive in the years before World War II). Makiguchi believed that the educator's fundamental obligation was to equip students with a sense of purpose so that they would be empowered to both discern and create value in their lives and communities. To explain his philosophy of education, Makiguchi wrote and spoke extensively on pedagogy. He argued that the teacher should be an intellectual and moral role model and should seek to develop genuine dialogue with students rather than force-feed them facts and information. Moreover, as Gebert and Joffee suggest, Makiguchi advocated a close interaction between the teacher, school, home, and local community. In his view, all play a dynamic role in fostering individual development and flourishing. Makiguchi's influence remains strong today in the lay Buddhist organization he founded in the 1930s, Soka Gakkai International (Value Creation Society), with some 12 million members around the world, as well as in Soka schools now in operation in several countries.

In Chapter 5, Charlene Haddock Seigfried elucidates the American Jane Addams's (1860–1935) influential creed that education is a lifelong endeavor grounded in experience. For Addams, education extends well beyond the confines of school. In many respects, it finds its fullest expression outside the school walls, in the ways in which people actually work, interact, spend their time, and focus their energy. Addams argued that all experience could be educative if approached in an open-minded, experimental spirit. She sought to support that spirit through the settlement house movement she launched in the United States in the 1890s. For example, at Hull House, in Chicago, she and her colleagues initiated countless programs that engaged new immigrants in activities through which they learned new ideas and skills and also shared with others their knowledge and expertise drawn from life experience. Moreover, Addams worked to connect Hull House activities with other civic developments in Chicago. She encouraged native-born citizens and new immigrants to regard one another not as aliens but as fellow Americans with whom they could work to bring forth a more democratic society. Seigfried shows that Addams's vision embodied a powerful idea of civic education. Addams articulated a public process through which all members of society educated themselves about one another, about what would improve peoples' opportunities and life chances, and about what would support a more just and efficacious approach to social problems and difficulties. As an aspect of her extensive educational and social work, Addams worked tirelessly against war and violence. Her efforts resulted in her being awarded the Nobel Peace Prize in 1931.

Wang Weijia and Zhang Kaiyuan demonstrate, in Chapter 6, why Tao Xingzhi (1891–1946) is widely regarded as "the father of modern Chinese education." The authors show that Tao exerted an enormous influence on the 20th-century movement in China to bring formal education to all people regardless of class or economic status. In a pioneering way, Tao fused Deweyan and traditional Chinese educational ideas. He spent several years studying with Dewey in New York City, even as he systematically examined Chinese philosophies of education. He articulated an original and expansive philosophy of education pivoting around the value of rendering human activity thoughtful. He advocated educating people to approach their work and lives as free and independent agents, acting out of intelligence, imagination, and resolve. Centering his initial approach around the promotion of literacy, Tao founded and led numerous regional and national educational organizations to advance public education, which was a controversial idea in his time and place. He also founded an important teacher education institute, wrote textbooks, and devoted much effort to establishing educational programs in rural areas. He was convinced that rural development was crucial for the eventual emergence of a democratic society in China. Wang and Zhang show why Tao's ideas remain vibrant and pertinent in today's educational and social climate, in which countless children throughout the world still lack basic education and fundamental freedoms.

In Chapter 7, Jacqueline Cossentino and Jennifer Whitcomb examine the peace-centered educational philosophy of the Italian educator Maria Montessori (1870–1952). Although Montessori is best known for her approach to early childhood education, Cossentino and Whitcomb show how what is today simply called Montessori education spans human development from infancy to adulthood. Montessori articulated a philosophy of education centered around her abiding conviction that if education is genuinely responsive to the developmental needs of children—emotional, intellectual, spiritual, and moral—it can lead to a more peaceful world. She elaborated a comprehensive approach to early elementary education in which she articulated views about the role of the teacher, the nature and place of the curriculum, the qualities of the physical environment, the nature of assessment, and the dynamics of student agency and freedom. She also established a program for later elementary education, for children ages 6 to 12, that would draw them into what she called a "cosmic" outlook on the world. Through the study of world history, the structure of language, the forms and evolution of nature, and more, combined with social inquiries undertaken outside the school, Montessori argued that children at this stage could begin to discern how they themselves might grow up to make a difference in the world. They would begin to conceive how they could employ their education to help remake the world, into a more democratic, fair, and peaceful place for all. Cossentino and Whitcomb demonstrate that Montessori's philosophy of education remains extremely influential today in a vast number of schools, both public and private.

Kathleen O'Connell examines, in Chapter 8, the educational work of Rabindranath Tagore (1861–1941), who spent most of his life in his native Bengal, India. While best known as a prolific poet, playwright, essayist, and novelist—he received the Nobel Prize in Literature in 1913—Tagore articulated and put into practice a pioneering vision of education centered around the arts, communication, and freedom. He believed that formal education all too often snuffed out the creative impulses of students and teachers. He viewed students as capable of adding to the richness of the world in endlessly diverse ways so long as they receive the right encouragement and support. He viewed the teacher as a creative facilitator and moral guide. For Tagore, the ideal teacher would be an artistic person, in the sense of being able to perceive the potential in students regardless of the subject matter at hand. At the same time, the teacher would combine a focus on learning with a vision for youth, of how young people would regard and treat one another, and the world itself, in an ethical manner. Tagore brought his ideas to life in the establishment of an innovative and influential educational center for children called Santiniketan, and he and others disseminated information about it in an effort to reform schooling across India. At the same time, as O'Connell points out, Tagore focused on higher education, convinced that both India and the world needed enhanced global exchange and mutually enlightening communication. He articulated a cosmopolitan idea of a university-educated person. That individual would have scholarly training linked with a philosophical, moral, and aesthetic education that would fuel a broad-minded outlook on the problems and prospects of humanity. Tagore established a university cum cultural center based on this vision.

Austrian-born Rudolf Steiner (1861–1925) founded what has come to be called Waldorf education, an educational approach that finds expression today in some 1,000 Waldorf schools around the world. In Chapter 9, Bruce Uhrmacher elucidates Steiner's distinctive idea that education entails the holistic cultivation of a person's mind, body, heart, and spirit. Steiner fused notions of intellectual, aesthetic, emotional, and spiritual education into a systematic program for schools in which teachers would work with children as the latter progressed through what he called "stages" of human development. Uhrmacher analyzes these stages and outlines the many sources of Steiner's ideas, which ranged from theosophy (a combined study of world religions, ancient mystic outlooks, philosophy, science, and psychic investigations) to anthroposophy (the study and practice of spiritual development, rooted especially in Christian traditions). Steiner sought to link his belief in both a physical and spiritual world with a vision of how educational practice could equip the young to live morally and spiritually fulfilling lives characterized, in turn, by a fundamental respect for nature in all its wonder. Uhrmacher highlights contemporary features of Waldorf education, illustrating the approach by focusing on how Waldorf teachers center their pedagogy around story and narrative and on how they assess and evaluate students using artistic methods rather than traditional letter grades.

In the final chapter of the book, A. G. Rud examines the humanitarian ideas and actions of Albert Schweitzer (1875–1965). Born in the Alsace region of France, Schweitzer is best known for his contributions to global public health and nuclear disarmament, which together earned him the Nobel Peace Prize in 1952. However, Rud shows in detail how Schweitzer's conduct and his philosophy of "Reverence for Life" have valuable educational consequences. Rud focuses especially on three of these consequences: education in the name of service to humanity, education for environmental awareness, and education for hospitality and community. He shows how Schweitzer modeled in his life all these educational ideas. Schweitzer abandoned a materially comfortable and secure way of life to serve others, and in so doing realized a far deeper meaning and sense of personal fulfillment. He articulated a vision of human life as embedded in nature rather than as standing apart (or over) it; he worked toward a holistic image of humanity and the world. He developed what remains a world-renowned hospital in Gabon, Africa, that serves the people in the surrounding region regardless of income or status. His approach to institutionalized medical practice centered less around technological expertise, although it incorporated that, than around ideals of rendering health service hospitable and supportive of human community.

## A WAY TO APPROACH THE TEN EDUCATORS
## AND THEIR WORK

As this overview makes plain, the individuals featured here differ markedly, not only in terms of national background but also, and more dramatically, with respect to the educational ideas they conceived and the activities they promoted. This diversity in philosophy and action forms an important criterion of selection for the book. As I argued at the start of this introduction, ideas and philosophies of education are dynamic and subject to transformation. If they are not, they reduce to inert and perhaps stultifying facts and information. This claim implies that there can be no one philosophy of education. There is no definition of the purposes of education that can terminate further discussion and inquiry.

Correspondingly, just as nobody can hand over an idea to another person, so nobody can give another educator a philosophy of education. Every teacher must work out his or her own ideas and educational philosophy, a process that necessitates thinking, careful study, experience with students, and dialogue with other educators. I urge readers not to approach the chapters ahead as if they were encyclopedic entries of fact and information. Rather, the chapters constitute deliberate attempts to provoke readers to think imaginatively and deliberately about education.

In addition to the important criterion of differing philosophies of education, five other criteria inform the selection of the figures in the book:

- Their work generates ideas and practices pertinent to today's world.
- They provide more than a theory about education; they articulate and enact an educational philosophy that can be lived in practice.
- They contribute to a common moral compass to guide educational work today, even while they emphasize quite different tactics and strategies.
- They represent an international scope, while demonstrating how good ideas can transcend borders in their beneficial consequences.
- They are remarkable, unusual human beings whose example edifies while it also educates.

In the remainder of this chapter I will address each of these criteria.

The 10 thinkers and activists featured here show us that human striving across the generations remains a timeless, wondrous source of learning for the present. The intellectual and programmatic resources they cultivated speak directly to contemporary challenges and offer a host of strategies that might be useful to teachers in the 21st century. Worldwide, educators are currently under tremendous pressure from efforts to standardize teaching and schooling, from market forces elbowing their way into schools and into the lives of teachers and students, from ongoing attempts to politicize education and put it in the service of selfish interests, and other sources. These circumstances are likely to continue into the foreseeable future. Each of the 10 individuals highlighted in this book faced equally formidable pressures. Although they dwelled in a different historical era, their work remains vivid and dynamic because it reminds us of a crucial truth that is easy to overlook: Individuals do make a difference in the course of events through their ideas and actions. For educators, whether experienced or in preparation programs, this familiar but sometimes unarticulated fact is powerful. Every educator can make a difference. Every educator has untapped resources for contributing to human good.

A key to employing such resources is understanding that challenges, obstacles, and frustrations, form an organic part of the world and are not, as such, things to resent. People grow and become accomplished, while helping others do so, by confronting difficulties rather than complaining about them or running from them. The figures in this book show time and again that engaging problems fuels human growth, imagination, and effective ideas and practices. Readers may find their efforts all the more illuminating because their ideas and actions may seem, at first (and even second!) glance unfamiliar, strange, even alien. Perhaps a well-known adage bears inserting here: The only way to become educated is by engaging that which is new. Our most influential educational experiences derive from the violation of our expectations, not from their confirmation. To consort solely with ideas one already knows can lead to intellectual stasis and fixed mental habits, rather than growth in one's knowledge and outlook. The juxtaposition in this book of strikingly different philosophies of education renders all of them new, in the sense of fresh, revitalized, and provocative.

A second criterion of selection, touched on in a previous section, is that the 10 individuals articulate and enact philosophies of education. They do not merely offer a theory of education. The difference between *theory* and *philosophy* is purely semantic if both terms are reduced to how one perceives the world. However, it is possible to have a theory of economics, of politics, of society, of the universe, and of the meaning of life without that theory having any influence on one's conduct. A physicist may change her theory of space and time, but meanwhile remain a Democrat or Republican, an honest or unscrupulous friend, a loving or distant parent, and so forth. But a change in one's philosophy implies a corresponding change in the things that one believes, values, and does. I encourage readers to examine the philosophies of education in the chapters ahead as possible ways of *living* while one is in the role of an educator, rather than solely as theories *about* education.

As discussed above, an educational philosophy provides educators with an articulate sense of values, with a moral compass, and with an engine of ideas for use in the actual work of teaching. The 10 luminaries featured here differ in their fundamental values. Some advance political values and concerns first and foremost. Others foreground religious and spiritual values. Still others spotlight aesthetic and artistic values in education. In addition, the ideas that spring from their differing philosophies of education are, unsurprisingly, also distinctive. Their specific ideas about teaching, curriculum, schooling, and so forth differ in sometimes striking and incompatible ways. Dewey and Makiguchi, for example, would not agree with the idea put forth by Steiner and Montessori that human beings go through various predetermined "stages" or "planes" of development. For Dewey, all people, ideally, grow throughout the course of life experience. He suggests that differences in their growth are a matter largely of degree rather than of kind. Makiguchi suggests that children are as capable of value creation in their lives as are adults—indeed, in some respects they are better equipped, since they do not feel as strongly the press of custom and convention. In contrast, Montessori and Steiner argue that children and young people do undergo identifiable, discrete stages of development that must be at the center of educators' planning and assessment if these teachers are to pursue their work responsibly. In short, the philosophers whose ideas are explored in this volume present incompatible conceptions of learning and human growth, or so it seems, and their proposals regarding educational practice differ accordingly. Such differences in values and ideas will, hopefully, provoke readers to ponder their own philosophies of education that much more critically.

However, while the philosophies of education of these thinkers differ with regard to values and ideas, they point toward common moral ground. They contribute to the making of a shared moral compass, by which I mean a sense of direction that humanity might take in facing the problems of our dwelling together on the planet. That direction is toward greater justice, deeper freedom, and broader and richer meaning in human life. These are the core elements associated here with the idea of the "moral."

A common moral outlook does not imply shared values. As mentioned, the individuals profiled here, like people everywhere, differ in their political, religious, artistic, and other values as well as in their sense of how these ought to inform education. Moreover, according to various contemporary criteria of justice and goodness, there are limitations in their viewpoints. For example, it is possible to take Du Bois and Steiner to task for being uncritically gender-blind in their proposals. It is possible, on the one hand, to criticize Schweitzer and Tagore for not being more politically conscious and active and, on the other hand, to charge Dewey and Freire with politicizing educational practice. For such criticisms to be themselves reflective and justified, they would need to examine with care the full tapestry of each individual's ideas and actions.

However exclusive these thinkers' philosophies may be with respect to particular values, or to national or regional concerns and circumstances, their moral vision of a better world seems to me to be remarkably inclusive. They linked their proposals with a tough-minded critique leveled against those who held political, economic, and educational power. Each of these thinkers, in his or her own way, took issue with the status quo and in some cases paid a severe price for their resistance (for example, Makiguchi died of malnutrition in a Japanese military prison during World War II). In a test of their moral vision, one might ask, Would they have been willing to abandon their values and ideas if they were privy to a better way to move toward a more just, free, and creative world? I believe that each of them would have been willing to engage this question seriously—as in fact they did at various moments in their eventful lives. This claim is why I discern the makings of a common moral compass across their otherwise contrasting philosophies of education.

At the same time, I do not want to discount the differences in moral *emphasis* they express. For example, Tagore reflects a major theme running through some of the chapters when he writes that education's purpose is to bring people and the world into greater harmony:

> We have come to this world to accept it, not merely to know it. We may become powerful by knowledge, but we attain fulness by sympathy. The highest education is that which does not merely give us information but makes our life in harmony with all existence. But we find that this education of sympathy is not only systematically ignored in schools, but it is severely repressed. From our very childhood habits are formed and knowledge is imparted in such a manner that our life is weaned away from nature and our mind and the world are set in opposition from the beginning of our days. Thus the greatest of educations for which we came prepared is neglected, and we are made to lose our world to find a bagful of information instead. We rob the child of his earth to teach him geography, of language to teach him grammar. His hunger is for the Epic, but he is supplied with chronicles of facts and dates. . . . Child-nature protests against such calamity with all its power of suffering, subdued at last into silence by punishment. (Tagore, 1917, pp. 116–117)

While the other educators in the book might resonate with Tagore's vision, thinkers and activists such as Addams, Dewey, and Freire would emphasize the political potential in education to render human affairs more just, free, and meaningful. They might suggest that Tagore's outlook is necessary in a comprehensive philosophy of education, but not sufficient. They would suggest that the difference is more than a matter of tactics; rather, it is one of substantive consequences in the here and now. Tagore, Du Bois, Makiguchi, and others might reply that political transformation in the direction of democracy constitutes a profound value that they not only endorse but are, in their respective ways, striving toward. However, they might suggest that unless education is fueling children and youth—here and now—with creative imagination; a sense of beauty and harmony; an abiding respect for individual mind, heart, and soul; and care for nature and the world, political transformation may be either a will-o'-the-wisp or may backfire and produce new and unanticipated modes of oppressive conformity.

When I suggest that the 10 persons profiled in this book contribute to a common moral compass, I do not mean to say that they travel in the same way or with their eyes on an identical destination. I do think they would regard one another as worthy interlocutors in a dialogue about what are the best, most humane, and most efficacious constituents of a philosophy of education. No doubt they would vigorously dispute where the right or most timely moral emphasis should reside with respect to action. I hope that readers of this volume will subsequently feel motivated to ponder where their own emphasis lies—in individual freedom and creativity, in disseminating knowledge, in social justice, in humane interaction between people and with nature, or in all these goods. I also hope they will contemplate how to communicate effectively and respectfully with fellow educators whose emphasis differs from theirs.

My conjectures highlight another criterion of selection that also offers an appropriate conclusion to this introductory chapter. The 10 thinkers included here are, in a nutshell, remarkable and unusual human beings. While the chapters ahead highlight, by design, ideas and their consequences rather than biographical details, they do provide sufficient background for readers to get a sense of what the 10 persons were like. As readers will see, each sought to harmonize philosophy and action, theory and practice. Each was a person of ideas: a serious and probing thinker about the nature and purposes of education, and about values and the human prospect more generally. Each was a person of action: a dedicated and committed leader and participant in human affairs. Each responded in a determined, systematic manner to pressing educational, social, and political problems. Their ideas derived not solely from other ideas, indispensable as those sources were for them, but from life itself—from their experiences as thinkers and as doers and from their moral commitment to a more humane world. The ancient Greeks articulated a human ideal that helps capture the collective accomplishment of those included in this volume. The ideal for a human life comprised a fusion of what the Greeks called *logos* and *ergon*, the harmony of word and deed, of idea and practice. The meaning of an idea comes to life in action and conduct, just as action and conduct only become intelligent if informed by ideas. The persons featured in this book show us how to strive for such a harmony, itself an enduring educational aim across cultures and eras.

P A R T  I

# Foundational Perspectives
# on the Aims of Education

# John Dewey on Education and the Quality of Life

## David T. Hansen

PHILOSOPHER, EDUCATIONAL THEORIST, founder of a famous school, public intellectual, prolific writer, international lecturer, renowned professor, a figure both acclaimed and criticized—American philosopher John Dewey (1859–1952) was all these things and more. His conception of education has inspired generations of educators and his works continue to be studied in universities everywhere. As a philosopher, Dewey wrote enduring texts on art, ethics, the nature of inquiry, religion, and other topics. That body of work has enjoyed a considerable renaissance in recent decades, following a "wilderness period" (from roughly the 1940s through the 1970s), when analytic philosophy prevailed in the discipline. This renewal of interest, now worldwide, has coincided with the publication of Dewey's complete works in 37 volumes (several volumes of his correspondence are forthcoming). Virtually every aspect of his life and thought has been scrutinized; scholars have even paid systematic attention to his unpublished poetry.

No single essay, or indeed book, can do justice to the scope and range of Dewey's life and thought, a fact illustrated by the spate of recent biographies that have come out (see, for example, Martin, 2002; Rockefeller, 1991; Ryan, 1995; Westbrook, 1991). In this chapter, I will focus on his convictions about what it means to lead a meaningful life. I will begin with a sketch of his core educational and political ideas. This section will be the most lengthy in the chapter, if only to convey something of the power and originality in Dewey's outlook. I will turn next to an account of Dewey's public life, with special reference to his work in the Laboratory School, which he founded in Chicago. I will then conclude with a brief comment on the complex nature of Dewey's legacy.

## DEWEY'S PHILOSOPHY OF EDUCATION

At the core of Dewey's thoughts on education is his belief that life constitutes a generative gift. In his view, education should assist people in learning how to realize and extend this gift. Dewey envisions humanity's promise as limitless. He perceives no fixed boundary to human creativity and imagination, and no limit to how deeply and literally "meaning-full" human life can become.

For Dewey, the quality of life mirrors its aesthetic depth, understood as the extent to which it embodies grace, artfulness, and appreciation, whether in maintaining a home, a classroom, a business, or a government. The quality of life also reflects its emotional maturity and attentiveness, which Dewey contrasts with sentimentality or superficiality. Moreover, the quality of life displays its moral depth, which encompasses considerations of freedom, justice, compassion, humility, and personal as well as social responsibility. Finally, the quality of life mirrors its intellectual scope and discipline, the extent to which intelligence rather than caprice, routine, or blind habit guides its trajectory. For Dewey, a fulfilled life features a deepening of quality, however subtle, through each experience. Education constitutes the pathway of such a life.

As Dewey elucidates these ideas and addresses how to translate them into educational practice, he also analyzes why humanity has not yet learned, intellectually and morally, how to realize the gift of life. While there may be no limit to human potential, there is also no limit, or so it appears, to the dispiriting, demoralizing, and often violent ways in which people stunt their own or others' possibilities. Dewey is ecumenical in tracing the sources of humanity's still unrealized ability to fulfill life's promise. He points to the class system perpetuated by a capitalist economy with its attendant inequities and strife; to the collectivist system generated by communism with its smothering of individuality; to various forms of ethnocentrism; to modes of bigotry and intolerance such as racism; to schooling centered around rote learning and conformity; and to the tremendous acceleration of history as seen in rapid technological, scientific, and economic transformations around the globe, which Dewey believes generate as much fear and uncertainty as hope. These are among the forces that weigh humanity down and prevent it from reaching its boundless promise. In works such as *Democracy and Education* (MW9) and *Experience and Education* (LW13), Dewey articulates an educational approach that he believes can address the situation.

## The Indirect Approach to Education

Dewey proposes an indirect rather than direct assault on the conditions that undermine human possibility. He is not a revolutionary. Rather, he is what we might call, for heuristic purposes, a reconstructionist. He urges people to build upon what is efficacious in the system even while moving it in new directions. That posture is consistent with how he urges educators to work with the young. In *Democracy and Education*, his penultimate educational treatise, he writes that "frontal attacks are even more wasteful in learning than in war" (MW9, p. 176). Dewey means that it is impossible to educate another person *directly* in the sense of unilaterally transforming his or her knowledge, perceptions, insight, and dispositions. Metaphorically speaking, a teacher cannot reach into a child's mind or heart and rearrange the intellectual, emotional, moral, or aesthetic wiring. Moreover, a teacher cannot "give" a student an education as if handing her or him a set of objects. Nor can the student "get" an education as if reaching for something on a shelf. As Michael Oakeshott puts it, "A picture may be purchased, but one cannot purchase an understanding of it" (1989, p. 45). A person can earn a high school or college degree, but that fact says nothing about whether the person has become educated.

For Dewey, the indirect way to teach entails focusing directly on the environment in which teaching and learning take place, whether it be a classroom, school auditorium, sports field, graduate seminar, or computer workshop. The environment includes the curriculum, instructional methods, and physical setting. Educators should take pains to select rich curricular materials and activities. They should cultivate the pedagogical talent necessary to engage students creatively with the curriculum. On the one hand, that talent encompasses the capacity to listen patiently, to speak clearly and honestly, and to be acutely attentive to students' responses to the curriculum. On the other hand, pedagogical talent includes a command of time-honored instructional methods such as the capacity to give a good lecture, to lead a thoughtful and sustained discussion of a text, and to organize effective small-group or individual learning activities. "A large part of the art of instruction," Dewey writes, "lies in making the difficulty of new problems large enough to challenge thought, and small enough so that, in addition to the confusion naturally attending the novel elements, there shall be luminous familiar spots from which helpful suggestions may spring" (MW9, p. 164). This grasp of method is both practical and intellectual. It is practical in the technical sense of knowing how to employ instructional approaches, and intellectual in the sense of understanding why and when they can stoke genuine educational experience.

Educators also need to consider how the physical setting may support or hamper learning. The arrangement of space, materials, light, and so forth will play a role in the course of experience. According to Dewey, both mind and body are always implicated in education, whether in a kindergarten, medical school laboratory, or 10th-grade poetry class. Moreover, the mind and body always dwell within a physical medium and are always influenced by it, usually unawares. Thus, the physical environment will factor into the quality of teaching and learning.

When juxtaposed with the term *direct*, the *indirect* may connote passivity, tentativeness, caution, or circumspection. However, Dewey's indirect approach to educating places much more extensive and far-reaching obligations on the educator than any direct method that comes to mind. For one thing, in Dewey's conception the educator must have a command of subject matter. This readiness means more than a knowledge of fact and information, indispensable as that is. Rather, it entails a grasp of the logic in the subject matter, a sense of its history and trajectory, and a feeling for the human interests and creativity that gave rise to the very existence of the subject in the first place. Dewey's approach also obliges the educator to become a permanent student of students. The educator must learn how to recognize and respond to the distinctive and varied ways in which students engage the curriculum. That process means learning how to heed students' thinking and incipient ideas as well as learning how to fuel them, and, given the rapidity of classroom activity, doing both often within the very same moment.

A fundamental aspect of being a student of students is being attuned to their powers of expression and understanding (Garrison, 1997; Latta, 2002; Van Manen, 1991). Attunement calls upon the teacher's growing aesthetic, emotional, moral, and intellectual sensibility. It means noting students' present capacities to put facts and ideas together in addressing issues and problems; to manipulate instruments and tools; to discern patterns, whether in color or logic or language; to communicate with others; and to bring their thought into form, whether it be prose or sculpture or speech. Teachers need to cultivate their attunement continuously because students differ widely in their capacities and proclivities, and also because each individual student will always be changing and (hopefully) growing, however subtly and unpredictably.

Teacher educators have long appreciated Dewey's article "The Relation of Theory to Practice in Education" (MW3, pp. 249–272) because in it Dewey emphasizes that the most important outcome of any preparation program is not knowledge of instructional techniques per se, but rather such knowledge *bound up* in a larger commitment to studying how students think and engage the curriculum. Facility with technique comes with practice; but that facility will be hampered if it is not guided by a deepening "pedagogical" perception. In his widely read book for teachers *How We Think*, Dewey implies that if teachers were forced to choose between having dispositions such as open-mindedness toward students and a sense of responsibility for educating them, and having a comprehensive knowledge of instructional technique, they should unreservedly select the former. He also shows, however, why such a choice is not necessary if the educator comprehends the principles behind the indirect approach he articulates (LW8, p. 139).

Dewey puts forward the idea of *continuity* to assist educators in grasping the values inherent in being a student both of students and of subject matter. Just as subjects such as history, art, and science have a continuous trajectory, in the sense of one interpretation or work responding to prior views and accomplishments, so it is with human growth. Genuine human development always draws upon prior experience, and educators should act on that truth in their pedagogy. However, Dewey differentiates education from acquisition. His idea of educational continuity means something other than establishing routines and becoming habituated to environments. The latter may not involve education at all. For example, a person can be trained through a scheme of rewards and punishments to behave in a certain way. That person will have acquired a new behavior. But education would emerge only if the person began to think about the new behavior—to question it, reflect upon it, consider its rationale, and so forth.

The term that Dewey applies to the teacher's task in maintaining educational continuity is *reconstruction*. Education involves reconstructing prior knowledge, understanding, and insight as the student takes in new questions, problems, perspectives, and realms of activity. This process, according to Dewey, is fundamentally transformative. At every moment it features "an immediate end, and so far as activity is educative, it reaches that end—the direct transformation of the quality of experience." The process obtains throughout a person's life. "Infancy, youth, adult life—all stand on the same educative level in the sense that what is really *learned* at any and every stage of experience constitutes the value of that experience, and in the sense that it is the chief business of life at every point to make living thus contribute to an enrichment of its own perceptible meaning" (MW9, p. 82). For Dewey, education always involves thought and awareness, whether we have in mind the child coming to grips with addition or the adult comprehending the workings of a poem. These undertakings yield what he calls the direct transformation of the quality of experience. He pictures a person who has accomplished more than memorizing a new fact or piece of information, but who now has a new meaning in his or her life, however modest in scope that meaning may be when weighed against the totality of the person's background. Dewey's focus on meaning-making gives rise to the democratic aspect of his philosophy of education, to which I now turn.

## Education and Democracy

Unlike many political and social theorists, Dewey does not begin with a conception of a democratic society and then fashion an educational system to serve and sustain it. He does not believe that education should serve anything or anybody. According to Dewey, to put it in the service of an aim or purpose outside its own movement is to compromise and perhaps destroy it. On the one hand, if education is determined solely by the needs of the state, its substance may not cohere with the needs and interests of individuals. On the other hand, if education is guided merely by the individual's particular interests and desires, it may become a tool for self-promotion and self-aggrandizement at the expense of societal improvement.

It may sound strange and counterintuitive to suggest that education should not "serve" the self. However, Dewey has nothing esoteric or ascetic in mind in arguing that the purpose of education for each individual is not self-reproduction but self-transformation. The latter implies genuine growth in the range of contacts and meanings that a person experiences. It suggests that the person is continually engaging more of the world than before. For example, the construction worker who seeks to develop his or her facility with tools; grasp of form and fit; and feeling for brick, mortar, and wood is constantly transcending his prior self. This worker may not employ such language to describe his or her work and, in fact, might be stunned to hear it cast in such poetic terms. All the same, anyone attentive to the worker's day-to-day efforts will see that this individual's artfulness is being deepened and enhanced. Interacting with more and more of the world of construction work, the worker is constantly educating him- or herself into a more artful self. One day the worker may realize that, having been transformed to such an extent, he or she can now help others enhance their abilities, and thereby enjoy the same widening experience of meaning that the worker him- or herself has undergone. A comparable account holds for any person who grows through her or his work and play, whether parent, policewoman, teacher, or politician.

For Dewey, education constitutes its own end. Human growth has no higher aim than the capacity for further growth. In formal terms, Dewey writes, education "is that reconstruction or reorganization of experience which adds to the meaning of experience, and which increases ability to direct the course of subsequent experience" (MW9, p. 82). Dewey regards education as the deepening and enriching of the quality of life, by which he means its felt meanings and significance. At the same time, education equips people to direct or guide that very process into ever-widening realms of meaning.

Dewey does not believe that the self has a fixed nature. The self *is* what it thinks, feels, imagines, and does. It has no identity or meaning outside these modes of activity. This outlook means that the self is permanently engaged in a process of "losing" and "finding" itself. According to Dewey, every time the quality of a person's experience alters, so does his or her self. However imperceptibly, through the course of any meaningful experience, the self can become more knowledgeable, sensitive, and aware. That process means it has literally lost its prior identity in which it was *not* as knowledgeable, sensitive, or aware. At the same time, however, the self has found a new identity, or new quality of personhood, that is captured in those same terms. Moreover, the self can now better direct subsequent experience because it now brings to bear a deeper, broader capacity, once more captured in the phrase *more knowledgeable, sensitive, and aware.* For Dewey, this process constitutes the spiral of growth, whose end is never terminal or fixed, but always in continuous transformation. We discern again his belief that humanity has an unfathomable capacity to enrich its experience and to expand its realization of meaning.

*Meaning* remains a crucial watchword because it opens the door to Dewey's outlook on democracy. His large corpus is replete with expressions of moral outrage at how often social and individual practices constrain experience—and thereby narrow and diminish the quality of selfhood that people can cultivate. Too often, social circumstances smother the prospects for human growth, forcing persons into routines, ruts, and lowered expectations of the meaning of life. In the worst cases, injustice, bigotry, and violence damage or annihilate human prospects. Equally often, individual habits, outlooks, and desires narrow both the individual's and others' possibilities. Individuals accept truncated modes of existence that shut down outlets for human sympathy, grace, and meaning. Dewey poses the question, What kind of political arrangement will best draw *out* individual capacities for growth, while at the same time drawing individuals *into* the life of their society?

*Democracy* is his answer. According to Dewey, democracy is more than a form of government. It is more than a system of laws, institutions, and practices such as voting. Rather, democracy "is primarily a mode of associated living, of conjoint communicated experience" (MW9, p. 93). Democracy comes into being through expanded communication, shared experience, and an abiding disposition to seek interaction with others rather than to shun them. The construction worker developing the ability to communicate with fellow workers is fueling democracy. The parent who initiates a conversation with another parent in the public park is enacting democracy. The taxi rider and cabbie who swap experiences are realizing democracy. The teacher willing to hear out a student's explanation creates a democratic moment for both precisely because it is marked by sincere communication, shared experience, and a commitment to mutual engagement. None of these people must think in such terms. Their purpose is not "the growth of democracy." Rather, their direct aims are getting jobs done, sharing backgrounds, supporting others, and so forth. However, the indirect effect is that their willingness to interact with others in genuine rather than solely self-serving ways infuses the societal ethos, however microscopically in each particular case, with expanded communication and meaning.

For Dewey, a democratic society is characterized by a constant, open-ended, and unconstrained expansion in communication. It features ever-widening and ever-new channels for mutual contact and understanding. A democratic society is a growing, transforming society. This view complements Dewey's image of a growing, transforming self. One fuels and depends upon the other. A society that expands its communicative pathways draws out individual initiative, thought, and engagement. Thus, it constantly invites the individual to grow. At the same time, each individual's broadened participation immediately contributes to the widening of societal passageways. Thus, each person transforms society itself, however minutely in comparison with the whole. This image captures what Dewey means by democracy as a mode of associated living.

According to Dewey, a democratic society depends on formal education far more critically than does a society that seeks merely to replicate itself. In the latter, education is limited to bringing the young up to speed with convention and custom. It does not entail educating the young to take up hitherto unknown and unrealized possibilities. However, in a society that aspires to grow, people will "endeavor to shape the experiences of the young so that instead of reproducing current habits, better habits shall be formed, and thus the future adult society be an improvement on their own" (MW9, p. 85). By "better," Dewey denotes a society with enriched, expanding interaction between all its members. In such a society, people will find it important to ensure that resources are distributed so that all have the fullest possible opportunities to engage in the formative process of communication, interaction, and meaning-making.

Dewey argues that his approach to education, outlined in the previous section of this chapter, is indispensable to the emergence of a democratic society. "Since a democratic society repudiates the principle of external authority," he writes, "it must find a substitute in voluntary disposition and interest; these can be created only by education" (MW9, p. 93). But as suggested previously, Dewey has in mind more than the American Founding Fathers' ideal of an educated public equipped to influence the machinery of government. His conception is at once deeper and more thorough. It is that democracy cannot come into being without an abiding commitment to what he calls "an interest in learning from all the contacts of life" (MW9, p. 370). Dewey describes such an interest as "moral" because it means, literally, the willingness to learn from *all* rather than just *some* of the contacts that people have in life. That posture means remaining open, flexible, and responsive, including with those who may differ in values, outlooks, and hopes. This aim establishes a more profound public meaning to education than being able to control governmental processes. Education should form persons with a robust social disposition, even as it also equips each person to realize his or her personal talents and bent.

Dewey harbored no illusions about how difficult it is to cultivate and sustain democratic life. Nonetheless, he pushed his idealistic vision to the limit and in so doing invited others to articulate their hopes as fully as possible. That very act of invitation can build confidence and generate energy. Countless educators and citizens have been inspired by Dewey's call and example. In the following section, I will touch on his extraordinarily active life—he was one of America's last great public intellectuals—and on his pioneering work as founder of the famed Laboratory School in Chicago.

## DEWEY'S PUBLIC LIFE AND THE LABORATORY SCHOOL

Dewey's educational and democratic vision materialized in an historical moment as tumultuous and confusing as our own. He was born in 1859, when the United States was largely an agrarian society and on the cusp of a nearly ruinous civil war. By 1916, the year in which he published *Democracy and Education*, the United States had experienced massive industrialization and urbanization; rapid population growth; an enormous expansion in the provision of public schooling; a revolution in communications and modes of transportation; several overseas wars, including the cataclysm of World War I; and myriad scientific and artistic breakthroughs. An acute observer of these events, Dewey understood the uncertainty and fear as well as the excitement they triggered. He sought to elucidate an educational approach (outlined in the previous section), that would enable people to understand and to shape these prodigious changes rather than merely being shaped by them.

Dewey not only studied his contemporary times but also commented upon them in endless op-eds, magazine articles, and public speeches and in meetings with unions, political parties, and other groups. In 1915 Herbert Croly, Walter Lippmann, and the other editors of the newly launched and soon to be widely read magazine *The New Republic* invited Dewey to become a regular contributor. Over the next twenty years he published more than 150 articles in the journal on a wide range of national and international topics, ranging from education in China to politics in New York City. His writing on education and other topics brought him so much attention that by the 1920s it was said that no public issue in America was settled until he had commented on it (Commager, 1950, p. 100).

Moreover, because of his ideas and civic commitment, he was enjoined to support and participate in many newly formed institutions that would go on to have illustrious histories in American society. He gave a supporting address at the founding meeting of the National Association for the Advancement of Colored People (NAACP) in 1909. Guided by W. E. B. Du Bois and others, the NAACP gave critical voice to Black Americans' political, economic, and social aspirations. Dewey was active in the formation of the

American Association of University Professors (AAUP) and was elected as its first president in 1913. He accepted the office because of his fervent belief in the value of academic freedom, at that time under threat as university presidents and trustees engaged in arbitrary dismissal of faculty. Dewey also participated in the founding of the American Union Against Militarism (AUAM) in 1916 and for many years served on its national committee commencing right after the end of World War I, when it was renamed the American Civil Liberties Union (ACLU). In this and other capacities he became an articulate defender of freedom of speech and thought in public life. He joined and was an active supporter of the New York City teachers union, speaking out repeatedly on behalf of teachers, students, and public education. He traveled extensively in the United States and abroad, giving speeches to packed auditoriums; offering seminars; and meeting with politicians, educational leaders, and academics. He also sustained a regular teaching schedule, wrote numerous scholarly books, and maintained a family life as well as many friendships.

In the midst of these busy affairs, Dewey continued to think of himself first and last as a philosopher. In his view, philosophy is not the rarefied study of timeless truths and reality. It does not mean determining standards of what is good, right, just, beautiful, or the source of happiness, and then propounding these from on high. "Philosophical problems," he argues, "are in the last analysis but definitions, objective statements, of problems which have arisen in a socially important way in the life of a people" (MW3, p. 73). For Dewey, philosophy is an interactive practice of thought, study, and criticism. It focuses on the uses or absence of intelligence, creativity, imagination, and other generative capacities in human affairs, even while drawing upon knowledge of life to criticize such terms as *creativity* and *imagination*.

Dewey's underlying sense that genuine philosophical problems mirror problems in experience propelled him to accept the ambitious task of forming the Laboratory School at the University of Chicago. Dewey founded the school in 1896—its initial name was the University Elementary School—and remained intimately associated with it until his move in 1904 to Columbia University in New York. During these 8 years, Dewey gained enormous insight into the dynamics of teaching and learning. Certainly, he brought to the task a strong scholarly background in psychology, ethics, social theory, and more. He had also studied educational philosophy, had begun to publish in the area, and had become somewhat familiar with the workings of schools in the United States. But he had not, as yet, come fully to grips with the elements of a philosophy of education—among them, conceptions of teaching, learning, and curriculum—nor had he found a way to bring them into a critical, working unity. His years at the Laboratory School created conditions that led him to reconstruct his outlook. His experience gave him confidence that the vision he slowly but steadily propounded through speeches, publications, and teaching was right for both democratic society and for individual flourishing.

During Dewey's tenure the Laboratory School grew steadily, beginning with its initial enrollment in 1896 of 16 children. It retained throughout a faculty-student ratio of 9 or 10 to 1 (in marked contrast with many schools at the time with classrooms of more than 40 pupils). Most of the children were from local middle-class families, some being the sons and daughters of university faculty; Dewey's own children were among them. After it became permanently housed, the school enjoyed ample outdoor space for gardens and playing fields and also had state-of-the-art laboratories and workshops. At the same time, financial concerns were a constant worry for Dewey; for his wife, Alice Chipman Dewey (1859–1927), who served in a number of administrative positions in the school; and for Ella Flagg Young (1845–1918), who served as a general supervisor in the school beginning in 1901 and whose insight into the dynamics of teaching and learning had a marked and lasting impact on Dewey's philosophy of education (Blount, 2002; Lagemann, 1996).

In her detailed study of the Laboratory School's initial years, Laurel Tanner (1997) muses about what it would have been like to visit the place when the renowned philosopher himself walked its halls. Her account and those of others make it clear how truly experimental were the school's operations. Dewey conceived the idea of a "laboratory" school as a place to put on trial his provisional ideas and those of his faculty regarding education. During his sojourn it underwent significant changes in curriculum, pedagogy, evaluation, and administration. Those changes resulted from the communicative environment Dewey advocated and enacted through his own conduct. The teachers in the school had an active and sustained voice in determining every facet of the academic and social program. They were influential in bringing about major changes such as a shift from their working as "generalists" in the elementary grades to working as subject matter specialists; the school accordingly adopted a departmental structure (a rare sight in today's elementary schools).

However, Dewey and the teachers also retained a strong interdisciplinary, collaborative bent in their work. As emphasized earlier in this chapter, Dewey believed in working with the child *and* the curriculum. He urged a dynamic balance in the educator's focus, and his years at the Laboratory School helped convince him that genuine student learning best derives from engaging with the richest, most thoughtful curriculum the educator can conceive. His experience also clarified his view that subject matter comprises more than information in a textbook. It also includes students' and teachers' aesthetic and intellectual responses to what is encompassed in the disciplines, as well as the personal experience they bring to its study. Moreover, Dewey and his colleagues came to see how vital it was for teachers to develop a longitudinal view of the curriculum, to envision where students might be a week, a month, a year from the given lesson for the day. The teacher's direct focus is always on present conditions and how to fuel the richest possible experience in the moment. Indirectly, her or his concern includes students' deepening understanding and command of the curriculum over time.

Dewey came to believe that a school would function best if it could become a genuine community, a "miniature democracy" characterized by open channels of communication and interaction. He did not mean a democracy in an electoral sense; he believed strongly in the leadership functions of school administrators, teachers, and parents. Rather, Dewey believed the school could become a place of "conjoint communicated experience" (MW9, p. 93) that would generate meaningful social and personal growth. The school could become a vehicle for the enrichment of students' and educators' minds and hearts, an aim that embodies Dewey's fundamental concern for the quality of life. He and the faculty of the Laboratory School tinkered constantly with mechanisms and programs to bring this vision into being. The records of the school yield a story of meetings, hallway conversations, and enthusiastic correspondence. The records also show that the administrative running of the school was organically integrated with ongoing curriculum and pedagogical development (an achievement mirrored in many successful schools in operation today). This arrangement included communication with the university, thereby reflecting Dewey's hope that the school would "break down the barriers that divide the education of the little child from the instruction of the maturing youth, [thus demonstrating] to the eye that there is no lower or higher, but simply education" (MW1, p. 55).

## THE LEGACY OF DEWEY'S PHILOSOPHY OF EDUCATION

Dewey's school attracted an increasing stream of visitors and inspired many comparable educational experiments. Innovative and what came to be called "progressive" schools sprang up in various parts of the country throughout the early decades of the 20th century. Many of the founders, administrators, and teachers in these schools devoured Dewey's educational writings, and their enthusiasm spread quickly into schools and colleges of education as well as among many sectors of society. Countless progressive-minded educators in the public school system sought to bend its ways to accommodate Dewey's ideas. The upshot was that for many educators and members of the public, Dewey and progressive education became synonymous.

That fact complicates, and some would say compromises, Dewey's educational legacy today. For one thing, the very meaning of progressive education remains contested and confused. In the broadest sense, progressive education represents a commitment to the student as an individual rather than as a cog in the social wheel. It advances the notion that life in school can influence life in society, and that the school should therefore enjoy considerable autonomy. It stands for establishing democratic values throughout the educational process. However, many progressive educators have advanced a "student-centered" educational approach that is paired with a negligent if not suspicious outlook toward academic instruction, a posture that relegates teachers to the role of mere "facilitators" (Santoro Gomez, 2005). In other uses of the term, *progressive education* intimates a hostile, us-versus-them struggle between teachers and the system in the spirit of a wholesale rejection of school-based hierarchies and structures. In still other guises, progressive education means an integrated curriculum and pedagogy that seeks to challenge students intellectually while also proceeding organically with the adult-led operations of the school. This last mirrors the approach that Dewey and his faculty sought to enact in the early years of their school. However, in the public imagination Dewey often became associated with *all* these disparate and sometimes irreconcilable versions of progressive education. The upshot was that Dewey became the target of criticism from a variety of educational and political quarters, despite multiple attempts on his part to clarify his actual philosophy.

Dewey's school did not survive as a laboratory environment in the manner that he and his colleagues envisioned. Today it functions like many other independent college preparatory schools. Most of the numerous experimental schools founded along the lines of Dewey's undertaking have also not retained their laboratory character (see, for example, Semel & Sadovnik, 1999). These facts help account for why scholars continue to debate just how influential Dewey's ideas have been in American education. On the one hand, there is evidence that Deweyan imagination, creativity, and sophistication remain alive and well in American education. That influence sometimes saturates entire schools, while at others it characterizes a few classrooms or groups of educators in a given locale. Furthermore, Dewey continues to be read in schools and colleges of education, and the academy in general is at present focusing a great deal of attention on his work. At the same time, there is also evidence that many schools and classrooms today are not educative settings, and there is an equal amount of evidence that while Dewey is taught and read in colleges and schools of education it is at a superficial level.

It has always been hard to discern how many educators have actually studied Dewey's work, as opposed to merely citing it, as they convert him into either a symbol of their fondest aspirations or the embodiment of all that is wrong in American education. The other side of the equation is that anyone who does truly engage Dewey's thought will realize how formidable a challenge he presents to the educator. Some have concluded that education modeled after his philosophy is impossible to pull off; it simply expects too much of the teacher (see Schwab, 1978). For me, Dewey's elevated ideas render his philosophy of education endlessly fascinating and unsettling.

Rather than expecting too much of the educator, I do not believe he "expects" anything at all. He never asks his reader to agree with him. He invites the reader to think, to feel, to wonder, and to care for the quality of life, even as he enacts these traits in the very style of his writing. He offers little by way of concrete advice, despite the wealth of techniques and suggestions he had at hand. Instead, he invites people to use their intelligence and imagination in dealing with the concrete situations in which they find themselves, and which nobody knows better than they. I believe his philosophy will strike a chord with anyone who aspires to live fully and to assist others in doing the same.

# Paulo Freire's Politics and Pedagogy

## Stephen M. Fishman and Lucille McCarthy

> Education must begin with the solution of the
> teacher-student contradiction by reconciling the
> poles of the contradiction so that both are simul-
> taneously teachers *and* students.
>
> —Paulo Freire

SOCIAL HOPE—hope for a better, more equitable future—is crucial for all teachers, no matter their grade level. For who can teach effectively without a sense of optimism that his or her pupils live in a world that encourages an increase in justice, equality, and collaboration rather than in a world that earmarks these qualities for decline? In our present era—when expanding poverty, ecological damage, and international conflict have left social hope in short supply—Paulo Freire's voice is a treasured one. As we will show, this Brazilian philosopher and educator brings together the two great reform-ist visions of Western thought—Christianity and Marxism—in a way that demands all instructors' attention. That is, Freire's blend of these two visions can be a source of social hope for all of us as classroom teachers, a source we need if our practice is to be both effective and full-hearted.

We divide our essay into three sections. In the first, we present the intellectual movements that influenced Freire as he developed his politics and pedagogy. In the second, we discuss the influence of Freire's politics on his pedagogy. Finally, we present a brief overview of the worldwide impact of Freire's ideas.

## INTELLECTUAL MOVEMENTS THAT INFLUENCED FREIRE'S POLITICS

Four historically important intellectual streams circulate through Freire's work: Marxism, neocolonial critique, existentialism, and Christianity. Of these, the strongest is, arguably, Marxism, with its focus on antagonism between the working and owner classes.

### Marxism and Class Antagonisms in Freire's Politics

Paulo Freire was born into a middle-class family in Recife, Brazil, on September 19, 1921. Recife is a port city in northeastern Brazil, one of the poorest regions in the world. In 1960, 75% of this region's population was illiterate, and the life expectancy for men was 28 and for women, 32. The gap between landowners and peasants was enormous, with 50% of the land owned by approximately 3% of the population (Taylor, 1993, p. 17). Although Freire was born middle class, he and his family were seriously affected by the 1929 economic depression. His father lost his job and then died 2 years later, leaving the family in dire economic straits. It was then, as a young child, that Freire experienced firsthand the extreme poverty and intractable class antagonisms that still mark Brazilian society. Although in his early writings, such as *Education for Critical Consciousness* (1969/1996), Freire expressed the belief that Brazil would be able to move gradually and peacefully to a more "open" and democratic society (p. 8), his work takes on a more revolutionary tone after the 1964 military coup in Brazil. This coup leads to Freire's imprisonment, a brief time in solitary confinement, and a 15-year exile.

Freire's most famous post-exile work is *Pedagogy of the Oppressed* (1970/2003), a book that has sold nearly a million copies. In it, Freire's analysis of the ills of contemporary society and its educational institutions reflects the influence of Marx's view of social-class antagonisms. Freire, like Marx, sees class conflict as central to understanding human history, and he forcefully argues that only a fundamental, revolutionary transformation of society will bring about justice and equality for Brazilians. The bourgeois or oppressor class will have to be replaced, he tells us, and it will take the same amount of violence to do this that the oppressors have used to gain and maintain their grip on the poor (p. 56).

### Neocolonial Critique in Freire's Politics

Although Freire's analysis of social and educational ills in *Pedagogy of the Oppressed* employs the Marxist concepts of *bourgeoisie* and *proletariat*, his pre-exile years made him very much aware that the contours of these class divisions were often shaped by the legacy of colonialism. Portugal had dominated and exploited Brazil's native population during Brazil's colonial period, and Freire saw this exploitation continue in the decades after independence in the 19th century. Despite Brazil's separation from Portugal in 1822 and transformation into a republic in 1899, large landholders continued in Freire's time to control all aspects of their workers' lives: economic, political, judicial, and educational.

Freire's critique of neocolonialism comes through loud and clear in his writing. He tells us that the oppressed classes have an existence that is "a form of death in life" (1987, p. 147). He argues that many peasants have been so dominated by the large landowners that they have become totally passive. They see themselves as no more capable of influencing their fate than do animals or trees. For example, one peasant tells Freire, "I have no tomorrow that is any different from today that is any different from yesterday" (Freire, 1997/2000, p. 42). Thus, the reformer's task, as Freire sees it, is not simply to organize workers so they can wrest control from their masters. The more fundamental challenge is to help workers and peasants exorcise the attitudes they have bought lock, stock, and barrel from their oppressors. Workers need to overcome the idea that they are inherently inferior, cannot think for themselves, and are unable to do anything about their low station in life.

Thus, Freire's educational work with peasants focuses on helping them see themselves as fully human. He wants them to appreciate the wisdom they already possess by renaming the world in light of their experience of oppression so that they can end oppression. This effort to expunge from the minds of workers the oppressive myths perpetuated by the neocolonial ruling class relies on a method of critical thinking that Freire calls "conscientization." He describes it as the "stripping" down of reality in order to understand "the myths that deceive and perpetuate the dominating structure" (1972a, p. 6). This method of "conscientizing education" requires that teachers enable students to join them as active learners who name and critique their own economic and political circumstances.

During Freire's 15-year exile, he traveled widely, and he came to see Brazilians' neocolonial situation as typical of Third World people all over the globe. By *Third World*, Freire does not have in mind only people in countries that have not industrialized. He has also has in mind people in so-called First World countries, including the United States, who have minimal opportunities to escape their financial and cultural poverty (1970/2003, p. 157). Freire tells us:

> The concept of the Third World is ideological and political, not geographic. The so-called First World has within it and against it its own Third World. And the Third World has its First World, represented by the ideology of domination and the power of the ruling class. (1987, pp. 139–140)

Further, Freire came to see neocolonialism as responsible for not only the subjugation of the worker class but also the subjugation of "dependent" nations, among them Brazil, whose loans and trade arrangements are controlled by more industrially and militarily powerful countries. His most scathing social criticisms are directed at what he sees as the moral bankruptcy of the dominant nations, in particular, rich countries' indifference to the suffering of the world's poor. He never lets his First World readers forget that the earth only sustains their extravagant standard of living at the cruel expense of the Third World poor. As one example, he points out that the amount it would cost to avert the deaths of 10 million Third World children who die annually is no more than the amount that U.S. cigarette companies spend yearly on advertising (1992/1999, pp. 94–95).

## Existentialism in Freire's Politics

In addition to Marxian influences and neocolonial critique, existentialist thought plays an important role in Freire's analysis of the human situation and his ideas for social reform. As he develops his criticisms of the ruling class, Freire sees oppressors' behavior as not only an attempt to maintain their own interests but also an effort to deny the humanity of the oppressed. This effort, according to Freire, ends up damaging not only the humanity of the workers but also the humanity of the rulers. To explain the oppressor-oppressed relationship, Freire draws upon such key existential concepts as freedom, being, and having. According to Freire, humans have a fundamental desire—what he characterizes as an "ontological need"—to be free. It may be suppressed at times; it may be eclipsed at times. But eventually it comes to the fore. Our need to be free is understood by Freire as a need to create or, more specifically, to name oneself and the world in cooperation with others. As we have already seen, helping people fulfill their "ontological need" to be free is the object of Freire's educational initiatives with the oppressed class. As people gain their freedom, they become historical agents, reshaping themselves and their environment. Put another way, when we are free, we create what has not yet been. And as we create being, we discover our true nature.[1]

Freire continues to draw upon the existential themes of freedom and being as he analyzes the oppressor's mentality. In Freire's view, the colonial landlords and capitalist owners build their lives around "having" as opposed to "being." The desire to "have" is, for Freire, driven by fear and lack of trust. Oppressors' fears lead them to dominate things and people. They fear letting others have freedom because they do not trust the world and others. Echoing the work of Erich Fromm, Freire says the oppressor class is "necrophilic" rather than "biophilic" (1970/2003, pp. 59–60). That is, the ruling class, in its obsessive need to protect itself, ends up promoting death rather than life. Its efforts to control others denies them their right to be free, that is, to *be*, and, in the process, the dominant class destroys its own chances for true freedom and being.

How does Freire believe we can get out of this situation? How do we stop this apparently endless cycle of fear leading to domination leading to the destruction of freedom and our chance to truly be? We have already indicated part of Freire's answer: critical thinking, or "conscientization," a method that helps peasants and workers overcome their passivity by becoming conscious about and ridding themselves of myths perpetuated by the ruling class. This approach by Freire is in line with orthodox Marxist thought. But there is more to Freire's remedy for the poverty and injustice that haunt the modern world than just critical thinking. He wants nothing less than individuals' total transformation.

## Christianity in Freire's Politics

Freire (1970/2003) is not naive about the dangers of class revolution. He realizes that simply replacing the tyranny of the capitalist class with a tyranny of the worker class leaves us no better off than we are at present (pp. 44, 57). That is, tyranny and domination by one class—whether bourgeoisie or proletariat—over another leads to profound injustice and inequality. Freire is also aware of how someone like Stalin can betray the oppressed class for which he was, presumably, the standard bearer. As a result, what Freire wants—and what he hopes educational reform can help bring about—is individual as well as social revolution. He wants radical individual transformation as well as radical social transformation. Thus, the Christian idea of death and rebirth is central to Freire's thinking. He wants peasants to die to their passivity and be reborn as free, creative people. In parallel ways, he wants members of the oppressor class to die to their "having" ways and be reborn in solidarity with the poor (1970/2003, pp. 61, 133). Freire's belief that individuals can die and be reborn with new commitments—what he calls the Easter experience—reflects his strong Christian orientation. This orientation is also apparent in Freire's advocacy for the poor, an advocacy that reflects his appreciation of Christ's deep concern for those at the bottom of the social ladder. Freire's championing of the poor is seen in his appreciation of peasants' language, his faith in their wisdom, and his respect for the unique vantage point from which they view the inequities of modern society (1970/2003, p. 45).

In addition, Freire's Christian roots are evident in his claim that authentic dialogue is necessary if we are to establish a more just, equitable, and democratic society. He argues that such dialogue depends on the virtues of faith, hope, and love (*caritas*) (1970/2003, pp. 89–92). He says that authentic dialogue requires that we trust and put our hopes in others. He says, "Love is at the same time the foundation of dialogue and dialogue itself" (p. 89). This means being present to other persons and loving other persons without putting demands on what sorts of people they should be. Freire says this is important for teachers as well as revolutionary leaders. Only leaders who trust and love the people—who are willing to listen to and learn from the people—have, in Freire's view, truly died to their oppressor ways and been reborn in solidarity with the oppressed. Likewise, only teachers who truly believe they can learn from their students, who trust them, and who give them the freedom to choose what they want to become are effective educators (pp. 68–69).

This Christian-rooted, sympathetic dialogue, with its emphasis on faith, hope, and love, blends with Freire's existential influences, particularly Martin Buber's concept of the I-Thou relationship (Freire, 1970/2003, p. 167). When we are in an I-Thou relationship with others, we treat others as free beings. We use our trust in them, our hope in them, and our charitable love for them, to help them recognize and fulfill their special potential. This sort of relationship respects another's being, and it is in sharp contrast with I-It relationships, in which we use others for our own benefit, treating them not as free beings but as objects.

## THE INFLUENCE OF FREIRE'S POLITICS ON HIS PEDAGOGY

Freire tells his North American audience that he cannot give specific pedagogical advice and that it is up to individual teachers to assess their school situations and experiment accordingly (Shor & Freire, 1987, p. 211). However, he dramatically articulates his fundamental teaching approach in *Pedagogy of the Oppressed*, and we believe that it presents useful cautions and guidelines for U.S. teachers. As we discuss Freire's pedagogy, we will show how the influences that shaped his politics also shaped his approach to the classroom.

### Marxism in Freire's Pedagogy

Influenced by Marxist thought, Freire emphasizes to his readers that teaching is always a political act (Freire, 1987, pp. 188–189). Educational institutions, as Freire sees them, are very much controlled by the ruling class. The dominant group tries to use schools to develop pupil attitudes and beliefs that legitimize the prevailing social structure and help those in power maintain their power. This means, for Freire, that all teachers, whether they like it or not, are involved in politics when they enter the classroom. Even instructors teaching such apparently politically neutral subjects as math and psychology, according to Freire, need to be aware that if they do not discuss the ways in which their students' mathematical and psychological skills will be used by their prospective employees, teachers, by omission, bolster the status quo. In adopting this stance, Freire follows in principle the attitude reflected in Marx's famous comment about educators in his *Theses on Feuerbach*. In his Third Thesis, Marx writes,

> The materialist doctrine that men are products of circumstances and upbringing, and that, therefore, changed men are products of other circumstances and changed upbringing, forgets that it is men who change circumstances and that it is essential to educate the educator himself. (1888/1978, p. 144)

In an important sense, Freire sets out to "educate the educator." He sets out to exorcise a myth fostered by the ruling class that the structure of schools and teachers' subject matter and instructional approaches are politically neutral and without bearing upon the perpetuation or reform of the prevailing social order. He points out that most contemporary classrooms are exemplifications of "banking" education and, thus, serve to perpetuate the status quo. Freire writes,

> Education thus becomes an act of depositing, in which the students are the depositories and the teacher is the depositor. Instead of communicating, the teacher issues communiques and makes deposits which the students patiently receive, memorize, and repeat. This is the "banking" concept of education, in which the scope of action allowed to the students extends only as far as receiving, filing, and storing the deposits. (1970/2003, p. 72)

We can see in this passage Freire's effort to educate the educator about the political ramifications of keeping students docile, of viewing instruction as something to be done *to* students rather than something to be done *with* them. This sort of banking approach, according to Freire, plays into the hands of the ruling class, since it keeps students unaware of their own critical abilities and the power of their own language and voice. By contrast, teachers should be "problem-posers." That is, they need to pose problems that they cooperatively explore with students rather than dictate solutions that have been unilaterally derived. Teachers should become co-learners with their pupils, genuinely valuing students' skills and wisdom instead of treating them as empty vessels to be filled. However, since most teachers do not engage in this sort of problem posing, they work, often unintentionally, in the interests of the ruling class. In this situation, Freire tells us, teachers who rely on banking education and students whose docility they promote are in "contradiction," and overcoming this contradiction is the primary task of "libertarian" pedagogy:

> In the banking concept of education, knowledge is a gift bestowed by those who consider themselves knowledgeable upon those whom they consider to

know nothing. Projecting an absolute ignorance onto others, a characteristic of the ideology of oppression, negates education and knowledge as processes of inquiry. The teacher presents himself to his students as their necessary opposite. . . . The *raison d'être* of libertarian education, on the other hand, lies in its drive towards reconciliation. Education must begin with the solution of the teacher-student contradiction, by reconciling the poles of the contradiction so that both are simultaneously teachers *and* students. (1970/2003, p. 72)

### Neocolonial Critique in Freire's Pedagogy

Freire further shows how political he believes teaching to be when he compares teachers and clergy in neocolonial, capitalist societies with the police and soldiers in colonial societies. He suggests that whereas the colonial landlord used police and soldiers to keep the natives in check, neocolonial capitalists use teachers and clergy to keep the poor and working class in check (1970/2003, pp. 62–63). In other words, the dominant class tries to use educators to convince students that the social and economic system that provides some people with enormous wealth and others with grinding poverty is a just system. Similarly, the dominant class tries to use clergy to convince the poor that their struggles are either God's punishments or their God-given chances to accept suffering and purify their faith (Freire, 1987, p. 131). Of course, Freire sees these views as oppressive myths that need to be dispelled by teachers and their students through the collaborative use of critical thinking, or conscientization.

### Christianity and Existentialism in Freire's Pedagogy

Why does Freire argue so strongly that these capitalist myths need to be exorcised? Why does he believe that capitalism and its inequities cannot be justified? Freire says that the usual attempt to justify the enormous differences between wealthy and poor on the grounds that, under capitalism, everyone has an equal right to compete for wealth does not hold up. He argues that people with little money and cultural capital cannot compete on an equal footing with those who have great amounts of both. In addition, Freire rejects the view that democracy is primarily about the freedom to earn and keep as much money as one can. To the contrary, he believes that the only just society is one based upon the idea that what matters most is giving people a chance to help one another realize their full potential. Thus, as he notes in the passage from *Pedagogy of the Oppressed* that we quoted above, educational reform begins by replacing the egoistic, dominating I-It relationships that characterize most classrooms with loving creative, I-Thou relationships. It begins by solving the "teacher-student contradiction."[2]

## FREIRE'S INFLUENCE WORLDWIDE

Freire's philosophy of education has had significant global impact because of the power of his ideas and his exile-enforced international travels. His initial influence was in Brazil, where he helped establish the Movement of Popular Culture in 1960 and then, in 1961, became the first director of the Department of Cultural Extension Service at the University of Recife. These programs had unusual success, with large numbers of rural peasants learning to read and write in just 45 days. Freire employed a phonics and illustrations method that allowed his adult students to write and discuss their own words and sentences. In addition, he focused on words such as *favela* (slum), *trabalho* (work), and *riqueza* (wealth) and illustrations of situations that were important to his students. That is, Freire followed his own dictum that education is always political. Because he began with words and concepts that had social and political meaning for students, instead of decontextualized words such as *tree* and *bird*, pupils were not only more attentive but also more likely to be active and critical learners. Freire's work was so successful in northeastern Brazil that he was asked to direct the National Literacy Program by Brazil's Ministry of Culture and Education in 1963 (Freire, 1969/1996, pp. 41–84).

However, the following year, the Brazilian military staged a successful coup. Because this conservative junta saw Freire's success with adult literacy and his political pedagogy as a threat, he was exiled. After spending 5 years in Chile, where he worked at the Chilean Institute for Land Reform and composed *Pedagogy of the Oppressed*, Freire went to Harvard in 1969 and taught there for 10 months. At Harvard, he influenced numerous American scholars who subsequently became important in the education field. These figures include Antonia Darder, Henry Giroux, bell hooks, Peter McLaren, Ira Shor, and Kathleen Weiler.

After his time at Harvard, Freire went to Geneva to become director of education at the World Council of Churches. In this position he had opportunities to discuss his educational philosophy and put it into practice on the international scene. He was especially active in the mid-1970s in helping to rebuild the school systems of former Portuguese colonies in Africa: Guinea-Bissau, São Tomé and Príncipe, Mozambique, and Angola. His work with the revered African revolutionary Amilcar Cabral is well documented in Freire's *Pedagogy in Process: Letters to Guinea-Bissau* (1978). Finally, in 1979, after 15 years in exile, Freire was able to return to Brazil, where he could once again exert a direct influence on his own country's educational practices. He did this as adult education supervisor for Brazil's Workers' Party (1980–1986); as minister of education for the city of São Paulo (1988–1991); and as professor of education at the Catholic University of São Paulo, where he taught until he died on May 2, 1997.

Besides taking into account Freire's international travels, we trace his worldwide influence to two features of his work. The first is his ability to blend the two great utopian visions in Western thought: Christian and Marxian. Freire is able to blend these visions, which are often seen as contradictory, because he finds Marx's efforts to build a classless, poverty-free society fully compatible with Christ's goals of equality and justice:

> I am convinced that we as Christians have an enormous task to perform, presuming that we are capable of setting aside our idealistic myths and in that way sharing in the revolutionary transformation of society, instead of stubbornly denying the extremely important contribution of Karl Marx. (1972b, p. 11)

In other words, Freire does not see Christians who work for greater earthly justice as mistakenly taking on this-worldly causes that are best left to secular people. Quite the contrary, he believes that those who toil for justice in this world are sharers in God's creative work. They carry on the tradition established by Christ's championing of the poor as reported in the Gospels. As he says, "Christ was no conservative" (1987, p. 139). That is, Freire does not view Third World poverty, as some Christians do, as God's will and its acceptance as a sign of one's renunciation of material pleasures. Rather, he sees poverty and injustice as inimical to living as human beings. Thus, the true work of all of us, for Freire, is the active promotion of greater earthly equality and democracy rather than passive waiting for transcendent eternal bliss. It is this worldly work that, in his view, should unite all Marxists and Christians. His blend of these two visions not only shaped education projects worldwide; it also had a formative influence on one of the most powerful reform movements in the world today, namely, liberation theology (see Berryman, 1987; Cone, 1986; Gutierrez, 1973).[3]

In addition to Freire's powerful blend of Marxism and Christianity, his substantial influence results from his ability to speak for people who have long been silenced. The African American educator bell hooks initially heard Freire lecture when she was a graduate student at the University of California, Santa Cruz. For the first time, hooks explains, she felt that someone was speaking about her and her experience as a member of an oppressed group in an oppressive society (1994, pp. 45–58). In sum, although Freire was writing primarily in the context of neocolonial South America, his work has had far-reaching influence because oppressed people around the world have found their own voice in his language. He has enabled countless people to see and name their world for the first time, and in helping them speak about their world, he has helped them take their first steps toward changing it.

## CONCLUSION

Freire's ability to weave together diverse traditions—Marxist, neocolonial, Christian, and existential—gave him a fruitful, critical perspective on contemporary education. It enabled him to make clear the ways in which the intellectual habits and beliefs of both teachers and students are shaped by the dominant class and an oppressive social structure. Working from this perspective, he was able to contribute to the ongoing efforts of educational reformers to better understand human nature and the conditions that promote intelligent reordering of oneself and one's culture.

Regarding Freire's impact upon politics and social change, his work gave theoretical underpinning to successful revolutions in Cuba, Nicaragua, and Guinea-Bissau as well as reform efforts by liberal factions of South America's Catholic and Protestant churches. However, despite these positive results, Freire, at the end of his life, was not naive about the actual progress that had been made toward his libertarian goals. In his last book, *Pedagogy of the Heart* (1997/2000), he laments the ongoing and pervasive corruption of Brazilian officials and the terrible poverty and illiteracy that still existed in the northeastern province where he was born. Yet while continuing to publicly and courageously denounce this social injustice, he also lauds the steps toward democracy that Brazil had taken since instituting a system of representative, regularly elected government.

Although the specific political and educational advances that can be directly credited to Freire's work are limited, we believe that this fact should not be cause for pessimism. The heavy weight of custom is always on the side of the status quo. This tendency means that while Freire would have us never forget the encompassing, long-term goals of educational reform, he would also remind us not to overlook the small immediate gains that individuals can make in their own classrooms. These, for Freire, often have important positive repercussions. Further, he reminds us that social reform occurs one act at a time and that every classroom, no matter the grade level, is a potential source of social hope.

# W.E.B. Du Bois and an Education for Democracy and Creativity

### Rodino F. Anderson

WHENEVER SOCIETIES are beset by challenges that test the very foundations of their ideals, education emerges as an aid for the adjusting and readjusting of cultural values. In this sense, education appropriately relates to the challenges of war, revolution, economic instability, and social justice. Much of the history of the United States is a testament to the central role that education has played in shaping its democratic, pluralistic culture. One of the most challenging tests of the underlying principles of the nation resulted from President Abraham Lincoln's 1863 Emancipation Proclamation. With the stroke of a pen, a once-enslaved people were suddenly declared to be "human citizens." But how could the rights and responsibilities of citizenship be achieved without education? And how could White society be educated into a new understanding of race? Clearly, the transformation of Black Americans into citizens could not be legislated into being, especially given the fact that for centuries they had been systematically denied any formal education. To make good on the Emancipation Proclamation, the country would need to formulate a vision and support an unprecedented investment of material and human resources. It would also need to call on the leadership and imagination of Black leaders such as W.E.B. Du Bois. In the face of this challenge, one often called "the Negro problem," in which moral, political, economic, and social questions were entwined, Du Bois wrote an imaginative and powerful response in 1903, in *The Souls of Black Folk*. In this chapter I will explore this response as a work of educational philosophy and read it as a relevant and practical text that advocates aesthetic education as a path to human dignity.[1]

Identifying that the "problem of the Twentieth Century is the problem of the color line," Du Bois sought to transform the impoverished identity of the American Negro. Doing so would signal a Copernican-like revaluation of the very meaning of race, culture, and morality at the foundation of citizenship in American democracy. At the heart of Du Bois's re-visioning of democracy was his ardent belief that education could address this by making possible "the sharing of gifts" between the cultures that constituted the nation and thus redefining the Negro race as a people worthy of full citizenship. In particular, he believed that education would position the Negro race to generate and contribute to a shared culture by putting forward its deep, unparalleled consciousness of the value and beauty of freedom. Du Bois's tireless, long life of 95 years constituted a sustained attempt to articulate and present the gift of the American Negro with the larger purpose of a full-fledged democracy in mind.

Du Bois's voluminous writings range from philosophy, sociology, and history to poetry, fiction, and autobiography. He published neither a formal treatise on education in general, nor a proposed curriculum in particular. His only book-length study of education was his reflection entitled "Seven Critiques of Negro Education," unpublished in his lifetime.[2] For this reason, it comes as no surprise that Du Bois's educational thought has not been the subject of systematic scholarship, unlike, for example, his political and social analysis. As recent scholarship has shown, however, he has bequeathed to his country and the world a rich vision of educational possibilities.[3] And we find a remarkable portrait of the meaning and power of education in his trilogy of works that "center around the hurts and hesitancies that hem [in]" Black Americans' quest for freedom (1940/1986, p. 551). These books include *The Souls of Black Folk* (1903/1994), *Darkwater: Voices from Within the Veil* (1920/1996), and *Dusk of Dawn* (1940/1986).

While these writings, combined with "Seven Critiques," offer a wealth of insight into Du Bois's thought, in this chapter I will confine my examination to themes from *The Souls of Black Folk*. *Souls* is widely regarded as Du Bois's most poetic, most philosophical, and most prescient analysis of race, education, and the American prospect.[4] As such, it serves as an important window on his view of important aspects of American society and democracy. In the first section of this chapter, I chart the educational odyssey of a young Du Bois, leading up to his famous 1903 publication. This analysis will help shed light on certain fundamental and recurrent themes of that book. The second section elucidates Du Bois's liberal arts educational philosophy and his provocative parallels between what he thought of as "the liberal arts spirit" and the Negro soul. A third section introduces *The Souls of Black Folk* in greater detail and analyzes its importance in Du Bois's educational thought. In a concluding section, I consider Du Bois's enduring significance for the philosophy and practice of education.

## ON A LIFE MISSION

From his birth on February 23, 1868, in Great Barrington, Massachusetts, 5 years after the Emancipation Proclamation, to his death in Ghana on August 27, 1963,[5] Du Bois's life spanned one of the most violent times in White-Black race relations in the United States. In an America where the Negro was often seen as a "problem" or, worse, a being "somewhere between men and cattle" (Du Bois, 1903/1994, p. 63), Du Bois knew at an early age that he wanted to dedicate himself to the mission of changing the very concept of race. Somehow, he sensed early in his career that he would be able to do this through the written word. "It had always been my ambition to write; to seek through the written word the expression of my relation to the world and the world to me," he says (1940/1986, p. 750). Focused on his path, Du Bois would encounter many obstacles, including institutionalized codes of oppression that were denigrating to the psyche of the Negro people; a pseudoscience of racial categorizing that prevailed in his day; a White (mostly Southern) public that thought his moral ideas too radical; and his so-called nemesis, the preeminent Negro leader of his day, Booker T. Washington. Later in this chapter, we will explore some of the ways in which Washington and Du Bois agreed and differed in their shared vision of a more democratic America.

Du Bois ardently believed that only through education would he have the opportunity to strengthen his mind and form his character to meet the challenges of his Herculean task. The story of his journey was to be a beacon of inspiration to others throughout his life, as well as a source of pride and renewal in his own life. To illustrate, we will consider three profound, educative moments in his educational odyssey that established the foundations of Du Bois's educational thinking. Each of these find commanding expression in *The Souls of Black Folk.*

Du Bois showed great intellectual prowess as a child, and in high school he had his mind set on attending Harvard College. Because of lack of money, full academic credentials, and the impending death of his mother, Du Bois held off on applying to Harvard. After a year of hard work building houses, and several churches contributing to his academic cause, he was given the opportunity to attend college for fall 1885 on sophomore standing at Fisk University in Tennessee. Suddenly, the northern boy of mixed ethnicity was on his way to a southern Negro college.[6] Up to this point, Du Bois had never experienced strife-ridden race relations like those he encountered in the South. Social oppression, legalized discrimination and segregation, poor economic conditions, and a generally inferior quality of education were now part of young Du Bois's reality. While undertaking a rigorous, classical liberal arts curriculum at Fisk, Du Bois sang with the Mozart society,[7] and, already armed with considerable oratorical skills, he further developed his talent as a writer and editor at the school's newspaper, the *Fisk Herald*. He also made time to be politically active in the struggle for the Negro's democratic equality by urging a Black student convention "to vote independently of the Republican Party in pursuit of black interests" (1940/1986, p. 1283). Throughout his career, he would make use of the skills he developed at Fisk University to create and edit many critical political magazines, newspapers, and journals to help improve the American Negro's existence.

Du Bois initially thought that a more liberal-minded North would act upon the dehumanizing social practices of the South once it fully grasped the scope of injustice. Graduating from Fisk in 1888, Du Bois finally made it to Harvard by securing a Price-Greenleaf grant, and later a Matthews scholarship. His experiences there proved decisive in the development of his intellectual powers as he interacted with some of the leading scholars of the day, most notably American philosophers William James and George Santayana and economist Frank Taussig. James, in particular, would become mentor and dear friend to Du Bois through some tough years at Harvard. Although Du Bois was privileged to have great minds invested in his success, his eyes were opened by the ugly presence of racist attitudes in a supposedly more enlightened North. What he saw and experienced drove home to him how deeply rooted were America's racial problems. Du Bois tells us that had he gone to Harvard before Fisk, he would have been "embittered by a discovery of social limitations" if he had "sought companionship with my white fellows" (1940/1986, pp. 578–579). He tells us of how his "better than the average voice" was rejected by Harvard's glee club, for "it posed the later problem of a 'nigger' on the team." In spite of unsettling experience like this, Du Bois pressed on and threw himself into his studies, in part because he was not active in the social-, political-, or public-writing scenes there—a stark contrast to his sociopolitical activism at Fisk. He earned his BA in philosophy, cum laude, in 1890.

If two starkly different social and educative worlds were not enough for Du Bois, his next educational achievement would come to be his most daring and ambitious undertaking. Although he was accepted to continue studying at Harvard at the graduate school in political science, Du Bois instead made his way to the University of Berlin—now Humboldt University—where he pursued a doctoral degree. This period in Germany was an awakening for Du Bois. Away from the oppressive racism of the United States, inspired by European culture (especially its art and music), acutely observant of German political affairs, and living in the birthplace of much of the philosophy and science he had studied at Fisk and Harvard, Du Bois was able to flourish in an untrammeled manner. Some scholars refer to his time in Germany as a romantic escape from American realities while others, among them Appiah (2005), believe that Du Bois's experience abroad powerfully shaped his nascent cosmopolitan thinking.

Du Bois's unique, worldly vantage point allowed him to think broadly and deeply about the struggles of the American Negro. Formed by three very different educational climates, Du Bois returned to the United States with a renewed determination to transform American democracy by addressing the Negro problem through education. He returned to Harvard, where he continued to hone his historical and sociological skills, and became the first Negro to obtain a PhD from the university in 1895. The power and promise in his scholarship was so apparent that Harvard published his dissertation, *The Suppression of the African Slave Trade*, as the very first volume of its Historical Monograph Series in 1896. His ideas were informed by an education rarely equaled by his contemporaries, Black or White. He saw racism as a threat to democracy and believed that if true democracy were ever to flourish, a penetrating vision of how to deal openly and honestly with racism would have to be offered. Du Bois's most vivid, grave, and haunting work, *The Souls of Black Folk*, was intended to provide this vision.

## THE POWER OF A BOOK

*The Souls of Black Folk* is a unique amalgam of philosophical, political, historical, sociological, and literary analysis.[8] In trying to communicate the "strange meaning of being black here in the dawning of the Twentieth Century" (1994, p. v), Du Bois writes with such emotional vigor and eloquence that it is easy to be seduced by the work's bittersweet ruminations, forgetting its overall message of cultivating a race to help create democratic culture. In "The Forethought" Du Bois shares the architecture of *Souls*. There, he explains that it is divided into five major sections that deal with (1) "the spiritual world in which ten thousand thousand Americans live and strive"; (2) the perceptions that dwell on either side of prejudice with education being of central concern to aid in destroying this orientation; (3) "deeper detail" and elaboration of previous section; (4) an attempt to dignify the Negro's "religion, the passion of its human sorrow, and the struggle of its greater souls"; and (5) his recording of oral narrative into a canon for American culture. Clearly, this is intended as text of cultural observation. This architecture of *Souls* has been described as a *Bildungsbiographie* (an educational text composed of multidisciplined narratives) (Zamir, 1995, p. 100). I wish to go further and flesh out the aesthetic dimensions of this educational work for two reasons: It articulates the attainment of freedom through art and, at the same time, teaches us how to adjust our judgments of taste in order to receive its message.

For example, in the chapter titled "Of the Training of Black Men," Du Bois writes that the highest goal of education is to develop empowered individuals:

Above our modern socialism, and out of the worship of the mass, must persist and evolve that higher individualism which the centers of culture protect; there must be a loftier respect for the sovereign human soul that seeks
to know itself and the world about it; that seeks a freedom for expansion
and self-development; that will love and hate and labor in its own way, untrammeled alike by old and new. Such souls aforetime have inspired and
guided worlds, and . . . they shall again. (1903/1994, p. 66)

Du Bois does not think that all people are capable of reaching this lofty
"higher individualism." However, he does believe that the *opportunity* to
aim in this direction should be made available to the Negro. Du Bois articulates his idea of how an elite few might ascend to these sovereign ranks in
his controversial essay "The Talented Tenth" (1940/1986, p. 842). In his
view, this group will help carry the message of a people forward in order to
help cultivate a truly diverse, cosmopolitan culture in the United States. He
calls this message of a people its "gifts" (1903/1994, p. 163). Given the growing ethnic diversity of the United States, Du Bois thought that there could
and should be a sharing of cultural gifts in the name of a genuinely pluralistic,
democratic life.[9] Yet these gifts could not be properly presented or received
because of an existential orientation that all oppressed people unconsciously
or consciously suffered, a malady Du Bois termed "double-consciousness"
(1903/1994, p. 2).

For Du Bois, the double-consciousness of the American Negro people
sprang from the strange identity they were offered by Lincoln's 1863 Emancipation Proclamation. Extracted from their homeland to be made into
machinelike animals for the promotion of the United States's economic growth,
enslaved for more than 2½ centuries, American Negroes were now, in one
fell swoop, asked to think of themselves as free American citizens. However,
as mentioned earlier, neither citizenship nor education can be established by
fiat. Achievement of an empowered identity, full citizenship, and community responsibility would necessitate traveling a rough and "rugged" road:

Here at last seemed to have been discovered the mountain path to Canaan;
longer than the highway of Emancipation and law, steep and rugged, but
straight, leading to heights high enough to overlook life. (1903/1994, p. 5)

But before education could do its work, Du Bois knew that the fundamental reality of the American Negro had to be understood. One way in which
he illuminated this was through his familiar metaphor of the Veil. How were
Negroes to be counted as American when they were constantly reminded that
they were less than human because of the color of their skin? How could these
"nigger" folk work, sing, and dance with hope of a better life, when they did
not know how to study and compete in the society into which they were suddenly thrown? The complex and nuanced metaphor of the Veil represented

the constant multiple barriers the American Negro was to meet on the way to achieving full citizenship: racial prejudice, cultural divides, self-doubt, and the inability to see and think clearly in a chaotic world. In general, it marks a perceptual divide and represents a form of denied recognition. *Veil* is not simply a word to connote the reality of prejudice and segregation; it refers to a fundamental moral condition that Du Bois wants the reader to imagine and feel. The Veil is an ontological fabric that obscures sight from within and hides the wearer from clear recognition from those outside. Thus, the Veil partitions off the life-world of Opportunity (1994, p. 3). For Du Bois, White America is blind to the Negro's humanity and thus shuts the Negro off from what humanity deserves. At the same time, Black America is blind to its own potential gifts, powers, and promise, and so fails to grasp its historical moment generated by emancipation. All this is implied in his concept of the Veil, which works to have the reader feel the weight of the oppressive, existential question that opens the book: "How does it feel to be a problem?" (1903/1994, p. 1).

In *Souls*—with the elements of the problematic Negro soul enumerated, its unrealized gifts, double-consciousness, and veiled perceptions defined— Du Bois offers an educational philosophy that keeps these elements in dynamic tension even as he proposes a solution in the form of a classical liberal arts education. For him, the liberal arts path best responds to the underlying existential and moral conditions that give rise to the "problem of the color line." From one point of view, his abiding commitment to the liberal arts is no surprise, since such an education was historically intended to cultivate free citizens. However, in *Souls*, Du Bois transfigures the idea of the liberal arts in order to address head on the Negro's yearning for genuine liberation and fulfillment. Thus, in this book, the young, broadly educated American Negro in a troubled society responded to the challenge of his people and his time with a forward-looking educational philosophy.

## THE EMPOWERING VISION OF DU BOIS'S EDUCATIONAL PHILOSOPHY

### Education for Freedom

Liberal arts education, an education begetting free thinking, is an ancient discipline that Du Bois strongly advocated. In *Souls*, he writes of this approach to education as the means by which human thinking has always strived to emancipate itself from mental stasis and delve deeper into the meaning of life:

> Nothing new. No time-saving devices,—simply old time-glorified methods of delving for Truth, and searching out the hidden beauties of life, and learning the good of living. The riddle of existence is the college curriculum that was laid before the Pharaohs, that was taught in the groves by Plato, that formed

the *trivium* and *quadrivium,* and is today laid before the freedmen's sons by Atlanta University. And this course of study will not change; its methods will grow more deft and effectual, its content richer by toil of scholar and sight of seer; but the true college will ever have one goal,—not to earn meat, but to know the end and aim of that life which meat nourishes. (1903/1994, p. 51)

Guided by the principles of what the Greeks called the True, the Good, and the Beautiful, the liberal arts curriculum represents these "riddle[s] of existence" as best it can. The curriculum—literally, "the course" of study—constitutes more than amassing fact and information. It is not rigid in substance or presentation, since its methods and contents are always changing. What makes the liberal arts curriculum unique and powerful as a path to freedom is the *receptive attitude* it takes to learnable things. That attitude responds to the fact that the very meanings of truth, goodness, and beauty are constantly under adjustment as humans come in contact with one another.

For Du Bois, the American experiment, made up of diverse, pluralistic understandings, best comes to possess its unique, democratic identity by attempting to foster a mode of orientation that is receptive to the new. This posture includes being receptive to what each person can contribute to the preservation and expansion of the nation's principles of life, liberty, and the pursuit of happiness. As he writes in *Souls*, "Freedom, too, the long-sought, we still seek,—the freedom of life and limb, the freedom to work and think, the freedom to love and aspire. Work, culture, liberty, all these we need" (1903/1994, p. 7).

This receptive attitude toward readjustment is Du Bois's pragmatic rendering of the humanistic orientation of the liberal arts. However, Du Bois is aware that there is a challenge in transforming a discriminatory society into one that is receptive to all people. First, in order to open oneself to this vantage point, one must toil—"delve," as Du Bois states in the quotation above—to attain the substantive realities of the true, good, and beautiful. Du Bois reminds us that at the heart of a liberal arts education is "book-learning" (1903/1994, p. 5), a suggestive term whose etymological meaning he plays with in Latin: *liber* (book) and *liberates* (to set free).[10] Charting the 4 decades following the Emancipation Proclamation, Du Bois signals that the Negro's complicated spiritual striving for freedom could now be enhanced by the ideal of "book-learning." In other words, as the 19th century drew to a close, Du Bois believed that the time had come when education in general, and a liberal arts education in particular, offered an important path to spiritual and political freedom for the Negro race. Indeed, what the Negro gains by the toil of "book-learning" are the fundamental elements of freedom. Du Bois writes:

To the tired climbers, the horizon was ever dark, the mists were often cold, the Canaan was always dim and far away. If, however the vistas disclosed as yet no goal, no resting-place, little but flattery and criticism, the journey at least gave leisure for reflection and self-examination; it changed the child of Emancipation to the youth with dawning self-consciousness, self-realization, self-respect. (1903/1994, p. 5)

With the birth of self-consciousness and meaning made possible through "book-learning" and liberal arts education, Du Bois believed, the Negro would begin to understand the "burden he bore on his back," feeling his problems of social degradation, poverty, and ignorance and the weight of systematic crimes committed against him (1903/1994, p. 5). The Negro would gain insight, perspective, and knowledge that could usher in new ideas and actions in the face of widespread societal constraints and violence. At the same time, however, Du Bois emphasizes that "education among all kinds of men always has had, and always will have, an element of danger and revolution, of dissatisfaction and discontent" (1903/1994, p. 20). Du Bois knows that if the Negro critically examines his debased status, he might put up arms and fight the fundamental crimes of slavery and racism with violence, or take mental and spiritual flight from the nation's problem because he feels it is too overwhelming for him to do anything about it. For Du Bois, therefore, "book-learning" is a double-edged sword, bringing both freedom of thought and grave, tragic revelations for the Negro consciousness. He charts a difficult course between an education that would simply alienate the Negro further from society, and an education that would infuse the Negro with a new self-understanding, new self-respect, and new self-reliance.

As stated above, *Souls* is a work of educational philosophy that prepares the reader to receive its message. This claim echoes the ancient Greek idea that tragic drama is educational. Tragedy plays on the spectators' sense and sensibilities. In time it can transform them, converting the spectator into a participant in society—a participant who now cares more substantively for the future of his or her fellow beings, who brings to society a deeper, chastened compassion as well as determination to alter conditions that lead to tragedy. Du Bois is acutely aware of these classical Greek notions when he writes the tragic drama in the penultimate chapter of *Souls,* "Of the Coming of John." In the following section I will touch on this chapter's place in the architecture of *Souls*, linking it with the fact that Du Bois opens every each chapter in his book with one or more bars from a Negro spiritual song. From this analysis, we will take up one of Du Bois's larger educational themes: the creation of culture through aesthetic education.

## The Aesthetic Education of Humanity

In "Of the Coming of John," Du Bois writes about a Black boy named John who leaves the South to get educated in the North, only to return to his ruin and early death, just as the townspeople in the South (both Black and White)

predicted he would if he was foolhardy enough to enter another world supposedly not meant for him.[11] John's fate reveals a double tragedy: how the
Whites are sunk in their racist belief that Blacks don't merit and can't "use"
an education, and how Blacks are so oppressed beneath the Veil that they
too can't envision a "why-for" for gaining formal education. The tragic end,
in which racist attitudes find violent expression, and those oppressed by violence heroically accept their seemingly grim fate, is a resounding apex to the
wrought drama. The narrative's climactic end is arresting, but it immediately
gives rise to possibility. At our most vulnerable moment as readers, shattered
by the brutal end of John's hopeful life, Du Bois elects in the very next chapter of *Souls* to reveal the origins of those mysterious bars of music he places
at the beginning of each of the book's 14 chapters.

In the final chapter of *Souls*, he tells us that the "Sorrow Songs" carry
the message of a people who are heavy of heart but full of hope that one
day, "men will judge men by their souls and not by their skins" (1903/1994,
p. 162). Furthermore, Du Bois makes the bold claim that these Sorrow Songs
are the "sole [authentic] American music" and the most "beautiful expression of human experience born this side of the seas" (1903/1994, p. 156). In
his view, the songs are part of the gift of the Negro people to American culture.[12] The gift is not simply the singing of songs, but the message and the expression of human experience they express. This gift of the American Negro,
for Du Bois, constitutes the first genuinely aesthetic mark of American culture. To place the Sorrow Songs at the center of American culture is to place
the long, hard-fought struggle of a people for the very meaning of freedom as
*the* struggle of American society. For Du Bois, the songs epitomize beyond any
"Star-Spangled Banner" or waving flag, however revered, the fundamental
yearning for freedom that is at the heart of true American ideals. The Sorrow
Songs are, then, the freedom music of America, for it is those songs that always envisioned a better place for all in potent, poignant terms.

With this example of the American Negro's distinct music, Du Bois
suggests that the aesthetic education of humanity is what begets the creation
of moral culture. In his view, aesthetic education is the formation of the realities disclosed by liberal education. Since it is liberal education that allowed
for the sharing of gifts through its receptive attitude, there must be a formative power that shapes receptivity. Aesthetic education is the cultivation of
receptivity. As such, aesthetic education points to the possibility of moral
culture. This is why Du Bois says that the Sorrow Songs carry a message that
shatters prejudice:

> The silently growing assumption of this age is that the probation of the races
> is past, and that the backward races of to-day are of proven inefficiency and
> not worth the saving. Such an assumption is the arrogance of peoples irrever-
> ent toward Time and ignorant of the deeds of men. (1994, p. 162)

The aesthetic education into the Sorrow Songs allows for moral culture to emerge. By placing a bar or two of the Sorrow Songs at the beginning of each chapter, little by little Du Bois is trying to form our moral orientation. It is the revelation of the Negro aesthetic here in the Sorrow Songs that grounds the possibility of American democratic society to become a morally conscious culture.

Thus, *The Souls of Black Folk* as a text on the aesthetic education of humanity outlines the belief that the liberal arts prepare the way for a truly receptive human being to exist in the first place. The aesthetically educated person, shaped by a study of the liberal arts, can see clearly above false, conventional dichotomies as symbolized by the Veil. For Du Bois, seeing above false dichotomies positions people to create in "the kingdom of culture" that is the distinctively moral, human realm on the planet (1903/1994, p. 5). In one of the most quoted passages of *Souls*, Du Bois writes,

> I sit with Shakespeare and he winces not. Across the color line I move arm in arm with Balzac and Dumas, where smiling men and welcoming women glide in gilded halls. From out the caves of evening that swing between the strong-limbed earth and the tracery of the stars, I summon Aristotle and Aurelius and what soul I will, and they come all graciously with no scorn nor conde-scension. So, wed with Truth, I dwell above the Veil. (1903/1994, p. 67)

Du Bois aspires here to be in an ahistorical, atemporal, aracial, transcendent space with other great minds. The movement in his picturesque portrait symbolizes liberation, for it reaches beyond unnecessary existential divisions. What begets this movement for Du Bois is classical education. His "book-learning" (*liber*), constituted by his imaginative recalling of a range of poets and philosophers, is the genesis of his freedom (*liberates*), which is evidenced by his choice words of *smiling, gliding, swinging,* and *dwelling*. He evokes a culture above the Veil where all can move "arm in arm." Du Bois believes that this moral possibility borne out of aesthetic education is precisely the message the Negro race has to offer America.

### Booker T. Washington in a New Light

Most works that address Du Bois's educational philosophy present his educational thought as deeply commingled with that of Booker T. Washington. Moreover, *The Souls of Black Folk* is often regarded as Du Bois's impassioned reaction and alternative to what he perceived as Washington's narrow ideas. It is, therefore, important to address the differences in these two important thinkers as a means of deepening our understanding of Du Bois's philosophy of education.

As the inscription on the Booker T. Washington monument, called Lifting the Veil, at Tuskegee University makes clear, Washington "lifted the veil of ignorance from his people and pointed the way to progress through education and industry."[13] Indeed, Washington's version of progress was predicated on industrial training, while Du Bois's conception of progress called for liberal arts education. Both were cognizant of the same problem, but what became clear as their debate developed is that the two had different presumptions about what course the creation of both Negro and American culture should take. However, their respective emphases need not be seen as mutually exclusive, since each sought to conceive how the gifts of the American Negro could best be realized.

Understanding that Negroes would have to learn how to compete with their White counterparts, in his educational thinking Washington called for racial uplift by means of economic stability in American society. He sought to transform what once was degrading slave labor into industrious, self-respecting, paid work. His educational program aimed to readjust the Negro's perception of material life, taking account of food, shelter, and mobility. In order to build community and remove the Negro from the center of political conflict, since Negroes were often physical targets of violent ramifications, he accommodated the segregationist idea underlying of mostly southern ways of thinking, evidenced in his 1895 "Atlanta Compromise." His belief in the construction of a segregated society gained strong support from politicians and he became widely accepted by Blacks and Whites as the voice of the Negro race. Washington's vocational educational program was accepted by many, White and Black alike, as the solution to the Negro problem.

Du Bois worked with Washington at the beginning of the former's academic career and was even offered a teaching position twice (1894 and 1902) at Tuskegee Institute in Alabama during Washington's presidency of the college (1881–1915). However, Du Bois gradually grew suspicious of Washington's accommodationist position on Negro education.[14] It was that very attitude that Du Bois wanted to combat, not the notion that some individuals may be best suited or interested in life-sustaining pursuits other than contemplation and studying great books (1903/1994, p. 54). As stated above, for Du Bois, the Negro was gaining ground in apprehending the "kingdom of culture," however slowly, after Emancipation, and it was this book-learning that would usher in a true revolution in Negro consciousness and American culture. In contrast, he regarded Washington's accommodationist standpoint as unsuitable for sparking and sustaining a heightened consciousness of culture creation. For Du Bois, the Negro must press onward with books in hand and with eyes on the Promised Land. He bitingly asks,

> Is this the life you grudge us, O knightly America? Is this the life you long to change into the dull red hideousness of Georgia? Are you so afraid lest peering from your high Pisgah, between Philistine and Amalekite, we sight the Promised Land? (1903/1994, p. 67)

Du Bois's disagreements with Washington deepened his resolve and presaged his eventual disenchantment with the United States itself. He became impatient with what he saw as complacency, as well as complicity, on the part of Whites and Blacks alike, with a political and economic system that valued stability and comfort more than justice. His many travels abroad after World War II, especially to the so-called developing world, only heightened his alienation from a nation he saw as losing its soul through its fixation on the Cold War and on consumerism, both reflections of economic power and competitiveness rather than the humanistic culture he had hoped for. In 1963, Du Bois became a citizen of Ghana and settled there for the remainder of his days. In one of those anomalies of life where the ironies of reality are far stranger than fiction, Du Bois passed away on the eve of the greatest civil rights march in American history, on August 27, 1963.

## FINDING DU BOIS TODAY

Although he turned away from his country in the end, Du Bois left behind an enduring legacy. For example, his vision of the Negro race and its gifts for humanity had an immense impact on one of America's most remarkable cultural movements, the Harlem Renaissance (1920–1930). Centered in New York, energetic groups of Negro writers, artists, scholars, and politicians created an empowered culture of personal expression. At the heart of this movement was the high value it placed on the aesthetic education of Black Americans to promote social and cultural change. The movement is indebted to the sustained, poetic efforts of Du Bois to dignify book-learning and inspire what he called "a catholicity of taste" in all who would create culture in the world. The manifold aesthetic flowerings of the Harlem Renaissance, represented by Countee Cullen, Zora Neale Hurston, and Langston Hughes, to name but a few, have had an incalculable influence on White and Black perceptions of the capabilities of a once-enslaved people (Appiah & Gates, 1999, p. 926).

Du Bois's enduring place in American social and educational thinking is also evident institutionally. The Du Bois College House (University of Pennsylvania), the W.E.B. Du Bois Institute for African and African American Research (Harvard University), and the Du Bois Library (Amherst College) are only a few of the places where serious study of his legacy continues. Moreover, as indicated at the start of the chapter, there has been considerable scholarly attention to his life and work. Recent studies range from a Pulitzer Prize–winning biography (Lewis, 2000) and analyses of his philosophical, sociological, and historical work on American society (Outlaw, 2000; Zamir, 1995), to the realization of Du Bois's encyclopedia *Africana* (Appiah & Gates, 1999).

Most of Du Bois's explicit educational philosophy centers on the function of Negro colleges and universities, and his legacy continues to thrive
in these settings.[15] Their curricula continue to mirror Du Bois's argument
that the seven classical liberal arts (*trivium* and *quadrivium*) should help
guide the Negro college and university, for such institutions are "to be the
organ[s] of that fine adjustment between real life and the growing knowledge of life, an adjustment which forms the secret of civilization" (1903/
1994, p. 52).

Du Bois's pragmatic and poetic vision of the liberal arts finds expression in the mission statements of many historically Black institutions of higher
education. For example, the Fisk University mission statement includes the
following passage:

> Fisk also is committed to involving both its faculty and its most advanced
> students in original research—since the passing on of the liberal arts tradi-
> tion is not merely the transmission of dead or static knowledge; rather
> the liberal arts tradition involves the recognition that knowledge is continu-
> ally developing. . . . The ultimate goal is to prepare students to be skilled,
> resourceful, and imaginative leaders who will address effectively the challenges
> of life in a technological society, a pluralistic nation, and a multicultural
> world.[16]

One of the most time-honored, if today hard-pressed, liberal arts is music.
It is perhaps the most ancient liberal art, and yet today is often the first to go
in American schools when budgets are tight. Du Bois argued in *Souls* that a
signal gift of the Negro, the world-historical "seventh" race, as he puts it
(1903/1994, p. 2), is its extraordinary expression of music, which is one of
the seven classical liberating arts. That legacy, too, continues at such institutions as Fisk.

Furthermore, Du Bois makes clear that one of the functions of the Negro
college is to *gather* a once-dispersed people back together again. His notion of
gathering has strong ethical overtones in that he regards the Negro colleges as
places for truly forming individuals. In the wake of formal emancipation, Du
Bois writes, the Negro colleges can function as "social settlements" (1903/1994,
p. 62). I have argued elsewhere (Anderson, 2006) that these communities offered more than the toil of letters, crucial as that was; they also fostered supportive communities that could shape character itself. Moreover, as V. S.
Walker (1996) reminds us, educational institutions for Black Americans before the civil rights era often provided spaces for more than just pushing back
against a still-racist society. Rather, they provided genuinely formative environments characterized by what Du Bois called the creation of culture.

Regarding elementary and secondary education, Du Bois's belief in the
formation of moral character can be seen at places such as the Talented Tenth

Academy and the W.E.B. Du Bois Scholars Institute, both in Brunswick, New Jersey.[17] Both institutions strive to form good character and leadership qualities in their students so as to meet the challenges that face many African American and Latino American communities. These institutions for high school students evoke the reciprocal relationship of moral character and community that Du Bois articulated in his writing on education.

Although Du Bois's educational philosophy is mostly mirrored in higher educational practice, he leaves us with imaginative ways of conceiving K–12 education. In particular, the curriculum that many public school students undertake in this country has its roots in liberal arts education. Required math, science, reading, social studies, and history courses aim at molding a well-rounded student. What we often forget is that these many fields of human endeavor are guided by the search for truth, goodness, and beauty. The subject matters, Du Bois would say, are deep expressions of human searching that are under constant renewal. They cannot be conceived just as an accumulation of facts that remain static. In this way, a distinctly American curriculum as an expression of human striving should be open to multiple voices. As we have seen, Du Bois championed the inclusion of the marginalized perspective of the African American as fundamental to the understanding of American letters. His provocative insights allowed for the birth of something we might call multicultural education.

Moreover, his demonstration of the Sorrow Songs as a canon of American culture places moral possibilities at the center of American education. From a Du Boisian vantage point, we should rightly be unsettled by the constant cutbacks in arts education, especially in predominantly impoverished socioeconomic areas. Perhaps the arts are viewed solely as forms of entertainment. However, Du Bois makes clear that freedom of expression is necessary for a genuine democratic culture to flourish.

## CONCLUSION

This chapter has touched on one aspect of Du Bois's multifaceted career and life, namely, his philosophy of education as expressed through his seminal work, *The Souls of Black Folk*. As we have seen, he sought in that work to confront in a frank, critical manner the pervasive injustices of slavery and racism in America. He sought to contrast this grim legacy with a vision of the possible, one that echoes the spirit of promise in the nation's founding documents such as the Declaration of Independence and the Gettysburg Address. Most important, he sought to include in that promise an educational path to moral, spiritual, and political freedom. For him, that path was the humanizing study of the liberal arts. While Du Bois himself concluded, perhaps tragically if also with reason, that the "possible" was in fact improbable, his writings surpass him in ways he might have found delightful. As we live with his legacy through the ongoing struggle of Black "souls" in America, we find that in the richness of his thought and action, W.E.B. Du Bois's own "gifts" of culture continue to show us how to create culture in our time.

PART II

# Political Pressures, Educational Responses

C H A P T E R   F O U R

# Value Creation as the Aim of Education: Tsunesaburo Makiguchi and Soka Education

**Andrew Gebert and Monte Joffee**

THE IDEAS OF Japanese educator and philosopher Tsunesaburo Makiguchi (1871–1944) have had an enduring impact in Japan and elsewhere in the world. His influence, which would not have seemed likely at the time of his death, occurred through two related developments. One has been the post-war revitalization and growth of the movement he established in 1930, the Soka Kyoiku Gakkai (Value Creation Educational Society). This has grown into today's Soka Gakkai (Value Creation Society), a lay Buddhist organization that is the largest and most influential movement of its kind in Japan, and the Soka Gakkai International (SGI), which claims memberships in 190 countries and territories. The second development has been the growth of a global movement known as Soka (value-creating) education. These are all the more remarkable because during his lifetime Makiguchi's ideas failed to gain widespread acceptance. His educational and religious convictions, a fundamental critique of the period of Japanese militaristic nationalism prior to and including World War II (1931–1945),[1] led to his arrest as a thought criminal and death in prison. The tensions between Makiguchi's ideas and the dominant ideologies in Japan predated this final confrontation, however. Thus, Makiguchi's life serves as a cogent example of how imposed societal regimentation can become a crucible for the development of individuals capable of giving birth to powerful ideas.

Central to Makiguchi's educational approach is his philosophy of value, which stresses the importance of human agency in creating the values of "beauty, gain, and good" to enhance the personal and collective lives of people. Makiguchi positions the creation of value as the ultimate purpose of human existence, defining a happy life as one in which the capacity to discover and create value has been fully deployed. Considering the lifelong happiness of learners to be the authentic goal of education, he structured his educational philosophy and efforts toward developing the value-creating potentialities of students.

Soka education has been refined and given institutional form by Makiguchi's successors, Josei Toda (1900–1958) and Daisaku Ikeda (1928–  ). In its practice today, Soka education is a secular approach that contains elements of curriculum, pedagogy, professional development, and standards for interpersonal relationships within schools; it embraces aspects of both progressive and traditional educational ideologies. Soka education is grounded in a belief common to most humanistic philosophies and religions. Among them Nichiren Buddhism, which Makiguchi came to embrace, holds that a determined individual has the inherent ability to significantly influence the interconnected web of life. Nichiren Buddhism rests on qualities such as hope, courage, and compassion—qualities that cross philosophical and religious lines. Soka education emphasizes and nurtures the idea that students should live out their lives as the protagonists of both personal and societal transformation.

Today, examples of Soka education can be found in a network of more than a dozen schools that stretch across three continents and that cover a range from kindergarten to university. It has inspired several independent private schools, such as the Soka Ikeda College of Arts and Science for Women, attached to Madras University in Chennai, India, and educational initiatives such as Brazil's Makiguchi Project in Action (de Melo Silva, 2000). Most significant, Soka education informs the professional endeavors of thousands of "Soka educators," who are inspired by its theories and seek to apply them in a variety of educational settings.

## MAKIGUCHI'S LIFE: THE PURSUIT OF VALUE

Dayle M. Bethel has been largely responsible for introducing the life and ideas of Makiguchi to the English-speaking world. His intensive research on Makiguchi began in 1969 and culminated in the publication of a biographical work, *Makiguchi the Value Creator* (Bethel 1973) and in later editions and translations of Makiguchi's major works (Bethel, 1930/1989, 1903/2002).

The descriptor "the value creator," ascribed to Makiguchi by Bethel, is apt because it reflects the centrality of value creation to Makiguchi's pedagogical work. It was a concern that was apparent in his early experiences and research and that continued to draw his interest through to his activities in the last decade of his life.

Makiguchi's felt need to create value was perhaps shaped by the historical setting in which he lived and the particular circumstances of his youth. Makiguchi was born during the early days of the Meiji period (1868–1912), which marked the end of Japan's feudalistic and isolationist policies and its rapid transformation from an agrarian into an industrial society. The population of the small coastal village where Makiguchi was raised experienced significant dislocation during this time of transition. Governmental pressure to increase farm output resulted in a farmer rebellion that was forcibly suppressed by the authorities and led to the execution of seven farmers (S. Ikeda, cited in Bethel, 1994). Raised by an uncle after his father deserted the family and his mother felt incapable of caring for him, Makiguchi's unsettled early life matched the turbulence of his times.

Makiguchi's own education took place in the midst of the cross currents of Japanese historical transformation as well. Japan's first national system of compulsory education was instituted in 1870, an event followed by the Education Law of 1872, which declared that the purpose of education was to enable students to lead fulfilling lives (Kumagai, 2000, p. 33). In the decades that followed, official Japanese educational policy underwent rapid shifts of direction, culminating in the Imperial Rescript on Education of 1890, which went so far as to codify the purpose of education as the production of subjects loyal to the emperor and the state (Kumagai, 2000, pp. 33–34). Although there is often a gap between an intended curriculum and what is actually taught in a classroom (Cuban, 1992), Makiguchi's early schooling took place during a time when educational policies that stressed the development of children's rational and critical faculties held sway; the curriculum in the prefecture where Makiguchi attended elementary school contained elements of a very open and enlightened approach to education (Saito, 1981, pp. 302–303). Receiving only the short formal primary education that was standard at the time, Makiguchi worked in his uncle's shipping enterprise ("Tsunesaburo Makiguchi," 1996). It is possible to conjecture that the informal education he received from this hands-on and community-based work shaped his later views on the need to fuse practical experience in life with structured processes of learning.

In later years Makiguchi often found himself on precarious ledges—geographical, educational, and spiritual—from which he was compelled to "create value." At the age of 14, he emigrated by himself across the Tsugaru Strait to the frontier region of Hokkaido, Japan's northernmost island. Then, at 30, with a young family in tow, he moved from Hokkaido to Tokyo with the ambition of publishing his studies on geography, as will be discussed below. Later, as an elementary school principal, he took great personal and professional risks in challenging the inequities and dehumanization of Japanese primary education. Finally, during the years leading to World War II, he confronted the spiritual regimentation of Japan in which the militarist government forced State Shinto religion and emperor worship on the entire population through acts of injecting this official dogma into the most intimate spheres of people's lives.

Creating value out of difficult circumstances is an arduous process. From a young age Makiguchi faced challenges with both courage and integrity. For example, upon moving to Hokkaido, he worked as an errand boy in the police department of the city of Otaru, where his hard work quickly earned him the respect of his superiors. Saito (1989, p. 760) documents that the Otaru civil service was rife with nepotism and patronage and Makiguchi's ties with influential local people could have surely led to advancement in the ranks of Hokkaido administration, business, or politics. Instead of choosing this route, however, Makiguchi enrolled in the Sapporo Normal School, a training school for teachers.

After graduating, Makiguchi taught for 4 years in a "multigrade classroom," a Japanese experimental equivalent of the American rural one-room schoolhouse (Kumagai, 1978, p. 35; Sharma, 1998, p. 11).[2] Beyond his classroom work, he demonstrated a commitment to reaching out to other teachers, publishing frequently in the local educational publication, *The Journal of the Association for Education in the Region of Hokkaido.* In 1898, as an editor of the journal, he came to be regarded as a leading figure among his colleagues (Kumagai, 1978, p. 33; Sharma, 1998, pp. 11–12).

During this time he also taught at the normal school from which he had graduated, and in this work he demonstrated a strong sense of justice. Saito (1989, p. 765) traces school and student records surrounding an incident in which Makiguchi supported a large group of students who struck against several excessively oppressive school policies. As a consequence of their actions, 43 students, out of a class of 50, were dismissed from the program and Makiguchi resigned in apparent protest.

While in Hokkaido, Makiguchi also undertook an intensive study of geography, which led to his concept of "the geography of human life" (*jinsei chirigaku*). Rather than merely examine physical geography, Makiguchi probed the dynamic relationship between geography and the psychological aspects of human life. Bethel describes in poetic language the picture of life he believes Makiguchi envisioned: "The earth, for Makiguchi, was a miracle. Life was a miracle, and he saw life vibrating through all phenomena" (1903/2002, p. xiv). Makiguchi held that education based on an awareness of the connections between human life and the natural and social environment could help develop the moral character of students. He hoped that people educated this way would construct an interdependent and harmonious world wherein military and economic competition between nations would be supplanted by "humanitarian competition" based on a recognition of mutual interests and benefit.

His research resulted in the 1903 publication of *A Geography of Human Life,* which was to become a standard text in Japanese teacher education. In 1910 Makiguchi became a field researcher for the Ministry of Education and in 1912 published *Research into Community Studies as the Integrating Focus of Instruction.* According to Saito (1989, pp. 771–772), Makiguchi's scholarship earned him the respect of several prominent scholars, government officials, freelance intellectuals, and journalists who met regularly as a group called the Group for the Study of Local Communities (Kyodokai). With his reputation and record of scholarship, he was able to obtain an elementary school principal's appointment in Tokyo. However, rather than use his connections to seek a plush assignment, he chose a position at an elementary school in a poor neighborhood that also included the duties of managing a night school.

Makiguchi continued to develop his philosophy of value through his educational praxis. S. Ikeda (1969), Bethel (1994), and Saito (1981, 1989) develop a portrait of him as an educator by piecing together school records and impressions of his former students and colleagues. What emerges is a profile of a stern and dignified person who was also extremely kind and deeply aware of the difficult circumstances of his students (Bethel, 1994, p. 39). As a teacher in Hokkaido, he would greet students in the morning with warm water for their cold hands and escort them home when it was snowing (D. Ikeda, 2006, p. 13). Makiguchi prepared meals of bread and soup for the children whose parents could not provide them with lunch and he discretely placed the food in the janitor's room so that needy students would not feel ashamed (D. Ikeda, 2006, p. 14). He is said to have bought stationery at reduced prices from wholesalers for his students' use (Kumagai, 1978, p. 60; Sharma, 1998, pp. 14–15). He also had strong regard for parental involvement and conducted many home visits (Kumagai, 1978, p. 60; Sharma, 1998, p. 15). It is documented that in schools under his leadership there was a considerable decrease in the numbers of cases of both juvenile delinquency and skin disease (Kumagai, 1978, p. 66; Sharma, 1998, p. 15). Makiguchi's school leadership style was controversial, however, because he refused to honor the favoritism and privileges that were typically accorded to the children of wealthy and influential families.

Thus, as seen through his career as an elementary school principal, the main outline of Makiguchi's personality comes into view: an impassioned drive to study and create change, a deep empathy for students, a willingness to take risks, and a desire to construct pioneering theories to explain sociological phenomena. Saito (1989) uses the term "radicalist" to describe Makiguchi's independent and critical frame of mind. In Saito's usage, this term suggests a clear demarcation from the word *radical,* which is frequently ascribed to political orientations that often ossified in Japan into rigid dogma. Although during his early years in Tokyo Makiguchi conducted dialogues with a group of socialists committed to democracy and pacifism (Miyata, 2000, p. 23), he did not agree with their call to break down existing systems (Makiguchi, 1983–1988, vol. 6, pp. 22–24).[3] Rather, Makiguchi continued to choose to be a change agent working within established structures. By temperament, and as an elementary school principal by profession, forbidden by law from participating in political activities (Gluck, 1985, p. 52), Makiguchi always kept in mind what could be realistically implemented. His "radicalist" vision of the way the world should be was always balanced with a keen pragmatic awareness of how it actually was. The dynamic tension between these two aspects of his thinking—radicalist and pragmatic—gave rise to an approach to educational reform that was at once visionary, gradualist, and doggedly determined.

Starting in 1913, for almost 20 years, Makiguchi served as the head of five different schools and became known as a gifted and dedicated educator; his work, in fact, attracted the attention of several prominent liberal thinkers of that time (Bethel, 1994, pp. 95–96).[4] Under his leadership, the Shirogane primary school, in particular, rose to a level of prominence (Kumagai, 1978, pp. 66–67). Many parents living outside the school district apparently wished to have their children transferred to the school and were willing to pay extra fees to this end (Makiguchi, 1983–1988, vol. 6, p. 92). During this time, he continued to develop his educational theories about value creation, which were to form the basis of his most important work, *The System of Value-Creating Pedagogy* (Soka kyoikugaku taikei), published in 1930. Makiguchi's understanding of happiness as the goal of both life and education begins with the recognition that although humans cannot create matter:

> What we can create, however, is value and value only. When we praise persons for their "strength of character," we are really acknowledging their superior ability to create value. (1983–1988, vol. 5, p. 13; in Bethel, 1989, p. 6)

Unfortunately, at the time of the publication, Makiguchi's book did not receive the attention or have the kind of impact for which he had hoped. After repeated clashes with educational authorities, Makiguchi was forcibly retired from his final school principalship in 1931.

A few years prior to this, in 1928, at the age of 57, Makiguchi had embraced Nichiren Buddhism. The conversion was not the result of a solitary epiphany but a gradual process that occurred in the course of sustained and intense discussions with a fellow principal, Sokei Mitani. Mitani convinced Makiguchi that the spirituality of Nichiren's teachings rose above mere personal sentiment; was aligned with rational, scientific, universal laws; and was meant to be fully engaged and integrated with the realities of life in society (Sato, 2000, pp. 53–54). Makiguchi saw a strong and natural connection between his new spiritual interest in Buddhism and his previous work in developing his philosophy of value:

> When, however, I reached the point of encountering the Lotus Sutra, I was astonished to discover that it in no way contradicted the scientific and philosophical principles which form the basis for our daily lives. . . . With a joy that is beyond the power of words to express, I have completely renewed the way of life I had pursued for almost sixty years. (1983–1988, vol. 7, pp. 405–406)

It is clear that, for Makiguchi, this newfound Buddhist faith provided a powerful spiritual grounding for the implementation of his educational and philosophical theories. Rejecting either a solitary or temple-centered spiritual practice, Makiguchi founded an independent lay organization, the Value Creation Educational Society (Soka Kyoiku Gakkai) to promote the practice of Nichiren Buddhism among educators and others with the goal of enhancing the ability of people to create value. Increasing the number of people skilled at creating value would realize Makiguchi's stated educational goals as well as his vision for society.

A decade earlier, Makiguchi had developed a close relationship with a young teacher, Josei Toda (1900–1958), becoming the younger man's mentor. The two came to collaborate in a mentor-disciple relationship to develop Makiguchi's pedagogical theories. For example, after teaching in two of Makiguchi's schools, in 1923 Toda established a private school, the Jisshu Gakkan, largely to implement Makiguchi's pedagogical theories free of the government's ever-present interference in public schools (D. Ikeda, 1968). Makiguchi, in turn, referred to the Jisshu Gakkan as the realization of his own vision for elementary schools and as the greatest realization of his work (D. Ikeda, 2001, p. 86). Toda also helped edit Makiguchi's writings, a task made nearly impossible by the older man's commitments as a full-time principal. Makiguchi's expectations for Toda's future role are clear from this comment he is recorded as having shared with family members:

> In the future, there will be a school system that puts the methods of value-creating education into practice. It will span kindergarten to university level. Young Toda will see to it that my work is carried on. (D. Ikeda, 2006, p. 86)

After his retirement, Makiguchi concentrated his efforts on developing the Soka Kyoiku Gakkai, which was to grow to a membership of about 3,000 people by the start of the war in 1941. His people-centered message and the growth of his following attracted the interest of the Japanese Special Higher Police (Tokko) and his movements were subject to constant surveillance (Japanese Special, 1943a, p. 127). This led to direct intimidation, beginning in the early 1940s, as Tokko officers conspicuously attended many of his speaking engagements and interrupted him when he strayed from government-sanctioned positions. Undeterred, Makiguchi kept up an intense schedule of travel and speaking.

Makiguchi was adamant in his stand against the collusion of Japanese political, military, and religious authority that wedded national policies to the cult of emperor worship embodied in the rites of State Shinto. Makiguchi opposed such official policies and beliefs even when virtually the entire religious and intellectual establishment of Japan, including the Nichiren Shoshu priesthood, with which he shared a nominal affiliation, capitulated to government pressure. Just a few days after the Japanese attack on Pearl Harbor on December 7, 1941, in an article carried in the Soka Kyoiku Gakkai's monthly periodical, *Value Creation (Kachi sozo)*, Makiguchi walked a line close to open sedition when he wrote,

> We must strictly avoid following ideologies of uncertain origin that cannot be substantiated by actual proof—even if they may be the most time-honored tradition—and thereby sacrificing the precious lives of others and ourselves. In this sense, the question of [compulsory worship at] Shinto shrines must be re-thought as a matter of great urgency. (1983–1988, vol. 10, p. 26)

In May 1943 the government banned the publication of *Value Creation* and in July Makiguchi and his disciple, Josei Toda, were imprisoned on charges of failing to demonstrate proper respect toward the emperor *(fukeizai)* and violation of the Peace Preservation Law, the core legal instrument for the suppression of dissent. From prison records, it is clear that Makiguchi's resistance continued throughout his ordeal; during interrogation sessions he referred to Emperor Hirohito as a "common mortal" *(bompu)* and described the war as a national disaster in contrast to the sanctioned description of it as a "holy war" *(seisen)* (Makiguchi, 1983–1988, vol. 10, pp. 201–203; Japanese Special, 1943b, pp. 151–152). On November 18, 1944, Makiguchi died in prison of malnutrition at the age of 73, but he left behind the seeds of a system of humanistic education that would be further cultivated by his successor, Josei Toda, and later by Daisaku Ikeda. Makiguchi's philosophy of value creation and his belief that this belonged at the center of teaching and learning remain his legacy today.

## MAKIGUCHI'S CONTRIBUTIONS TO EDUCATIONAL THOUGHT

Makiguchi's philosophy of value seeks to clarify the concept of *happiness* in terms of value.[5] Value, according to traditional Western philosophy, has three constituent elements—Truth, Beauty, and Good—and from the early years of modernization and Westernization in Japan, this triad was accepted in intellectual circles as self-evident. Miyata, in his analysis of Makiguchi's theory of value, notes that it represents a pointed critique of the neo-Kantian educational theories then predominant in Japan (Miyata, 1997, p. 31). These systems of thought and their highly abstract related pedagogical theories are compared by Makiguchi to "the winds that violently roil the stratosphere but leave the lower reaches of the atmosphere unmoved" (1983–1988, vol. 5, p. 16) or to "applying eye drops from a second storey window" (1983–1988, vol. 5, p. 38). Makiguchi was particularly disturbed by the sight of teachers struggling to absorb and implement the latest theories from Europe and the United States—introduced by the professional theorists ensconced in Japan's universities—while the lessons of actual educational practice in Japan went unmined. Thus, Makiguchi urges teachers to engage in collating, analyzing, and distilling their own experiences in order to "inductively establish principles" (1983–1988, vol. 5, p. 17) that could be fed back into their daily praxis.

A reflection of his intellectual autonomy, Makiguchi maintains a critical eye towards the authority of the ideas of Japanese educational theorists—an authority that rested on their ability to read in the original the even more authoritative ideas of Western philosophers. His core stance is always one of scrupulously choosing which ideas he will accept and on what terms; so, while he eagerly embraces the tools of analytical rationality from the West, he remains in many ways rooted in an Eastern worldview. Makiguchi's seemingly effortless grasp of interdependence—between humans and nature and among humans in their social relations—may be understood as a reflection of this Eastern worldview (Matsuoka, 2005, p. 202).

The linchpin of Makiguchi's theory of value centers on his questioning of "Truth" as a value. For Makiguchi, truth is found in the correspondence between an objective reality and the words and concepts applied by humans to that reality. As an educator, Makiguchi was thoroughly committed to the pursuit of knowledge and truth as it was embodied in the student's interaction with experience. Still he argues that "Truth" should not be conceived as a constituent element of value.

To illustrate this distinction, he offers the example of people hearing a report of a disastrous earthquake or fire. The report itself is either true (i.e., corresponds to objective reality) or false. But the truth or falsity of the report is independent from the question of value—*its positive or negative impact on people's lives* (1983–1988, vol. 5, pp. 222–223). Thus, in developing his critique of Japan's neo-Kantian theorists' conception of value, Makiguchi first sought to bring abstract and disembodied "Truth"—largely prior to and outside of lived experience—firmly back to earth.

Whereas Makiguchi considers truth a matter of "qualitative equivalence," value for Makiguchi must be seen as the "relational power of the object measured by the quantitative response of the subject" (1983–1988, vol. 5, p. 219). Value thus arises from the interaction between humans and their surroundings and it is only in this sense that value can be created; truth cannot then be a component core of value. Therefore Makiguchi proposes a change and reordering of the three elements of value. "Beauty" (and its opposite) is a measure of partial, sensory response within an individual. "Gain" is the measure of a relationship that extends and expands the total vital experience of the individual ("loss" is that which shrinks and limits this). "Good" is to the life of social collective what gain is to the life of the individual ("evil" is the societal equivalent of individual loss). Grounded in these definitions, Makiguchi's reordering of "beauty," "gain," and "good"— which, taken together, constitute his understanding of "value"—represents concentric circles of expansion from within the life of the individual to the life of the community.

In terms of his notion of "good" pertaining to the social collective, it should be noted that while Makiguchi acknowledged the importance of particular societies and cultures as the site and context of life, he never regarded these as absolute. In his 1903 work on geography, he proposed a three-tiered scheme of identity, urging that we be aware of ourselves as simultaneously citizens of a local community, the national community, and of the world. Thus Makiguchi's positing of "society" as the arbiter of moral judgments does not assume separate, incommensurable moral universes for different cultures, but is implicitly open to the idea of intercultural negotiation toward the formation of a larger moral consensus.

Makiguchi's philosophy of value, therefore, is a call for individuals to create "beauty," "gain," and "good"; it represents an invitation for open-ended engagement with a complex and difficult world. Through such engagement, individuals can create potentially limitless value.

It is also important to note that Makiguchi denies the idea of "the sacred" as an independent field of value (as was proposed by some neo-Kantians). He asserts that even the claims of religion should be assessed by the measure of value creation:

> Other than freeing people and the world from suffering, what meaning could there be for the existence of religion in society? Isn't freeing people from suffering the value of gain? Isn't freeing the world from suffering the moral value [of good]? (1983–1988, vol. 5, p. 356)

Makiguchi likewise rejects any conception of "happiness" that is solely personal. "Individual well-being entails cooperative and contributive existence within society," he argues (1983–1988, vol. 5, p. 129):

> Thus, genuine happiness requires sharing the sufferings and joys of the larger public as a member of society; and it can easily be understood that full and

harmonious life within society is an indispensable element for any concept of authentic happiness. (1983–1988, vol. 5, p. 131)

Makiguchi believes deeply that it is possible—even vital—to harmonize personal "gain" and social "good." He is also keenly aware that this cannot be done without enormous effort. This interplay loosely corresponds to the dynamic tension between his radicalist and pragmatic perspectives. His philosophy of value creation thus has the potential to provide a conceptual and practical framework for bringing into dialogue what, in today's parlance, are the often opposing viewpoints of traditional and progressive education. Makiguchi criticizes both as incomplete approaches. He decries traditional education's penchant to simply convey knowledge:

> The aim of education is not to transfer knowledge; it is to guide the learning process, to enable the acquisition of [the methods of] research. It is not the piecemeal merchandizing of information; it is to enable the acquisition of the methods for learning on one's own; it is the provision of keys to unlock the vault of knowledge. (1983–1988, vol. 6, p. 285; in Bethel, 1989, p. 168)

At the same time, Makiguchi rejects recklessly individualized conceptions of learning. For him, contemporary pedagogies devoted to such abstract goals as "self-realization" were essentially "methodless" (1983–1988, vol. 6, p. 272).

For Makiguchi, the tug between radicalist and pragmatic perspectives can be resolved through the efforts of teachers to probe the actual roots of individuality. In other words, an educator's responsibility lies in awakening and encouraging individual interests that connect the student with broader human concerns, rather than uncritically accepting whatever students happen to desire or want to do. Makiguchi likewise emphasizes the importance of educators' clearly thinking out formulations of the purpose of education (1983–1988, vol. 5, p. 110). He holds that "the purpose of education should be derived from the purpose of life itself" (p. 111).

Makiguchi's vision presents teachers with a rich but challenging image of their work and requires authentic and courageous teachers who themselves are value-creating individuals living within and contributing to society. In this sense, Makiguchi's philosophy speaks to the art of teaching as well as to the process of learning:

> Just as an artist realizes his/her ideal on canvas or in marble, educators should offer to the impressionable minds of children an ideal of life as well as the capacities necessary to realize that. . . . Educators, regardless of their actual success or failure, must be able to envisage being a paradigmatic personality of the first order in society. (1983–1988, vol. 6, p. 32)

Teachers must be able to catalyze meaning in the lives of students and "guide unconscious living to consciousness, valueless living to value, and irrational living to reason" (1983–1988, vol. 5, p. 405; cf. Bethel, 1989, p. 90). As Makiguichi said, "When we realize this, a teacher comes to a humble appreciation of his/her true position, which we can never forget is to be that of an aide, guide and midwife, empowering and assisting the activities of the learners themselves" (vol. 6, p. 54). Teachers must first "practice and experience in their own lives the principles and techniques of learning that they are seeking to help their students understand and acquire" (p. 330; in Bethel, 1989, p. 179).

But teachers are not the only guides in the adventure of learning. Makiguchi holds that the active roles of home and community are also necessary to nurture happy, strong, and contributive youth. He regrets the extent to which the home and community have abdicated important educational responsibilities to the school, with the effect of "turn[ing] young people's entire childhood and adolescence into a study hall at the expense of all else" (1983–1988, vol. 6, pp. 195–196; in Bethel, 1989, p. 151). In Makiguchi's view, the resulting apathy leads to a loss of physical and emotional well-being. To counteract this, Makiguchi strongly calls for the unification of life and learning, as well as of school and community. As early as his 1903 work on human geography, Makiguchi maintains that "the lofty insights, understandings, and principles of the universe are revealed in every tiny village or hamlet" (1983–1988, vol. 1, p. 23; in Bethel, 2002, p. 21). In his 1912 work on community studies, he proposes that students directly observe the complex relations between people and their physical and social world as a foundation for academic coursework. He suggests, for example, that the costs of running a school, as well the sources of funding in taxes and donations, be made known to children, as an object lesson in economics (1983–1988, vol. 3, p. 276).

With this important community connection in mind, Makiguchi recommends (but was not able to implement in his own schools) a program of half-day schooling. He argues that half-day schooling would be more effective academically and more economical as well. The time students spend outside school in family, community, or vocational pursuits would instill an "appreciation for work" (1983–1988, vol. 6, p. 213; in Bethel, 1989, p. 156) and would, he believes, revitalize and redefine the purpose of study:

> Study is not seen as a preparation for living, but rather study takes place while living, and living takes place in the midst of study. Study and actual living are seen as more than parallels; they inform one another intercontextually, study-in-living and living-in-study, throughout one's whole life. (1983–1988, vol. 6, p. 212; in Bethel, 1989, p. 156)

Thus, Makiguchi's philosophy of value, forged out of the dynamic tensions of his own work and experience, provides a basis for an approach to teaching that guides the processes of learning inherent in life and living, and through it, Makiguchi seeks to develop the core human capacity to generate meaning.

## SOKA EDUCATION IN PRACTICE

Makiguchi's legacy has endured through the efforts of his closest disciple, Josei Toda, who survived the ordeal of imprisonment and, in the chaotic years of occupation and postwar Japan, went on to rebuild the organization his mentor had founded. A crucial part of Toda's genius, according to Richard Seager (2006), a historian of religion, was his ability to reframe abstract Buddhist theory in practical ways. He conceived of the Buddha as the highest potentialities inherent in human life and "enlightenment" as an inner-motivated process of self-transformation or "human revolution." Propelled by Toda's passionate determination to empower the common people, who had borne the devastating brunt of war and defeat, the organization grew rapidly, claiming a membership of more than 750,000 families at the time of Toda's death in 1958.

Soon after assuming the presidency of the Soka Gakkai in 1960 at age 32, Daisaku Ikeda began to bring an international dimension to what had until then been a Japan-based movement. At the same time, he launched a concerted effort to actualize the vision for education set out by his two mentors, Makiguchi and Toda. In a memoir-style essay, he records the words of Toda as he shared with him the "flame" of Soka education:

> Daisaku, let's establish a university, Soka University. I hope this can be achieved in my lifetime, but that may not be possible. Should that be the case, Daisaku, I'm counting on you to do it. . . . Let's make it the best university in the world! (D. Ikeda, 2006, pp. 10–11)

Inspired by Toda's vision, Ikeda went on to open Soka Junior High School and Soka High School in 1968, followed by Soka University of Japan in 1971. Currently, there are 12 additional Soka schools: five Soka kindergartens in Japan, Hong Kong, Singapore, Malaysia, and Brazil; three Soka elementary schools in Tokyo and Kansai, Japan, and in Brazil; an additional Soka junior high school and high school in Kansai; a Soka Junior Women's College in Tokyo; and Soka University of America in California, which received accreditation from the Western Association of Schools and Colleges (WASC) in 2005.

In founding the Soka school network, Ikeda provided only broad guidelines about the core principles and goals of each school and emphasized that capturing Makiguchi's spirit was more important than following the specificity of his proposals. Beyond this, the staffs of the schools were given considerable discretion to plan the details of their programs.

Asian studies scholar Daniel Metraux (1994) points out that the staffs of Soka schools were aware of each school's potential impact on the public's perceptions of the Soka Gakkai (p. 104). Perhaps as a result of cultural pressure to conform to societal expectations, the academic and departmental structure of Soka University of Japan, for example, has evolved into one quite similar to that of other Japanese universities. In Japan, private K–12 schools are highly regulated by the Ministry of Education, Culture, Sports, Science, and Technology (MEXT) and the degree of supervision also limits the abilities of educators to experiment with substantive changes to the educational program. The Soka schools have, therefore, sought to demonstrate their uniqueness in other ways. T. Miller (personal communication, Feb. 9, 2003), a teacher and observer at various schools within the Soka school network, notes the humanistic quality of student-teacher relationships in the schools; he traces this tradition to the example set by the founder, Daisaku Ikeda, who through his many visits, gifts, and messages to students, has modeled humanistic educational interactions for faculty members (Gebert interview with I. Katagiri & Y. Ushiyama, Tokyo, November 2005).

Among the first Western observers to visit and study Soka schools was Carl Gross (1970) of the Institute for International Studies at Michigan State University College of Education, who reports on "a definite relationship between the philosophy of education underlying the schools and the practices which have been established" (p. 56). In a departure from the drab appearance of many Japanese urban schools at that time, the Soka schools had beautiful artistic landscaping, truly impressive buildings and facilities, and a student-teacher ratio that was—at a little more than 20 to 1 considerably smaller than the then national average of 31 to 1 (elementary) and 40 to 1 (secondary) (p. 59). Although they are inspired by the Buddhist orientation of the Soka Gakkai, the Soka schools have a completely secular curriculum (p. 59).

On the basis of 1967 planning documents that he studied, Gross indicates that the leaders of the Soka Junior High School and Soka High School were from the outset concerned with the equity of educational opportunity. Gross praises their admissions procedures, which incorporated a process of student interviews to "select individuals of character, who have leadership ability, and evidence creativity and initiative" (1970, p. 58); such practices contrasted with those at several other private schools in Japan at the time of his report that relied heavily on academic test or IQ scores and, therefore, disregarded many unique and personal qualities of potential students. Gross reports that the planners were, indeed, looking for "gifted" students, but their views about giftedness seemed highly compatible with interpretations about giftedness that have more recently emerged.[6] In other words, the first Soka schools seemed intent on attracting a student body made up of active young people with a wide variety of personal and intellectual strengths.

Richard Seager (2006) records his recent visit to Kansai Soka schools in Japan. He summarizes from an English brochure for the schools that lists the principles formulated by Ikeda: (1) Uphold the dignity of life; (2) Respect individuality; (3) Build bonds of lasting friendship; (4) Oppose violence; and (5) Lead a life based on both knowledge and wisdom. He also notes what he sees as a Buddhist influence in aspects of the schools—in their opposition to militarism, in their schoolwide campaigns against bullying, and "in the way harmony and helpfulness pervade the ideals of the school" (p. 108). He further relates an encounter that personalized the educational philosophy of the school:

> The idealistic streak in Soka education catches me off guard when, over a lunch of noodles, fresh vegetables and miso soup, a boy of about ten asks me, in a piping voice and amazingly good English, "Professor Seager, what is your dream?" (p. 109)

G. D. Miller (2002) analyzes the evolution of the theory of Soka education as distinguished from its applications. Indeed, the implementation of Soka education extends far beyond the network of Soka schools. Among the membership of the Soka Gakkai International are many thousands of educators throughout the world who are attempting to apply the principles of Soka education within their own cultural contexts. As a means of sharing pedagogical practice with this wider world of Soka educators, more than 20,000 field reports have been collected in Japan from educators working in pre-K–12 schools (both private and public), universities, and more independent settings such as after-school centers or tutoring (Soka Gakkai Educators Division, 2000).

While the reporters frankly reference their Buddhist practice, the frameworks of the teachers' approaches are essentially secular in nature and replicable by people of all persuasions. For example, there are frequent references to "praying for a student's happiness," but this should be interpreted as the focusing of the psychic energy of caring for students and their problems rather than as appeals to a higher, external power.[7] Several common themes emerge from the records that provide important glimpses into the nature of Soka education:

- A commitment to the happiness of individual children is reflected through often-repeated phrases such as "opening the heart of a problem child," "reaching the child," "learning to empathize and connect with the children," "never giving up on students," and "continuing to believe in students to the very end."

- A belief in the efficacy of dialogue is pervasive and includes an emphasis on one-on-one conversations; visiting children at home; reaching out to families; and using creative forms of communication such as writing comments in student diaries and journals, letters to students, and classroom newsletters.
- An acceptance of full responsibility as educators to solve classroom problems is viewed as a key component of the teacher's role. Ikeda's assertion that the teacher is the decisive force in the educational environment is frequently cited.
- There is recognition that personal development is crucial to the teaching process. In almost all the reports, teachers describe inner conflicts, efforts to challenge the urge to run away, and finally learning to appreciate problematic children as spurs to their professional growth.
- There are frequent efforts to reach out and involve the wider community in all aspects of teaching.

Several examples drawn from the Japanese published collection of educators' experiences (Soka Gakkai Educators Division, 2000) also illustrate the broad role teachers can play:

- An elementary school teacher won the admiration of the community by working with students to clean up streams near his school in an effort to increase the local population of fireflies, a traditional symbol of natural beauty in Japan.
- An elementary school teacher was able to restore order, morale, and a positive learning environment among her third-grade students who had been involved in a series of thefts. The turning point was the teacher's success in making a breakthrough with the ringleader of the group.
- The director of a rural kindergarten forged valuable intergenerational ties by encouraging the young families of the students to participate in traditional rice planting and harvesting ceremonies carried out by members of the older generation.
- After being transferred to a difficult school in Osaka, a middle school teacher had his students write their own script for a play about the dangers of sniffing paint thinner, which they then performed throughout the community. The actions of the teacher had the wider effect of inspiring a demoralized teaching staff.
- A high school teacher challenged student apathy by developing a

culture of volunteer activism. As a result, the students held a charity bazaar and collected goods for a school in the Solomon Islands.

From these brief accounts, it can be seen that Soka education stresses the power of the individual teacher to challenge educational difficulties through his or her personal efforts. In each of these cases, much as in the example set by Makiguchi, teachers personally undertook difficult challenges and created a pathway to learning and happiness by dint of personal courageous action. Each of these efforts constituted a "microsolution" rather than a "macrosolution." One can only conjecture what impact widely practiced efforts of this nature could have on a demoralized educational system.

Soka educators are making similar efforts in countries outside Japan. In 1995 Soka educators in Brazil launched the Makiguchi Project in Action (de Melo Silva, 2000). As of 2005, members of Brazil Soka Gakkai International, often retired citizens, have served as volunteers in more than 221 partnership schools. For a 3-month period in each school they organize student-interest activities such as handicrafts, art, horticulture and gardening, culinary arts, and environmental education and plan professional development sessions for teachers and activities for parents. These interventions help to break destructive and despair-inducing patterns of teacher-student relationships as teachers begin to observe and foster the positive characteristics, creativity, and healthy interactions of their students. Questionnaire responses received from participating teachers over the course of the 6 years of the de Melo Silva research document that the interventions cause significant student gains in learning, creativity, motivation, and the quality of interpersonal relationships. This model is currently being replicated in Panama ("Makiguchi Project in Panama," 2001).

Several private schools around the world have also been founded—at least partially—on Soka education principles, including the New School of Collaborative Learning in Beijing, the Centro de Orientacion Infantil in Panama, and the Learning Centers of the International University Asia Pacific. In the United States, the Renaissance Charter School in New York was founded in part on Makiguchi's theories (Joffee, 2006). This school's motto, "Developing Leaders for the Renaissance of New York," is a call to nurture students who are capable of creating value in their community. Visitors to the school have remarked on the overall sense of happiness and engagement among students, and this is supported by data from Indiana University's High School Survey of Student Engagement (Joffee, 2004). Parent satisfaction is an exemplary 93.7% as measured by a recent school survey (Kadamus, 2005).

Indeed, scholarly research and documentation are beginning to emerge from the work of educators in several countries who are applying concepts of Soka education. In her doctoral dissertation, Iris Pagan (2001) narrates her efforts to employ the principles of "Makiguchian Pedagogy" in a middle school science classroom of a private school in New York. Her findings, which have much to offer to middle school science teachers, suggest that a Makiguchian approach to learning can enhance socially situated learning while also sustaining adequate mastery of science content. Principal Marita Bombardieri was able to transform a problem-ridden vocational high school in Como, Italy, into a center of peace and dialogue in a community beset with the task of integrating a large influx of immigrants (Marrazzi, 2001). Projects such as these test the principles of Makiguchi's thoughts in various global settings. An online quarterly, *Newsletter of International Soka Educators* (www.eddiv.homestead.com/newsletter.htm), highlights the work of practitioners throughout the world as they attempt to apply the principles of Soka education. In fact, the effort made by Soka educators to share their practices through Web sites, conferences, and correspondence is one of its most promising characteristics.

## CONCLUSION

In a conflict-ridden world full of philosophical and political strife, Makiguchi's notion of value creation is a call to educators and individuals to pursue both pragmatic and radicalist action through a unified theory of education. Rather than succumb to the confusion and paralysis of the educational system today, Makiguchi would urge educators to find ways to create value to improve rather than dismantle the system. As an ordinary citizen living in a perilous time, Makiguchi provided an example of a contributive life as he walked courageously along treacherous paths, seeking always to find a way out of chaos through value creation. The legacy of his struggle is seen in the great number of people who are now working with excitement and ardor throughout the world to realize his vision. By insisting that value creation is a path to human fulfillment regardless of oppressive forces, internal or external, Makiguchi defines the aims of education and speaks to our own time in a clear and compelling voice.

# Learning from Experience: Jane Addams's Education in Democracy as a Way of Life

**Charlene Haddock Seigfried**

JANE ADDAMS (1860–1935) was among the first generations of women in the United States to receive a college education. Unlike educators who believe that the mass of humankind could not have worthwhile experiences and that all valuable ideas have to come from outside the neighborhood, "and almost exclusively in the form of books" (Addams, 1902/2002a, p. 194), Addams believed that education was a lifelong endeavor because it was grounded in experience. Eager to make a difference in a world that offered women few opportunities, she and Ellen Gates Starr founded Hull House (1889), one of the first American settlement houses, in a poor, ethnically diverse, immigrant working-class district of Chicago during the tumultuous years of the Industrial Revolution. The settlement attracted an extraordinary group of women, who made major contributions to reforming social and civic institutions.[1] They founded the first kindergartens and public playgrounds in Chicago and the first juvenile court, they worked tirelessly to undermine the horrors of sweatshops and child labor, they lobbied for shorter working hours for women who were doing back-breaking labor both at home and outside it, and they supported workers' rights to organize and protest inhumane working conditions. Besides being a center of social experimentation and reform that predated the opening of a department of sociology at the University of Chicago, Hull House offered classes in art, music, drama, sculpture, philosophy, and literature to its immigrant neighbors.

Addams was both the dynamic force that held the settlement together and its spokesperson to the outside world. Her philosophy and social theory were developed through many lectures and books on such issues as social ethics, pacifism, juvenile delinquency, the settlement movement, social democracy, and feminism. She was a founding member or early supporter of the National Association for the Advancement of Colored People (NAACP), the National American Woman Suffrage Association, the American Civil Liberties Union, and the Women's International League for Peace and Freedom. In polls she was voted the most respected woman of her time, until she was vilified for her steadfast pacifism during World War I and became a victim of the Red scare for supporting radical causes. Eventually, common sense prevailed, and she was awarded the Nobel Peace Prize in 1931.

## WHY EXPERIENCE MATTERS

All of us are involved in transactions with the natural and social worlds of which we are a part. When such involvements cease to be merely customary and repetitive and instead become matters of care and concern, then learning can take place. For pragmatists like Addams, learning requires intelligent engagement with the world, which means approaching experience experimentally.[2] Such engagement is optimized through sympathetic understanding, an attitude that both opens the inquirer to new perspectives and encourages receptive responses. Education is an ongoing process transforming both those engaged in it and the situations in which it takes place. Knowledge is not a passive affair or the accumulation of facts, but the outcome of inquiries into problematic situations with a view to alleviating their negative aspects and producing better outcomes. Unless such inquiry is care-ful and concerned that the outcomes of investigations be just as well as successful, they are more likely to favor the few rather than the many and to be socially destructive rather than constructive.

As a result of her years of living and working in the midst of an immigrant community whose members were considered by the established population to be inferior because of their foreign origins and languages, their Catholicism or Judaism, and their differing customs and food, Addams was acutely sensitive to the multiplicity of outlooks and values that characterize our complex, modern world.[3] She soon recognized the tendency of all levels of society to privilege their own perspectives, deeply rooted as they are in class, race or ethnicity, religion, and gender. Native-born citizens, especially those better off financially and educationally, were in the habit of making righteous or one-sided appeals to the obvious truths and unquestioned values as they saw them in order to justify their sense of superiority to the immigrant laboring population. These attitudes served to solidify entrenched views and provided no means for getting beyond limited perspectives to more equitable and justifiable beliefs and actions.

To counter such unrecognized prejudices that fueled class animosities, Addams advocated the development of a sympathetic understanding that includes recognizing the difficulty of overcoming the biases that inform who we are and grasping the necessity of listening to others differently situated. These efforts to take seriously what are initially alien practices and puzzling points of view have the potential to expand our horizons and can contribute to the resources required for overcoming complex social and political problems. Sympathetic understanding motivates the need for working with others as equal partners, a motivation sustained by a profound belief that each human being has a right to develop to his or her utmost capacity (Addams, 1930, p. 199). Addams believed that cooperative rather than top-down solutions were more likely to satisfactorily resolve such widespread problems of the time as political corruption, exploitation of workers, poverty, overwork, sickness, crime, domestic violence, and child neglect.

Addams makes the startling claim that we are responsible for choosing our experiences. This is because our moral judgments are filtered through our experiences. To the extent that our experiences are one-sided and limited, so too will be our moral judgments. It is therefore incumbent on us to actively seek out those experiences that will enlarge the depth and scope of our moral understanding. Unless we reach out beyond our comfort zone, we will not be able to take account of others differently situated, nor accurately grasp the motivations for their actions, and thus we will inevitably misjudge them and act with insufficient evidence.

## LEARNING AS TRANSFORMATIVE

Schools and universities often fail to recognize that for learning to take place, students' attention must be engaged and they must be challenged to participate in transforming for the better situations of mutual concern. Instead, institutions tend to treat knowledge as merely a collection of detached bits of data in one subject area after another or as rote learning suitable for machine testing. Addams indicted the technocratic model of education that has only become more entrenched in our own times. She insightfully remarked:

> As the college changed from teaching theology to teaching secular knowledge the test of its success should have shifted from the power to save men's souls to the power to adjust them in healthful relations to nature and their fellow men. But the college failed to do this, and made the test of its success the mere collecting and disseminating of knowledge, elevating the means into an end and falling in love with its own achievement. (1930, p. 199)

She complained that already in her day "the habit of research and the desire to say the latest word on any subject" overcome "any sympathetic understanding" of the audience addressed (1930, p. 199). She illustrated her claim by recalling an invitation she made to an anthropologist to help bewildered night school teachers of new Greek, Armenian, Bohemian, and Italian immigrants to better understand their students and to help rid them of their bias that equated lack of English proficiency with ignorance. The professor was initially willing, but then admitted that he did not have the information necessary for such a talk. Instead, he later sent three of his students to her at three different times to get help in identifying people in the neighborhood who had six toes or whose relative had! No wonder Addams thinks that "the best trained scientists are inclined to give themselves over to an idle thirst for knowledge which lacks any relation to human life, and to leave to the charlatans the task of teaching those things which deeply concern the welfare of mankind" (pp. 196–197).

## EXPERIENCE AS EXPERIMENTAL

Experience becomes the basis for knowledge and intelligent action to the extent that it is experimental. In her autobiographical account of the Hull House settlement, *Twenty Years at Hull-House*, Addams (1912/1981) presents Hull House as a sustained demonstration of the value of a cooperative experimental approach to social problems. The value of cooperative experimentation was impressed on her from navigating the dire economic, social, and cultural straits of the immigrant population in Chicago from the end of the 19th century until after World War II. Concerned persons and organizations sought various ways of aiding the victims of unbridled laissez-faire capitalism by changing the conditions under which they lived and worked. Addams's approach was to ask of any perplexing situation: "Has the experience any value?" (1902/2002a, p. 63).

By sharing her determination to make the most of the new experiences she was having in Chicago, Addams sought to draw attention to the importance of consciously seeking what could be learned from our everyday lives. This included reassessing long-held values and reimagining what actions could be taken and what results would follow from taking one course of action rather than another. In her view, perplexities about situations that confound our expectations and yet do not suggest any viable course of action are often a signal that hidden biases are operating that are obscuring the facts of the situation. Such perplexities can either remain frustrations or they can become incentives for opening up new perspectives and values and thus lead to personal growth and more intelligent actions.[4] In *How We Think* John Dewey introduces his chapter on the five stages of reflective thinking by echoing Addams's insights, saying that when we find ourselves in a perplexing situation, we may dodge it and turn to something else, we may indulge ourselves in merely imaginative solutions, or we may face the situation. Only in the last case do we begin to reflect.[5]

The close connection between experience and experiment as the basis for theory is brought out by Addams's consistent claim that it is dangerous to administer "any human situation upon theory uncorrected by constant experience" (Addams, 1935/2004, p. 50). She introduces this principle by an anecdote taken from the life of her fellow resident and good friend, Julia Lathrop. In an essay on the Cook County Charities, Lathrop describes the dire poverty and suffering in Chicago caused by the general economic depression of 1893, which included the castoffs attracted by the Chicago World's Fair. The Cook County relief agencies, including the infirmary, the insane asylum (as it was then known), the hospital, the detention hospital, and the county agency, were institutions of last resort, and the poor dreaded ending up in any of them. Describing one of the hospital wards as a place "with beds crowded together, others laid upon the floor and filled with a melancholy company of feeble and bedridden men and idiot children," Lathrop added that "it must haunt the memory of whoever has seen it" (Addams, 1935/2004, p. 50). But what really bothered Lathrop, Addams reports, was the regulation that separated patients by sex, regardless of their circumstances. Particularly affecting was the plight of an old couple who had spent every day of their long married life together and who could see each other only once a week in their institutionalized surroundings and then only for a half hour and through a screen of heavy netting. Addams and Lathrop thought it was absurd not to try to correct these practices in view of the human suffering they produced and that would have been obvious to anyone who experienced these results.

But they were also aware that experience is mediated through what has already been experienced and through preconceptions and learned beliefs. In giving other examples of practices and regulations that were blindly followed without regard to their dreadful consequences, Lathrop mentions that doctors were not allowed to bring their students into the wards for instruction, thus neither exposing them to the conditions there nor instructing them about how to respond. Yet, despite such ignorance, as soon as they received their medical degree, "the word of the newest and rawest medical graduate might reign supreme." If such inexperienced young men were either following set practices or even setting the standards, then it was unlikely that they would have sufficient imagination or insight to realize that the results of their actions were not the only ones possible or desirable. Therefore, a corollary of the principle that it is dangerous to administer any human situation upon theory uncorrected by constant experience is that each person's experience needs to be expanded and corrected by the experience of others differently situated. Those in authority often ignore or dismiss the experiences of those under their authority, to their own detriment and also to that of those under them; to that of the institution in which both participate; and, ultimately, to the society that the institution represents.

The experimental method requires getting the facts straight through sharing perspectives and engaging in social inquiry and then taking practical steps to benefit from the insights gained. Instead, people too often fall back upon what they already know and take for granted, as they confidently and dogmatically assert opinions. Addams tried to encourage a more thoughtfully experimental approach in her dealings with people on all levels of the social ladder. As *Twenty Years at Hull-House* makes clear, this approach permeated the day-to-day life at the settlement. In her biography of Julia Lathrop, for example, Addams comments: "She is in no sense a propagandist but she is always determined to stand for getting the facts and to limit the application to the place where solid work can be done" (Addams, 1935/ 2004, p. 120).

## SOCIAL METHODS AND ETHICS

The methods that the Hull House settlement developed over the years were an important part of its educational mission. These methods were social, since, according to Addams, "the educational effort of Hull House always has been held by the residents to be subordinate to its social life, and, as it were, a part of it" (1893/2002c, p. 36). She means by "social" method an approach of working with others "in a medium of fellowship and good will," rather than working for them or imposing knowledge and values on them (1935/ 2004, p. 294). The experiential and experimental basis of lifelong education was guided by a social ethics grounded in Addams's profound attachment to democracy as a way of life. She based her social ethics on the interdependency of persons, from the intimacy of the family to the relations among nations. Interdependency was both a fact of life and a goal to be achieved. Addams was an ardent pacifist who remained steadfast despite severe criticism and social ostracism during World War I. In *Newer Ideals of Peace*, she argues that the social point of view should be kept paramount. Although she believed that there was a growing cosmopolitan interest in human affairs that would lead to an increase in social sympathy, she also recognized that "the social sentiments are as blind as the egoistic sentiments and must be enlightened, disciplined and directed by the fullest knowledge."[6]

Addams illustrates what she means by a social method by recalling how Hull House workers, under the guidance of a physician, worked with Italian immigrant women to help them take better care of their underdeveloped children (Addams, 1899/1982, p. 198). The problem was not a lack of knowledge on the part of the settlement workers, as she admits it often was, but how best to communicate known benefits to recent immigrants who were understandably reluctant to change traditional beliefs and patterns of conduct. It was useless to just distribute written information concerning recently collected scientific data about the relation of poor diet and unsanitary conditions in tenement houses to problems such as childhood malnutrition. The problem was not just one of illiteracy or not understanding English, but was of deep-seated cultural differences and suspicions. Rather than lecturing about nutrition or directly attacking superstitious beliefs about the evil eye causing disease, she invited a group of Italian women and their children to join the Hull House women in festive Sunday morning breakfasts and they were given access to public baths at the settlement house. Knowledge was gained in the process and Addams says that soon the intelligent care of children learned by this group was passed on to the women's friends and neighbors in the Italian community. To avoid misunderstanding, this example must be balanced with many others in *Twenty Years at Hull House* where Addams demonstrates how the knowledge of the better-educated settlement workers was really White, middle-class bias in disguise and needed to be corrected by their immigrant neighbors, who held different and often superior views and values.

## EDUCATION BY CURRENT EVENTS

When Addams was nearly 70 years old, she described her theory of education at some length in "Education by the Current Event," the last chapter of *The Second Twenty Years at Hull-House*. Unlike research universities, the Hull House settlement in its early years saw its mission as bringing into the circle of knowledge men and women who would otherwise be left out, whether because of ignorance, or because their lives of hard work narrowed their interests, or because their curiosity was as yet unawakened and just needed friendly encouragement. The means for wider inclusiveness was the use of current events.

Addams also acknowledges, in retrospect, that Hull House and other settlements, such as the Chicago Commons, did engage in original research, and she even sets the record straight that they were the actual pioneers in field research, antedating the first sociological departments in the universities by 3 years. The earlier and later claims are not at odds, because the gradual development of the settlement creed rejected violent revolution in favor of gradual change in bettering social conditions. Knowledge consists not in mere accumulation of facts, but in intentionally gathering information for a worthwhile goal.

The goal Addams advocates is a full life for all persons in a society that recognizes the dignity of everyone and the right of all to participate fully in establishing the conditions of their associated lives. Since the cooperation of as many persons as possible in resolving social, economic, cultural, and political problems is desired, education consists in developing a sympathetic understanding of the ways that issues affect all members of society, high and low, and providing those who have been left out with the means of fully and knowledgeably participating.[7] According to Addams, in their various activities over the years, settlements were trying to "build up a technique, although with only a few scientific generalizations to go upon[,] in order to use the group itself for educational ends" (1930, p. 410). To that end, many cooperative efforts were undertaken, involving sociologists, psychiatrists, artists, economists, gymnasts, caseworkers, dramatists, musicians, and anthropologists. The tremendous increase in understanding and methods of inquiry and resolutions that multiple perspectives make possible reflects the complexity of life itself and ensures that no one group or set of values will dominate all others.

With these philosophical foundations, Jane Addams's educational theories assert that in a democracy education is lifelong and involves transformative growth in personal understanding and ever-renewed care for ascertaining the particular factors influencing situations instead of decision making out of self-interest or a one-sided perspective.[8] Addams sums up this approach as "education by the current event" and explains that from time to time some issue dominates the news and arouses intense passions and desires in the community. What before was one worn-out theme among others suddenly takes fire as a "newly moralized issue . . . lighting up human relationships and public duty with new meaning" (1930, p. 381). Such occasions are examples of intensely lived experience, that is, they fuse the experiences, knowledge, and affections of a society into a whole, and therefore concentrate attention and energy in a way conducive to education and reflection and concerted action. Among examples of such events, Addams cites the Scopes trial in Tennessee, over the issue of evolution and creation; the coming to power in England of the Labor Party, which provided a useful counterpoint to the way the United States envisioned the general welfare of labor in the ever more powerful industrial system; and the problem of race relations epitomized by the great urban migration from the South.

It is not hard to envision similar sources of debate that have rocked the public more recently, including controversies over teaching creationist as well as evolutionary accounts of development in school biology classes, the increasing loss of business-sponsored pensions and health care for workers, and clashing views on Mexican immigrant workers and illegal immigration. These recent phenomena, like the ones Addams develops, have the potential to arouse public interest in a way conducive to their finally being addressed carefully, thoughtfully, and effectively. Addams gives detailed and insightful analyses of her three examples as she elaborates them in view of achieving socially better resolutions reached by social methods. She uses them to educate the public about the importance of cooperative solutions in which all can share and that recognize the mutual dependence of all sectors of society on the others, as well as the need to examine all sides of the issue and to develop a willingness to experiment and try new solutions instead of falling back on old patterns of action and prejudices.

What is different from the anecdotes of Hull House activities in the case of events that are significant enough to arouse whole communities is that Addams wants to extend to a larger public the attitudes and methods that settlement workers and other reformers have been evolving over decades of work. Her own interests had grown to international dimensions through her working to prevent war between nations and secure peaceful resolutions of disputes, and she was more convinced than ever that care and concern for the common welfare was not the business of only a small group of dedicated community activists. She concludes a book chapter by quoting John Dewey's recently published (1927) book, *The Public and Its Problems*, to the effect that social intelligence requires involving the public in resolving the critical issues of the day, and she extends this insight by pointing out that the public stretches from the local neighborhood to the whole world (Addams, 1930, p. 413; Dewey, LW2, p. 372).

Despite Addams's usual mix of astute analysis, description of background conditions, disclosure of judgments marred by unwitting bias, listing of the contributions of institutional resources, pleas for cooperative methods, and suggestions for improvements, she expresses some reservations about whether the public can actually be educated in the way she suggests. She recognizes that her enthusiastic expression of these charged moments made such opportunities for educating the public seem possible, but then adds, "And if the community had been able to command open discussion and a full expression of honest opinion the educational opportunity would have been incomparable" (1930, p. 381). Addams can point to stirring events as being of significant magnitude to become sources of education, but whether they would actually be depends on the public's willingness to engage in open discussion and honest opinion and—most important—to learn from one another. Since such events where personal experiences blossom to comprehend a wider situation call for new adjustments, one must be prepared to have one's protective cover of offhand and instinctive responses shattered. Such is the challenge thrown down by Addams to the public: Which will prevail, complacency and prejudice or sympathetic understanding and imaginative reforms?

## THE ROLE OF CONVERSATION IN MEDIATING PERSPECTIVES

The social method and education by the current event come together in the lively practice of conversation as practiced in Addams's life and in that of the settlement life of Hull House.[9] Dewey singled out the centrality of conversations to both Addams and Hull House when he said:

> And we all know that the work of such an institution as Hull House has been primarily not that of conveying intellectual instruction, but of being a social clearing-house. It is not merely a place where ideas and beliefs may be exchanged, not merely in the arena of formal discussion—for argument alone breeds misunderstanding and fixes prejudice—but in ways where ideas are incarnated in human form and clothed with the winning grace of personal life. (MW2, p. 91)

Since they are easy to mistake, Dewey carefully differentiates conversation from argumentation, which can increase instead of lessen misunderstanding and can exacerbate rather than undermine prejudice. Where Plato had praised true knowledge as residing in an ideal realm of pure Forms, Dewey praises the way ideas are literally embodied in human form, and shine in the lives of the Hull House residents. He points out that the classes held at Hull House are exceptional precisely because they bring together people of many different ethnic backgrounds and across a whole range of social classes and enable them to communicate across seemingly unbridgeable boundaries. Communication becomes communion. Dewey thus elevates the art of conversation at Hull House to the level of genuine social reform and explains the important functions that conversations at their best can have.

Addams gave us a straightforward description of the importance of conversation in education. Conversations are for the most part spontaneous and free floating. But they can also be productively structured, as was the quaintly named Everyday Club, which Addams and her fellow Hull House residents Julia Lathrop and Ella Flagg Young belonged to. The Everyday Club "was a group of forty civic minded women who met at luncheon whenever called together by a committee of three to discuss current topics when in the opinion of the committee an interesting matter was before the public" (Addams, 1935/2004, pp. 118–119). This dependence on timely events for calling a meeting recalls Addams's insight that education by current events is most efficacious. She also explained the nature of the conversations desired and their potential impact on the participants:

> Julia Lathrop was at her best, perhaps, at such gatherings where her always keen mind was stimulated to its most alert expression. Such clear thinking on the part of one person has an enormous liberating power and taps new sources of energy in others. The result of a generous and fearless desire to see life as it is, irrespective of the confines and limitations which so needlessly divide it, can only be obtained at its best in a group of friends such as the Everyday Club became. (1935/2004, pp. 118–119)

Oddly enough, to see life as the height of clear-sighted subjectivity, a conviction upheld by such writers as Ralph Waldo Emerson, is understood by Addams as far more than a personal accomplishment—it requires the assistance of others. The confinements and limitations that divide us are not just external barriers; they are embodied in our own persons. We see life from a certain perspective, one that is determined by our past experiences and solidified by the beliefs and opinions we have learned or acquired. Such beliefs are dogmatic unless they are open to revision by changed circumstances, better reasons or explanations, and contrary facts.[10] Our differing perspectives, therefore, both define our identity and divide us from others. Such divisions are harmful to the extent that they solidify into positions of privilege and subordination through the attitude of taking one's own beliefs and opinions as obvious truths and those of others as questionable or false. Engaging in conversation that is open-minded and respectful is one of the best ways to sort through our various approaches and expand our horizons. We also liberate ourselves in liberating others from their preconceived notions and by responding in kind to their perspectives. The enthusiasm generated by such insights can be a source of energy enabling us to put them into practice. Since this whole process involves self-exposure, our willingness to take such a risk is bolstered by a secure environment such as the one provided by friends.

According to Dewey, "The only thing ruled out is the dogmatism and intolerance that would forbid discussion" (LW14, p. 234). In the same work, with deadpan humor, he points out that "communication is not announcing things, even if they are said with the emphasis of great sonority." In *Art and Experience*, he reimagines communication as

> the process of creating participation, of making common what had been isolated and singular; and part of the miracle it achieves is that, in being communicated, the conveyance of meaning gives body and definiteness to the experience of the one who utters as well as to that of those who listen. (LW10, pp. 248–249)

Addams explores in great depth and detail the ways that genuine communication, that is, communication that opens itself to the differing attitudes, values, and worldviews of others, profoundly changes the self-understanding, values, and experiences of those whose sense of moral superiority has habituated them to talking down to others. By implicating herself in this indictment, Addams slyly intimates that all of us are prone to fall into this sense of intellectual superiority and moral smugness without realizing it. In *Democracy and Social Ethics* she highlights this subjective aspect of the pragmatist method of inquiry through her emphasis on the perplexities inherent in it.[11]

Addams points out how misunderstanding inevitably occurs when middle-class women in their charity efforts encounter members of the underpaid and overworked laboring class. Not recognizing that they are seeing and judging the world from their own Protestant, feminine, and middle-class standards, they cannot understand the attitudes of their largely Catholic, ethnically diverse, poor clients and are often perplexed and offended by them, especially when the objects of their charity resent their own unconsciously superior attitudes. Such perplexity can be severe enough to cause some of the young women charity workers to quit in reaction to what they perceive as the obduracy and ingratitude of the lower classes. But others take their perplexity as an indication that hidden barriers exist in their efforts to communicate, and they persist and seek to examine their own attitudes and beliefs as well as those of the recipients of their charity. Only in this way will genuine communication become possible and lead to further insights and more successful ways of addressing the ills they encounter.

Addams paraphrases the insights of educational theorist Mary Parker Follett (1868–1933) to explain how the disorienting effects of diverse ways of understanding the world can either enhance or undermine communication, depending on whether one side seeks to subordinate the other or both sides merely compromise their positions, rather than seeking together for genuinely new possibilities (Addams, 1930, p. 202, citing Follett, 1924). Addams says that such possibilities occur, according to Follett, "in the sphere of activities, of desires, of interests, not in that of mere ideas or of verbal symbols" (1930, p. 202). Conversations, to be efficacious, must not get bogged down in verbal jousting, but seek out mutual interests as a prelude to cooperative actions. Addams envisioned such cooperative actions as extending from local to national to global issues. Starting from a wholehearted belief in the solidarity of the human race, she worked hard to help people understand that "without the advance and improvement of the whole, no[one] can hope for any lasting improvement in [his or her] own moral or material individual condition" (Addams, 1912/1981, p. 100).

# Tao Xingzhi and the Emergence of Public Education in China

## Wang Weijia and Zhang Kaiyuan

TAO XINGZHI (1891–1946), one of the most influential educators in modern China, devoted his whole life to the struggle for democratization of China's education and political life. The ideas of Tao Xingzhi—the forerunner and advocate of democracy and democratic education—regarding education have been very significant in his native land. Particularly influential is his theory of integrating education with life, whereby "life is education," "society is school," and there is a "union of teaching, learning, and doing." Just as his Chinese name, Xingzhi, which means "doing then knowing," would suggest, Tao's educational ideas emphasize the need for theory to be based on practice and then put *into* practice.

Tao's legacy is closely connected to the movement to modernize China through mass education or, as one would say in the United States, through *public education*. But in order to understand the impact of his work in this area, we must first understand the context of China during Tao Xingzhi's youth. Tao was born into a chaotic age, when China felt humiliated by a series of defeats in the two Opium Wars (1840–1842 and 1856–1860), the war between China and France (1883–1885), the war between China and Japan (1894–1895), and the defeat in the Boxer Rebellion by the Eight-Nation Alliance Expeditionary Force (1900).[1] Against the backdrop of successive military frustrations and deteriorating national power, a few liberal-minded officials began to recognize the advantages of Western technology represented by Western weapons. Some young intellectuals also started to feel dissatisfied with traditional Chinese education, which only focused on liberal arts.

As a result, the pragmatic theories of John Dewey became very popular in China, as Dewey's philosophy was rooted in broader ideas of science, democracy, and industrialism. His ideas, conveyed in such statements as "[Democracy is] a mode of associated living" (MW9, p. 239), resonated with Tao Xingzhi's aspirations for a modern China.

## JOHN DEWEY'S INFLUENCE ON TAO XINGZHI

The famous historian John King Fairbank[2] once said that Dr. John Dewey's most creative student was Tao Xingzhi (Zhou, 1991, p. 397). Indeed, Tao was such an excellent student that, in the manner of all good students, he moved beyond his teacher, and he eventually created a unique approach to education in China.

Born in Xixian, a rural part of Anhui Province, in 1891, Tao received a traditional education in old-style private schools during his childhood. These kinds of schools focused on the teachings of Confucius (551–479 B.C.E.), with the textbooks of Five Books and Four Classics.[3] Students like Tao were supposed to become government officials by passing through different levels of civil examinations. At the age of 15, he entered Chongyi School, which was run by China Inland Mission, and began to receive a new-style education with a more diversified curriculum that included mathematics, medicine, physics, and English.

In 1909, he enrolled in the preparatory school of Huiwen College in Nanjing,[4] which was run by a local Protestant church. Two years later, he became an undergraduate majoring in liberal arts at the University of Nanjing. It was during this period that Tao received a systematic Western higher education; he was able to expand his knowledge and develop new ways of thinking, and eventually, he formulated his belief in democracy. His experience in Protestant schools such as Chongyi, Huiwen, and the University of Nanjing helped broaden Tao's vision. From then on, he paid more attention to the relationship between Western education and Chinese traditional education.

In 1914, Tao Xingzhi went to the United States, where he received an MA in political science from the University of Illinois. He then transferred to Columbia Teachers College in September 1915 and applied for a PhD in education. This is where he met John Dewey. Although he stayed at Columbia for only 2 years, Tao was able to establish a lasting friendship with Dewey, who was at the height of his influence. The time at Columbia and the opportunity to know Dewey deeply affected Tao's thought and practice. As his awareness and knowledge deepened politically, educationally, and philosophically, he began to see the possibilities of educational reform. He wrote in one of his letters:

> My sole purpose in this life is to create a democracy by education and not by military revolution. After seeing the serious defects of the sudden birth of our Republic, I was convinced that no genuine republic could exist without a genuine public education. (document dated 1916; reproduced in Tao Xingzhi, 1991, vol. 6, p. 451)

And it was at Columbia under Dewey's tutelage that Tao adopted the philosophy of pragmatism, a philosophy that emphasizes the organic relation between theory and practice and that takes lived experience as the starting point for all social inquiry and reform. As he developed his ideas regarding education, Tao benefited from his interactions with Dewey. It is instructive to explore this influence as we seek to understand Tao Xingzhi's own philosophy.

When Tao came back from the United States in 1917, he was deeply concerned about the backward state of Chinese education. As he said in one of his speeches, "When I returned from abroad, I noticed that our school teachers were concerned only with lecturing, and students were concerned only with receiving what was taught; so I was convinced of the need for reform" (document dated 1927; reproduced in Tao Xingzhi, 1991, vol. 1, p. 125). According to Tao, the traditional Chinese teaching method of teachers' "pouring" knowledge into students and students' learning passively needed to be reformed, and the relationship between teachers and students needed to be one of mutual learning.

This could explain why Tao began to adapt Dewey's theories of education to the realities of modern China, where massive illiteracy was prevalent: about 200 million Chinese, or 50% of the population, never had any formal schooling. As soon as Tao returned, he published an article in the *Educational Weekly of the China Times* titled "An Introduction to Dewey's Educational Theories," in which he stated, "[Dewey] always advocates that the educational targets should be democracy, and the educational methods should be experimentation" (document dated 1919; reproduced in Tao Xingzhi, 1991, vol. 1, p. 300). However, Tao's theories would not be mere reflections of Dewey's thought. During the period when Tao ran the Xiaozhuang Experimental Village Normal School (1927–1930), which we will discuss below, he formed his own, distinctive educational theory.

## TAO XINGZHI'S THEORY OF EDUCATION

The educational theory of Tao Xingzhi can be expressed in three principles: *life is education*; *society is school*; and there is a *union of teaching, learning, and doing*. *Life is education* conveys Tao's view that learning occurs everywhere and throughout life. His claim that *society is school* builds on this idea as it looks outside the classroom to the wider world where, he believes, children learn constantly from many people. Finally, Tao's concept of the *union of teaching, learning, and doing* further reinforces his fundamental understanding of education as something that involves all aspects of experience.

## Life Is Education

"Education is life," a statement articulating one of the most important educational philosophies of Dewey, was revised by Tao Xingzhi to "Life is education." Dewey believed that genuine education was not a preparation for life, but had its own integrity as a part of life. In his words, "Education is a process of living and not a preparation for future living; education is life itself" (EW5, p. 88). According to Tao, life and education are the same thing. Tao once said, "Life and education are two names for one phenomenon, just as a person's nickname and official name refer to a single individual" (document dated 1931; reproduced in Tao Xingzhi, 1991, vol. 2, p. 649).[5] He went on to explain that life education means "an education of life, by life, and for life." (document dated 1934; reproduced in Tao Xingzhi, 1991, vol. 2, p. 633). Tao does not mean that everything a person undergoes is educative. Rather, he highlights the fact that education can only derive from actual lived experience, whether in the school or elsewhere. Education cannot be merely passive, any more than life is merely "existence." Tao argued that the claim that "life is education" could help to broaden the scope of education from books to real life. For this reason, he does a "half somersault" with Dewey's philosophy when he develops the view that "life is education." According to Tao, only when we consider life itself as the source of education can education manifest its power.

## Society Is School

Dewey also believed that "school is society," affirming the close relationship between education and society. He held that a school should set up certain recognized social patterns, and he proposed that the environment of the schools might function as a small society, with a lot of substantive interaction between all its inhabitants. Tao Xingzhi, by contrast, likened the school to a small birdcage. He believed that the birds (students) should be put in the air (society), where they would soar freely. That is, he wanted experiences in the classroom to be extended outward into the more spacious social realm because the outside world could also instruct: "The first step to being a human being is to be close to the masses; the first step to learning nature is to be close to the nature itself" (document dated 1929; reproduced in Tao Xingzhi, 1991, vol. 2, p. 443). Consequently, he called for the utilization of all available resources for the uplifting of the people, such as in employing temples, teahouses, and every possible vacant place for reading circles and discussion groups.

In the context of early 20th-century China, this approach was very unusual. With it, Tao strove to combine the idea of *society is school* with the scientific and democratic tradition of the May Fourth Movement of 1919, which we will discuss below.

## Union of Teaching, Learning, and Doing

*Learning by doing* is another cornerstone of Dewey's educational philosophy. Dewey believed that all learning was the byproduct of inquiry, which was a kind of action. As a result, he encouraged teaching methods based on action and performance as well as on the direct and concrete experience of students. Tao agreed with this idea, emphasizing that one could only learn how to plant crops if one was in the field or how to swim by being in the water. In addition, inspired by Zhang Boling, president of Nankai University, who advocated the "union of learning and action," Tao developed the idea of the "union of teaching, learning, and doing." He believed that only by striking this balance could the two propositions of *life is education* and *society is school* be transformed into reality.

Meanwhile, Tao also emphasized that the union of teaching, learning, and doing is not only a method, but also a description of a three-pronged relationship that is crucial to learning. Things must be done, individuals must learn, and those in relation to individuals must become teachers. Expressed somewhat differently, education is not only about teaching students to learn, but also about teaching them to engage actively in life through various physical labors (document dated 1930; reproduced in Tao Xingzhi, 1991, vol. 2, p. 557; Zhang & Tang, 1992, pp. 209–212). As we will see, these ideas informed the foundation of Xiaozhuang Experimental Village Normal School (1927–1930), where Tao sought to realize his three fundamental educational principles.

## THE RISE OF THE MASS EDUCATION MOVEMENT

During World War I (1914–1918), the Chinese joined the Allied side, which included Britain, France, and later the United States. A mass demonstration of about 3,000 students in Tiananmen Square was sparked on May 4, 1919, following the news that the Treaty of Versailles[6] had recognized Japanese claims to the Shandong Province, a former German territory, rather than returning it to China. Soon a nationwide student movement erupted. With "Science and Democracy" as their rallying cry, the leaders of what came to be called the May Fourth Movement had begun to advocate for mass education and carry out some experiments in education, which they believed would alleviate poverty and bring China into the modern world. These ideas were on the minds of the people when John Dewey arrived in Shanghai in 1919 and began his lecture tour. His first lecture was titled "Democracy and Education." In this discourse, he claimed that the solution to social problems was the dissemination of education to the masses (Zhang Baogui, 2001, p. 71). In the second lecture, titled "The Real Meaning of Education in a Democracy," he further described the educational model of a true republic (Zhang Baogui, 2001, p. 74). The goal, or "real meaning," according to Dewey, was to offer everyone the opportunity to receive an education while respecting individuality (document dated 1919; reproduced in Tao Xingzhi, 1991, vol. 1, pp. 27–34). These lectures aroused the attention of people from all walks of life and encouraged them to see education in a new way. Just as Tao said, "Since the May Fourth Movement, students came forward to carry out social services, to educate people, to set up mass schools everywhere" (document dated 1924; reproduced in Tao Xingzhi, 1991, vol. 1, p. 671).

As experiments in mass education were carried out in different places, Tao kept a particularly close eye on the work of another educator who also advocated mass education. Yan Yangchu (James Yan, 1893–1990) was born in Sichuang Province and raised a Christian, graduating from Yale University in 1912. Sponsored by the Young Men's Christian Association (YMCA), he went to France to set up night schools in Paris for Chinese laborers during World War I. In 1920, he returned to China. Again sponsored by the YMCA, he went to the large cities of Changsha, Yantai, and Jiaxing to continue his efforts in developing mass education. Unlike the previous teaching method in China, with teachers reading and students imitating and reciting, Yan used slides to present characters, pictures, and texts to the students. Thus, with limited faculties and few faculty members, he was able to teach a large number of students. Furthermore, his method of visual presentation often made it easier for the students to learn and remember their lessons (Zhang & Tang, 1992, p. 164).

From the beginning, Yan Yangchu and Tao lost no time in collaborating. In 1923, they established the action committee of the national Association for the Promotion of Mass Education, or Pingmin Jiaoyu Cujin hui (APME), in Shanghai. With Tao in charge of the project, they decided to start from Nanjing and Beijing, and then spread out to the other provinces. Supported by the committee, Tao began to compile textbooks for mass education. On June 20, 1923, the Nanjing APME was established. It soon raised 15,000 yuan and set up three laboratory schools with 50 students per school. At the same time, four other laboratory schools were set up in Beijing (Zhang & Tang, 1992, p. 164).

Proposals for a mass-education movement received a warm response from all levels of society, and in August 1923, the General Association for the Promotion of Mass Education, or Pinmin Jiaoyu Cujin hui Zonghui (GAPME), was established in Beijing, with Yan Yangchu as the director. Tao was in charge of daily affairs as the executive secretary of the board of directors. Under the GAPME, there were provincial, municipal, town, and village branches, which helped to promote mass education. Committees of Mass Education were also set up in the streets of the cities and villages in the countryside. A mass-education network was thus established nationwide.

For Tao Xingzhi, the purpose of extending education to the masses is very clear. China had been a military state since the 1911 revolution had failed to achieve unification, and the country was ruled by the warlords who governed territories beyond the control of the powerless republican central government in Beijing. Even so, Tao saw the opportunity for modernization in China through the education of the civilian population. In a letter to a family member, he explained what he meant by *modernization*:

> I want to use a vigorous, openly disseminated education to create a vigorous, openly communicating society. My career these years, such as setting up summer schools, preaching mutual aid between faculty and students, and advocating coeducation [for women and men], are all for this purpose. However, the large-scale performance focused only on mass education. I do believe that through mass education, a vigorous, openly communicating society will appear very soon. (document dated 1923; reproduced in Tao Xingzhi, 1983–1985, vol. 3, p. 41)

This "vigorous, openly communicating society" signified a modernized society. Tao explained this idea more explicitly in the "Declaration of the General Association for the Promotion of Mass Education," a document he assisted in drafting:

> Whether the foundation of a republic is solid or not, it is totally dependant upon citizens' knowledge. If the citizens have received a comparatively high education, and are able to collaborate together with one heart and are responsible for the nation, the foundation will be solid for sure. Otherwise, it is only a facade, without any use. (document dated 1923; reproduced in Tao Xingzhi, 1991, vol. 3, p. 665)

To this end, GAPME initiated a complex program. First, it invited experts to study various problems of mass education, including distribution methods; the organization of schools; and the administration of teachers, facilities, and textbooks. Second, it started various experiments of mass education, such as setting up night classes and organizing summer sessions. They initially experimented with the program in Beijing and Nanjing, cultivating personnel to help in future experiments. They also established schools in remote provinces and districts, including Mongolia and Tibet, and in places where Chinese populations lived overseas, such as in Southeast Asia. The GAPME also collaborated with people from different regions and different walks of life to help carry out the mass-education movement. This work included setting up the Chinese National Association for the Advancement of Education, or Zhonghua Jiaoyu Gaijin she (CNAAE), and distributing promotional material for the movement. Further, in China at that time, there were 100 million illiterate people between the age of 12 and 25, leading GAPME to draw up a feasible plan whereby a 4-month basic course was developed, to teach willing participants 1,000 Chinese characters. With estimated costs of only 0.6 yuan per person, it was expected that this plan would be carried out within 5 to 10 years. After the first period of study, which took 4 months, the second stage would focus on professional education (document dated 1923; reproduced in Tao Xingzhi, 1983–1985, vol. 3, pp. 666, 668–669).

Developing a textbook for the mass education of Chinese people was, perhaps, the most significant component of the movement's success. To this end, Tao and another educator, Zhu Jingnong, who had studied in the United States, compiled *Thousand Character Text*, publishing the first volume of this important series in August 1923 (Toa & Zhu, 1923). By November that year, the fourth and final volume was published. The complete textbook consisted of 96 texts and was designed for 1 hour's study a day for 96 days, or 16 weeks of use. The underlying purposes of this textbook were, among other things, to cultivate a democratic spirit and attitude among China's citizens; to train readers in practical matters, such as dealing with daily correspondence, accounts, and other material; and to give students the capacity and desire to read books and newspapers.

Starting in the autumn of 1923, Tao Xingzhi went to the provinces of Jiangsu, Anhui, Jiangxi, and Hubei, north and west of Shanghai in the Yangtze River basin, to promote his idea of mass education. In 1924, with the goal of spreading the movement all over the country, he began to pay attention to northern China. Wherever he went, he contacted individuals from diverse social circles and all levels of the workforce, emphasizing the importance of a grassroots mass-education movement to China's future.

His work met with a warm response. In the cities of Anqing and Hankou alone, 17,000 and 20,000 people, respectively, attended his assembly and the corresponding parade. This resulted in a great spectacle. After his painstaking efforts in 1923–1924, APME branches were established in 20 provinces, and 500,000 people were instructed in the *Thousand Character Text*, of which more than 3 million volumes had been published. The most successful region was Jiangsu Province, where the majority of its 60 counties set up APME branches. In Henan Province, 73 counties set up schools. In Hunan Province, 26 counties set up branch associations and 356 schools, while 140 public reading rooms were established (Zhang & Tang, 1992, pp. 168–169).

## MATURING IDEAS AND PRACTICES

For Tao Xingzhi, his work of advocating mass education came to life with the establishment of the Xiaozhuang Experimental Village Normal School in a small village near Nanjing in 1927. By August the following year, there were 120 students in total. In terms of enrollment, the school was not significant. However, regarding its quality of instruction, that was another matter. The students were inspired by Tao's educational ideas and their aspiration was the improvement of rural education. Among them, there were students from Tsinghua and Jinan Universities, leaders of a publishing house, and even teachers from several colleges. They were Tao's admirers as well as his collaborators. The faculty of Xiaozhuang was also unusual. Besides employing some famous professors, such as Zhao Shuyu, Shao Zhongchun, and Chen Heqin, the school invited some farmers and laborers to teach. According to Tao, "Farmers, countrywomen, and axmen could also be the teachers of our school" (document dated 1927; reproduced in Tao Xingzhi, 1991, vol. 2, p. 344).

The Xiaozhuang School was divided into two sections: one for training teachers of elementary schools, the other for teachers of kindergarten. At the very beginning, there was not even a schoolhouse. Teachers and students either slept in tents in the open air or lived with the farmers. Eventually, they started to build houses by themselves, with teachers' and students' own assiduous efforts. According to Tao, the school "should help to promote the productivity and self-defense of the farmers and contribute to the liberation of the farmers all over the world" (document dated 1927; reproduced in Tao Xingzhi, 1991, vol. 8, p. 152). This school was based on the spirit of fraternity and liberty, ideas that seemed to have nothing to do with the political parties active in China at that time. Tao published an editorial in 1923 titled "The Starting Point of the Social Reform" in which he pointed out that for "a person at a certain time in a certain place to do a certain thing is the one and only way" (document dated 1923; reproduced in Tao Xingzhi, 1991, vol. 2, p. 591). He believed that any kind of reform began with minor changes, to concentrate one's attention on certain specific actions, and then moved on step by step. For him, the career he wanted to "devote his whole life to" was the "education movement."

Tao Xingzhi was so immersed in his educational experiment that he did not have time for politics. Unfortunately, politics knocked at his door. The turmoil of the warlords in the 1920s and 1930s severely hampered the development of the mass-education movement. In April 1930, Xiaozhuang Normal School was closed down by Nationalist troops, and Tao was listed as a wanted man, forcing him to escape to Japan. As he became increasingly aware of China's deepening national and social crisis, he began to reflect upon his life, his educational practice, and the mass-education movement itself.

In the summer of 1930, before he escaped to Japan, Tao had gathered together some of the faculty of Xiaozhuang School, in the concession of Shanghai,[7] to discuss the work of the school. At this assembly, he lamented:

> From now on, we cannot sit calmly in the reading room to draw up plans or ideas, and we cannot do our experiments from village to village step-by-step. Instead, we should unite more people to work on it. Our basic army is the peasants. A Chinese revolution won't succeed unless all the peasants unite together! (quoted in Dai, 1982, pp. 49–50)

He had recognized that without fundamental social reform, his attempt to save China through education could not be achieved. As a result, he came to understand education as a tool of fundamental social reform and to believe that these two elements—education and revolution—should be combined. After the beginning of the Japanese invasion, on September 18, 1931, Tao anxiously sought a new, more radical path for Chinese education.

In February 1932, Tao was permitted to come back to China from Japan after two years in exile. He launched several educational projects, including the Gong Xuetuan (Labor Science Union) Movement, which promoted three central ideals: labor to nourish life, science to understand life, and union to protect life. This was a new educational entity combining teaching, learning, and doing in the villages and cities. Tao also launched the Xiao Xiansheng (Little Teachers) Movement, which would organize primary school students in teaching Chinese characters to adults, and the Nantong (Refugee Children) Education Movement, to bring life education and defending the nation together in one project. In this way the mass-education movement permeated China's entire society. During the years of war with Japan (1937–1945), besides taking part in the anti-Japanese and patriotic movements, Tao still concentrated on his educational reform movement. It was at this time that he set up both the Society of Life Education and the Yucai School, a primary school in Beipei, Chongqing Province.

Both these projects were important in the fulfillment of Tao's philosophical ideas. The aim of the Society of Life Education was "to discuss the most reasonable and efficient new educational principles and methods in order to promote the enlightening of consciousness, to cultivate creativity, to spread education and to improve life" (document dated 1940; reproduced in Tao Xingzhi, 1991, vol. 4, p. 447). The main goals of the society included investigating life needs, designing educational blueprints, editing educational materials, studying specific problems, experimenting in various educational methods, spreading the achievements of these investigations, introducing the members to useful forms of service, promoting the mutual aid of the society, and guiding the members to further study (Zhang & Tang, 1992, pp. 392–393). Following the establishment of the Society of Life in 1938, branches were set up in northeastern areas, including Sichuang, Zhejiang, Anhui, and Shanxi. Soon the number of registered members reached 2,400.

In July 1939, Yucai School was created in Beipei, Chongqing Province, in western China. This was a new style of special school for gifted refugee children. It was different in some ways from Xiaozhuang Village School, but seemed to inherit its spirit. After the students entered the school, they would first receive a general education following the Education Ministry standard, and then would be divided into different groups for special studies according to their own interests and aptitudes. For example, the curriculum of the natural science group included physics, chemistry, geometry, and calculus. The curriculum of the social science group included ethics, political economics, philosophy, and international relations. The literature group included literary criticism, world literature, rhetoric, and other similar subjects.

The aim of Yucai School was to train certain individuals of ability among the refugee children. The school emphasized that it was not seeking to merely train experts and specialists. Hence, besides the specialized training courses, rudimentary courses were also required to help the students acquire a broad, general knowledge. This was not an effort to train little aristocrats. The students of Yucai School came from the ordinary people and would go back to their communities to serve by putting to use what they had learned. Yucai was a program newly developed in his life education theory, and it continuously enriched and expanded upon the original plan of disseminating education (document dated 1940; reproduced in Tao Xingzhi, 1991, vol. 4, pp. 456–457).

In spite of the differences in approach between Yucai and Xiaozhuang, the goal was the same for both: integrating education with life. They were created to develop the creativity of both children and the common people. In the summer of 1941, Tao Xingzhi proclaimed that June 20 to July 20 would be the "month of collective creation." He called for people to create "a healthy stronghold, good artistic circumstance, a garden of production, and a climate of learning" during this month (document dated 1941; reproduced in Tao Xingzhi, 1991, vol. 4, p. 490). In August, based on the successful conclusion of this month of creation, Tao called for the start of the "year of Yucai creation" (Zhang & Tang, 1992, pp. 430–431). That year's aims were to develop and cultivate the spirit and ability of individual creativity in the children, from classroom teaching to extracurricular activities, from campus culture to social practice. A year later, great accomplishments were achieved, especially in music, art, and drama; "stars" were born and numerous new works appeared. For example, the students had produced 4 dramas, 27 songs, more than 10 research reports, and more than 30 research facilities, all of which were highly praised by a wide range of people. Yucai became a well-known and highly respected model school in China.

In October 1943, Tao Xingzhi published his "Proclamation of Creativity," in which he emphasized that the educator should not only "create the students whom he would venerate," but also "create the educational theories and techniques that he would venerate" (reproduced in Tao Xingzhi, 1983–1985, vol. 3, pp. 482–483). The ultimate aim—achieved through the union of knowledge, feeling, and consciousness combined with the union of wisdom, benevolence, and courage—was to cultivate the person of truth, kindness, and beauty. This "new" person would possess the qualities of a wise heart, an earnest enthusiasm to understand both society and ordinary people, and a spirit of self-sacrifice for the benefit of society.

In order to cultivate such a person of truth, kindness, and beauty, teachers were expected to first realize and discover the strength that resides within children. In 1944, Tao published an article titled "Creative Children's Education" in which he put forward the concept of "five liberations" as an important approach to learning. These are the liberation of children's heads, hands, and mouths as well as the liberation of space and time (document dated; reproduced in Tao Xingzhi, 1991, vol. 4, pp. 540–542). Following this idea, teachers would enable children to make full use of their heads to explore and think; offer them the opportunity to use their hands; give them freedom to ask questions; and liberate them, as though they were birds eager to fly from the birdcage of school and its frequent examinations. In essence, Tao wanted to develop and set free the creativity of children, to allow them to grow up, strong and healthy, on their way to realizing truth, kindness, and beauty.

## CONCLUSION: RENEWING TAO XINGZHI'S PHILOSOPHY TODAY

From mass education to creative education, from the dissemination of knowledge to the cultivation of the new person of truth, kindness, and beauty, Tao established an expansive theoretical system of life education. But this system was not merely theoretical; it came from practice and would return to practice. This, and his dream to reform the old China, were the ideals driving Tao Xingzhi throughout his life. As he said in one of his poems to a friend,

> I use my hands and head to knock at the door of knowledge.
> Only in the cold winter could the pine and cypress show their tenacity.
> I admire the collective creation, which might end in a failure, but success
>     will come at last. (document dated 1943; reproduced in Tao Xingzhi,
>     1983–1985, vol. 4, p. 590)

Tao was devoted not only to mass education but also to the democratic movement, as necessary to a modern China, and he expected to promote the modernization of China by this two-pronged effort. Tragically, he broke down from constant overwork and died suddenly on July 25, 1946. On that very day the famous Chinese writer Mao Dun wrote,

> Tao Xingzhi is like a soldier who had been fighting for a long time, and finished his last drop of blood and lay down gloriously. . . . His death will bring an earth-shaking sound that will echo in the hearts of millions of people and be echoed in the farthest corner of the land. (Mao Dun, 1946/1984, p. 22)

Tao Xingzhi would not see the establishment of the new China. Unfortunately, the new China did not recognize the true value of this great educator until the end of the Cultural Revolution in 1976 when more and more people of insight began to investigate the rich works of this remarkable educational pioneer. From 1983 to 1985, the Huazhong Normal University edited the collected edition of Tao Xingzhi's works and soon established the Tao Xingzhi Research Center, where the first doctoral dissertation on Tao Xingzhi has since been completed (in 1992). Meanwhile, many other provinces and cities have set up Tao Xingzhi Research Associations and started experimental districts[8] where his educational ideas have been put into practice. Learning and studying about Tao Xingzhi, as well as practicing and developing his educational ideas, has become a common practice nowadays in China. Indeed, Tao Xingzhi's thoughts on education are still valid and relevant to contemporary educational reform.

# PART III

# Unleashing Human Growth and Potential

# Peace as a Premise for Learning: Maria Montessori's Educational Philosophy

**Jacqueline Cossentino and
Jennifer A. Whitcomb**

MARIA MONTESSORI'S philosophy of education is much more than a set of ideas about curriculum and instruction. Rather, what has come to be known as the Montessori Method is a comprehensive, highly elaborated, and fully integrated system of intellectual, social, and moral development. Although she is perhaps best known for her approach to early childhood education, Montessori education spans human development from infancy to adulthood.[1] And while peace is central to her educational vision at every stage of development, it is her design for elementary learning that most vividly brings that vision to action.

It was during the 1930s as Europe experienced economic depression and saw the rise of totalitarianism that Montessori spoke most passionately and eloquently about the relationship between education and peace. In her lectures, delivered from 1932 to 1939, then collected and first published in 1949 in *Education and Peace* (1972), she outlined her optimistic argument that an education truly responsive to the child's psychological and spiritual development would bring an end to war. Later, while in India during World War II, she elaborated that argument into a fully integrated program for the elementary age child, which was published in *To Educate the Human Potential* (1967b). In the present chapter, we focus on Montessori's idea of the elementary curriculum, known as "cosmic education," that emerged at that time. We begin with an overview of her life, highlighting those experiences that gave rise to her ideas about peace and education; in the second section we outline three core constructs fundamental to her vision for elementary education; the third section describes her philosophy in action by illustrating a contemporary elementary classroom; and, finally, we speculate about the import of her ideas for educators in the 21st century.

## OVERVIEW OF MONTESSORI'S LIFE AND IDEAS

Maria Montessori (1870–1952) lived during a period marked by tremendous political, economic, and social upheaval.[2] She was born in the year of Italy's unification, and her youth and early adulthood were spent in a country seeking to establish itself as a modern nation-state on a par with its European neighbors.[3] Montessori, an only child, spent her early childhood in Chiaravalle, an agricultural town in the coastal province of Ancona on the Adriatic Sea. When she was 5, the family moved to Rome, where she attended school. While anecdotal accounts suggest that Montessori was not a particularly gifted elementary student, her desire to complete her secondary education, study engineering, and later enter a college of medicine was a radical departure from attendance at a conventional finishing school, which most middle-class young women experienced.

Montessori received training as a physician—itself a revolutionary act. Her subsequent academic study at the university provided her with an understanding of scientific thought as well as an acute capacity for empirical inquiry. During her formative university years, the ideas and ideals of socialism shaped the university's intellectual milieu. Her mother's influence and support along with Montessori's intellectual training led to Montessori's graduating in 1896 as a young woman with a radical, progressive commitment to improving the lives of those living in poverty or suffering neglect.

### Montessori Steps into the World

In her early years as a physician (1895–1900), Montessori held an appointment at the university hospital while also operating a private practice. As she practiced medicine among the poor in Rome, she was drawn to the condition of those children and youth who were called "feebleminded" or "deficient" and sent to asylums where even basic needs went unmet. Her belief that these children were capable of far more led her to study anthropology, educational philosophy, and pedagogy. The work of the French physicians and psychologists Jean-Marc Gaspard Itard and Edouard Séguin was particularly influential. Both men devoted their careers to working with people with disabilities and it was from this orientation that Montessori launched her own work with children. From Itard, Montessori adopted the practice of studying children's activity in their environment and then adjusting the environment based on those observations. Séguin, a student of Itard's, had begun developing instructional apparatus specifically for mentally impaired children. In addition to placing a focus on didactic materials, Montessori adopted Séguin's developmental orientation toward learning environments. That is, Séguin observed that the environment itself should be customized to the developmental needs of children at various stages. In Montessori's hands, the notion of a developmentally responsive environment, filled with carefully constructed didactic materials, became the "prepared environment," one of the cornerstones of the Montessori Method.

In 1906, at the age of 36, she became involved in an urban renewal effort in San Lorenzo, a poor quarter in Rome. There she opened the first school designed for "normal" children, and she named it the Casa dei Bambini, or "Children's House." The well-publicized success of her experiments in the Casa was a decisive turning point in her life. In 1907 she left the practice of medicine and devoted the remainder of her life to education.

The spread of the Montessori movement was swift and international in its scope. Starting in 1909, Maria Montessori began to travel the world giving lectures and demonstrations on her educational method. During this period she visited nearly every continent and established official residential status in Barcelona (1915–1936), England and Amsterdam (1936–1939), India (1939–1946), and again Amsterdam (1946–1952), thus giving rise to her claim that she was a "citizen of the world."[4] In 1909, confident that her method would have universal appeal and with the support of a wealthy patron, Montessori wrote, in one month, *Il Metodo della Pedagogia Scientifica applicato all'educazione infantile nelle Case dei Bambini*, whose English translation (Montessori, 1909/1912) is simplified to *The Montessori Method*. This seminal work is one of the few publications by Montessori that was composed by her in the form of a written text. Most of Montessori's published writings are actually transcriptions or recollections of her speeches by audience members.

Montessori typically approved such transcriptions for publication; however, it is important to highlight that Montessori was a woman of action, not a contemplative scholar. That her lectures and 3- to 4-month training courses were capable of transforming audience members into "believers" has led to the claim that Montessori's ideas spread because of a "cult of personality" (Cohen, 1969). It is important to discount neither the tendency among some Montessori teachers to revere her nor the control she and her son Mario exerted over the dissemination and implementation of her message. However, in our view the spread of the Montessori Method, which has unfolded over multiple generations and across multiple cultural contexts, suggests that the power of the ideas, rather than Montessori's personal magnetism, explains the method's popularity.

The two world wars of the twentieth century, the Spanish Civil War (1936–1939), and the rise of fascism in Italy all affected the spread of Montessori's ideas and her commitment in later life to the peace movement. She was thrice nominated for a Nobel Peace Prize: in 1949, 1950, and 1951. During World War I (1914–1918), with Barcelona as her official home, Montessori traveled to the United States, where she gave lectures and held training courses, which were covered extensively in the popular press. During these years her two major texts were translated into 11 languages. Inspired by the belief that education could heal the suffering that children experienced as a result of war, Montessori proposed the establishment of La Croce Bianca, the White Cross, in 1917. This would be an organization whose goal was "'to treat the children of war; to gather up the new human generation and to save it by a special method of education.' The plan was to train teacher-nurses to work with the depressed and frightened children of the war-ravaged countries" (Kramer, 1976, p. 253). Although the organization was never established, Montessori's concept did foreshadow England's plan for children during the blitz of World War II, and it contributed to the immediate opening of Montessori classrooms in France in 1917. More significant, the plan illustrates how Montessori framed, at least in part, the spread of the Montessori movement as a contribution to the restoration and maintenance of peace in Europe.

During the years between the two world wars, Montessori, now a grandmother, maintained an active travel schedule, offering international training courses every 2 years in England and in Europe and opening Montessori schools in Austria, England, Germany, Holland, Italy, and Spain. Both internal and external tensions shaped the movement's spread. Internally, Montessori's own desire and economic need to oversee the implementation of the Montessori Method led her to demand full control over all aspects of teacher training and production of didactic materials. Throughout her career, she cultivated a circle of loyal followers and was decidedly intolerant of experimentation with or modification of her method.

Externally, political tensions in Europe contributed to the closure of numerous Montessori schools. For instance, Montessori's schools in Barcelona were initiated and supported by Catalan leaders committed to social reform and to promoting the Catalan language and culture, a movement opposed by the leaders of Spain's "second republic." The turmoil of the Spanish Civil War led to the closure of these schools and, ultimately, to Montessori's departure from Spain altogether. Similarly, in Italy, the Fascist prime minister Benito Mussolini invited Montessori to open schools as part of his larger plan to promote the achievements of Italian culture. As she did in Spain, when pressed in Italy to align herself with the political party in power, Montessori refused, asserting that her cause was that of children. Ultimately, Montessori's refusal to cede authority to the Italian government led to Mussolini's closure of her schools, the suppression of the movement, and her permanent exile.

**The Cause of Peace**

It was during the 1920s and 1930s that Montessori elaborated her method for elementary and adolescent students. Her experiences in Spain and Italy, which were repeated in Austria and Germany, reinforced her belief that children's education was the means to social reform because they informed her argument that children were the greatest hope for peace. During the 1930s, as the forces of totalitarianism gathered strength throughout Europe, Montessori grew more active and vocal in the international peace movement, giving major addresses in Brussels, Geneva, and Copenhagen.[5] These lectures, first published in Italian in 1949 and later translated into English in the volume *Education and Peace* (1972), are her most direct statements of belief that a child, if given a proper environment, will develop to his or her fullest potential to be a citizen of humanity, transcending national and political boundaries.

In her address to the European Congress for Peace in 1936, Maria Montessori declared:

> Man now flies higher and more confidently through the heavens than the eagle; he has mastered the invisible secrets of the energy of the universe; he can look up into the skies and the infinite; his voice can cross the world's seas, and he can hear the echoes of all the world's music; he now possesses the secret powers of transforming matter. In a word, contemporary man has citizenship in the great nation of humanity. (1972, p. 29)

She goes on to underscore what she regards as the educational and political consequences of this sea change in the human condition:

> Our principal concern must be to educate humanity—the human beings of all nations—in order to guide it toward seeking common goals. We must turn back and make the child our principal concern. . . . The child is richly endowed with the powers, sensitivities, and constructive instincts that as yet have neither been recognized nor put to use. In order to develop, he needs much broader opportunities than he has been offered thus far. . . . Society must fully recognize the social rights of the child and prepare for him and the adolescent a world capable of ensuring their spiritual development. (1972, p. 31)

Here Montessori argues forcefully, even rhapsodically, for the necessity to awaken the child's potential and to honor its natural development.

At an address in Copenhagen in 1937, she was even more outspoken about the power of children to influence the world if adults took them seriously enough:

> In our experience with children, we observed that the human child is a spiritual embryo, endowed with mysterious sensitivities that guide him, with creative energies that tend to construct a sort of marvelous instrument in men's souls. . . . The child is also capable of developing and giving us tangible proof of the possibility of a better humanity. He has shown us the true process of construction of the normal human being. We have seen children totally change as they acquire a love for things and as their sense of order, discipline, and self-control develops within them as a manifestation of their total freedom. We have seen them labor steadily, drawing on their own energies and developing them as they work. The child is both a hope and a promise for mankind. If we therefore mind this embryo as our most precious treasure, we will be working for the greatness of humanity. (1972, pp. 35–36)

Thus, as Europe faced the inevitability of a second world war, in these and similar remarks woven throughout her various lectures, Montessori distilled her life's work into an argument for the fusion of education and peace.

Montessori spent the years of World War II in India and returned to Amsterdam in 1946 after the war. Although in her late 70s, she maintained a schedule similar to that of her youth: She supervised the publication of her many lectures, transcribed during various training courses; managed with Mario the Association Montessori Internationale (AMI); and gave numerous invited addresses, including those at three International Montessori Congresses (1949–1951) and at UNESCO's General Plenary Sessions (1947, 1950). Active to the end, she remained dedicated to her lifelong mission of service to social reform and to the rights of those with less power in society. She was a woman who both profoundly shaped and was shaped by the social, economic, and political context of the era in which she lived; more important, the legacy of her work lives on several generations after her death.

## THE CORE CONSTRUCTS: PLANES OF DEVELOPMENT, PREPARED ENVIRONMENT, COSMIC EDUCATION

### Planes of Development

The Montessori Method is a developmental approach to education founded on the close observation of the maturing child. In a sequence that foreshadows Piaget's four "stages" (sensorimotor, preoperational, concrete operational, and formal operational), Montessori outlined four "planes" of development. Like Piaget's stages, the planes map a progression from re-flexive motor activity to concrete and abstract thinking. But unlike Piaget's framework, Montessori's planes offer holistic renderings of the child at suc-cessive developmental passages. The child at 3, for instance, is said to be in the period of "absorbent mind." From 3 to 6 the child takes in the world sen-sorially. His or her drive to explore and experiment is fueled as much by spiri-tual as cognitive impulses. "The absorbent mind is indeed a marvelous gift to humanity," Montessori declared near the end of her life. "By merely 'living' and without conscious effort the individual absorbs from the environment even a complex cultural achievement like language. If this essential mental form existed in the adult, how much easier would our studies be!" (1949/1994, p. 64). Along with recognizing the cognitive power associated with the spongelike mind of the 3-year-old, Montessori identified a spiritual impulse in young children that, if properly nurtured, would mature into a powerful "inner guide" leading the child to peaceful, orderly, compassionate action. She called this impulse the "spiritual embryo" (1972, p. 35). Comparing the de-veloping child's spiritual/moral "potentialities" with that of the physical em-bryo, Montessori asserted that human capacity for purposeful living, creative energy, and compassion is present even in infants. If allowed to occur natu-rally, she claimed that the very process of development serves as a fulfillment of these capacities.

The key to fulfilling those developmental capacities, she further posited, is what she described as "freedom within limits." Elaborated in *The Discov-ery of the Child* (1962/1967a), Montessori distinguished freedom from lib-erty. The developing child must be free to carry out the process of "forming his personality," which is best achieved in an environment specially designed to meet that child's developmental needs. Within that environment, the child engages in purposeful activity, or the "work" (Cossentino, 2006) of devel-oping him- or herself. Within this scheme, the adult's role is to "follow the child." Montessori observed that children engrossed in work were peace-ful and contented, which she interpreted as evidence of the fulfillment of intellectual and social, as well as spiritual, potential. The notion of the "spiritual embryo," then, establishes both the purpose and the foundation for Montessori's framework of development.

Montessori's planes run in 6-year cycles in the age of a person (birth–6, 6–12, 12–18, 18–24), with each cycle subdivided into two distinct 3-year cycles. Moreover, within each developmental plane, but especially in the first plane, Montessori claimed that children pass through "sensitive periods" for particular intellectual, social, and moral awakenings. There are sensitive periods for language, movement, music, order, and so on. The central role of the adult, again, is to recognize these sensitive periods and direct the child to work designed to foster those awakenings.

By the time the child reaches the second plane of development (6–12) absorbency is replaced by deliberateness. The child becomes more task-oriented, more satisfied by completion, better able to map relationships between the parts and whole. What was the "spiritual embryo" has now matured into a being at the dawn of both abstract and moral reasoning. Identity begins to solidify during this plane and the child remains deeply invested in the work of formation. Montessori compared the mind of the child in the second plane to a "fertile field" where the "seed of everything can be sown," using this metaphor to illustrate the elementary child's unbounded curiosity to understand culture and the world/universe (1967b, p. 4). In addition, the child in this plane is more oriented toward learning and working in a community and toward moral reasoning, particularly the discernment of good and evil, an aspect of development that underscores her holistic point of view and a key difference with Piaget.

## The Prepared Environment

An even more important distinction from Piaget's theory is Montessori's deliberate association of each plane with an environment specially prepared to match the developmental needs of the child at each developmental epoch. Achieving the goal of "freedom within limits" rests on a subtle partnership between the child's spontaneous activity and an environment organized to frame that activity. "The first aim of the prepared environment," Montessori said, "is, as far as it is possible, to render the growing child independent of the adult" (1936/1966, p. 267).[6]

Environments are prepared differently for each plane, but they share similarities across the developmental spectrum. The prepared environment is, first of all, an orderly one. "Work" is arranged carefully in a developmentally progressive manner on open shelves so that children may have easy access to materials. In the elementary classroom materials are organized into disciplinary domains (e.g., mathematics, botany, geography, language) and children find a wide range of resources and materials, rather than textbooks, to draw from, thus reinforcing the critical role of choice and their responsibility to select materials.

Second, the environment is aesthetically pleasing, thereby instilling a sense of respect for the environment on the part of the children. Montessori was clear on this point:

> The environment should be "artistically beautiful" . . . not beauty produced by superfluity or luxury, but by grace and harmony or line and color . . . absolute simplicity. . . . No ornament can distract a child really absorbed in his task; on the contrary, beauty both promotes concentration of thought and offers refreshment to the tired spirit. (1917, pp. 144–146)

The teacher's attention both to the arrangement of materials and to the room's aesthetic qualities contributes to a sense of order that facilitates purposeful movement within the surroundings. In addition, Montessori envisioned that children would have immediate access to the outdoors and, when possible, a garden.

Finally, the environment should be a community shared and cared for by all its members. Sweeping floors, washing tables, watering plants, and feeding animals are all natural elements of the "practical life" aspect of the Montessori curriculum. Moreover, because environments are set up to accommodate multiage groupings (usually 3-year cycles), children establish bonds with one another, their teachers, and the physical space that serves as their "schoolhome" (Martin, 1992). For example, children do not have assigned desks; rather, they move fluidly from one area of the room to another, depending on the resources needed as well as their own sense of whether they require solitude or colleagues to accomplish a task. Thus, the features of the prepared environment—order, broad access to materials, aesthetic beauty, permeable boundaries, community responsibility, and flexible movement— all give the child the freedom to follow his or her curiosities, to marshal his or her intellectual energies to pursue questions, and therefore to construct integrated understandings.

## Cosmic Education

The particular manner of preparing an elementary environment is, perhaps, the most concrete manifestation of what Montessori referred to as "cosmic education" in *To Educate the Human Potential* (1967b). This is a relatively "late stage" elaboration of the Montessori system, developed in collaboration with her son Mario in India during World War II. Its purpose, like that of the rest of the system, is to respond to the unique developmental needs of the child between the ages of 6 and 12—to harness the combined forces of intellectual curiosity, physical stamina, and moral awakening. However, beyond this developmental approach is a more sweeping social agenda that Montessori always had in mind: to remake a world ravaged by war and injustice into a more peaceful, harmonious place.

Cosmic education holds as a central aim the child's discovery of his or her "cosmic task" (Duffy & Duffy, 2002; Montessori, 1973b). "Cosmic task" refers to one's particular role in the larger "cosmic plan" as a member of society whose collective impact is felt by all. The "task" of remaking the world, in other words, is the "great work" of humanity. It is a universal cause that requires both individual discernment and collective commitment. While the entire system is oriented toward this goal, discernment beginsin earnest during the second plane of development, between the ages of 6 and 12.

Here, Montessori's own cultural heritage, first as a Roman Catholic and later as a devotee of the mystical philosophy of theosophy, is most evident. She drew upon the Catholic catechism and upon theosophical reconstructions of ancient Indian doctrines of the union of the human soul with divine consciousness and karma. Her vision of cosmic education links the universal to the particular in the structure of the curriculum as well as the organization of the environment. Moreover, it instantiates the notion of harmony and situates it in the activity of learning.

> If the idea of the universe is presented to the child in the right way, it will do more for him than just arouse his interest, for it will create in him admiration and wonder, a feeling loftier than any interest and more satisfying. The child's mind then will no longer wander, but becomes fixed and can work. The knowledge he then acquires is organized and systematic; his intelligence becomes whole and complete because of the vision of the whole that has been presented to him, and his interest spreads to all, for all are linked and have their place in the universe of which his mind is centered. (1967b, p. 9)

Where the child from birth to 6 requires the carefully prescribed limits of the classroom environment, within which he or she masters the basics of independent living, the child from 6 to 12 requires a more expansive rendering of the wonders of the universe. In practice, this means, quite literally, presenting a picture of the whole—the whole sweep of human history, the whole structure of the English language, the whole image of the frog or fern—before exploring the smaller, more manageable parts. Montessori's assertion that a coherent picture of the whole is needed if one is to make sense of the parts distinguishes her educational vision from that of nearly every other major educational reformer, and most dramatically from Progressive Era contemporaries, such as John Dewey (Egan, 2002).

## THE PHILOSOPHY IN ACTION

Unlike traditional elementary curricula, the Montessori elementary program is driven by what in Montessori parlance are known as the "cultural subjects." These include history, geography, geometry, the arts, and the sciences. Study in these subjects is framed in an interdisciplinary mode that tends to revolve around the exploration of three fundamental questions: What am I? Where do I come from? What is my role in the universe?

These questions are, in Montessori's scheme, thoroughly appropriate for children who are at the dawn of moral and abstract thinking. Prior to the elementary years (birth to 6), the curriculum is driven by the development of fundamental sensory-motor competencies. Children are said to be given the "keys" to the world. By contrast, children in the stage she identified as "child-hood" (6–12) are ready to learn more about the world beyond their imme-diate touch. Children in this second plane of development are insatiably curious, have the physical stamina to explore a range of topics, have the concentration to stay with those topics over extended periods of time, and have the independence to manage their time and work within carefully con-structed guidelines.

In most Montessori elementary programs, children begin their day with 3 hours of uninterrupted, largely self-directed "work."[7] In addition to math and language work, a good deal of a typical elementary student's morning may be taken up with researching and writing a report on amphibians, con-structing a model of the Parthenon, or composing an original creation myth. Self-directed work entails variations on three primary activities: classifica-tion, sequencing, and exploration. Classification (in the form of charts pro-duced for the study of zoology, botany, and geology) and sequencing (in the form of time lines for all the cultural subjects, but especially history) provide structure for the creative and imaginative work of exploration.

The teacher, in this scheme, provides structure and guidance, but is not the source of knowledge. The preparation of an orderly, highly enriched environment constitutes one of three key activities distinguishing Montessori pedagogy from more traditional, transmission approaches to teaching.[8] In addition to preparing an environment specially designed to meet the intellec-tual, social, and spiritual needs of children at various stages of development, Montessori teachers base their instructional decisions on close observation of the child at work. Observation is the primary basis for assessing readiness; interest; and, ultimately, mastery. Invitation is a third core activity of Mon-tessori practice. Teachers offer lessons, both individual and group, based on interest and readiness demonstrated by the child; and the offer is just that: an invitation to work imaginatively within the structure provided by the environ-ment and the materials contained within that environment.

A key example of the balance of structure and imagination is the series of narratives that serve as touch points for the curriculum. Known as the Great Lessons, these five stories, told by the teacher to the students, col-lectively present a picture of the story of the universe. Beginning with the creation of the earth and progressing to the beginning of life, the emergence of humans, and the development of social life in the form of language and numbers, these lessons are designed to provide a compelling impression of the whole. Therein lies their "greatness." The picture of the whole of the universe then prompts students to wonder, to question, to seek to know more. Once the interest is sparked, work may begin. The stories themselves provide a scaffolding to support imaginative inquiry, which is then carried out in a varied series of extensions and experiments. Following the story of creation, for example, which tells of the formation of elements, the transformation of matter, and the manner in which chemical interactions gradually produced the earth, students may examine the composition of our planet, the force of gravity, and plate tectonics. Or they may conduct experiments involving the transformation of solids, liquids, and gases.

While the subjects under study are wide ranging, the nexus of exploration remains consistent throughout the 6 years of the second plane: Who am I? Where do I come from? What is my role in the universe? Within these questions Montessori presents peace as not just a goal of education, but its very context. To "give [the children] a vision of the whole universe" is to prompt holistic and generative exploration of a phenomenon that is at once limitless and orderly. Within the universe all things are connected. To examine the origins and purposes of those connections is to engage in activity that is both fascinating and consequential. According to Montessori, it is precisely the combination of vastness and order that appeals to the elementary child.

In other words, the child as a cosmic being is a child in search of meaning. Aiming to meet the needs of the child in search of meaning gained through knowledge of oneself and society, the curriculum for cosmic education not only provides a limitless course of study, it mirrors the order of the universe itself. The preponderance of charts and time lines provides, perhaps, the most concrete manifestation of this order. Children use these charts as reference tools, exemplars, and symbols of their work. Incorporating research material, drawings, and tracing, the charts are reproduced by the children, usually in groups. Once completed, the charts may be displayed in the classroom, where they become one of many artifacts of the collective work of the elementary community.

## Going Out

In addition to the structure of the curriculum itself, a key element of cosmic education involves learning beyond the classroom. While the prepared environment is rich in resources, venturing into the wider world is central to understanding one's role in that world. Elementary children go out individually, in small, self-directed groups, as well as on larger, more traditional field trips. Whether the trip is to purchase crickets to feed the classroom frog or an overnight camping excursion, the critical element of "going out" is the students' central role in planning and executing the event.

Ideally, going out is prompted by a genuine need that cannot be fulfilled within the classroom. For instance, in the course of a research project on turtles, a student may initiate a visit to a local university to interview a biologist who studies turtles. To carry out the trip, the student must contact the biologist to schedule the visit, arrange for transportation to and from the lab, and follow up the visit with appropriate correspondence. Students who are planning an overnight trip will research lodging possibilities and contact visitors bureaus to obtain maps and other information relevant to the trip. Overnight trips are often funded by money raised by the students themselves. In these cases, the fund-raising activities become practical life exercises with consequences. In most cases, regardless of the source of funds, students are responsible for creating and working within a budget. In every case, the child's agency, both individually and as a member of a group, lies at the heart of the enterprise. A final way in which children go out in the world is through service learning; for example, children may identify a social issue of interest, research that issue, and identify a way in which they may engage in social action to respond concretely to the issue explored. In some Montessori schools, such a project is viewed as the culmination of the 9-to-12 cycle, an experience that is foreshadowed as the younger students watch and listen each year as their older classmates conduct and share their research and social action activities.

### "We Declare Peace"

The notion of development as active and effortful reflects Montessori's perspective that peace is not a passive endeavor. Peace is made in daily interactions large and small. Along with lessons in grace and courtesy, which are introduced in the first plane of development, Montessori's most overt demonstration of peace education occurs in what is sometimes known as the "peace rose ceremony." Many Montessori classrooms include an area specially designated for conflict resolution. Usually this is a quiet space that may contain a rug or a table set up with objects designed to calm the spirit. There may be a Zen garden or beads for handling or a beautiful print for gazing. Children are free to spend time at the peace table when they are feeling out of sorts or need a break from the morning routine.

Often the area will contain a vase with a single rose. This is the "peace rose." Children who are engaged in a disagreement are encouraged to go to the table together, to take turns listening as each explains how he or she is feeling and, ultimately (and often with the guidance of an adult), to come to an agreement that each "can live with." At the conclusion of the discussion, the students are encourage to "declare peace," and younger students will often repeat the phrase "We declare peace," sometimes holding the rose together. Older students are more likely to offer the rose as an opening to discussion. A child may approach another child with whom he or she has had a conflict, hand him or her the rose, and ask for a solution to the problem. Implicit in the concept of the peace table is the notion that conflict is a natural part of community life. The very presence of a space in the classroom devoted to peaceful conflict resolution acknowledges that peace is a goal that requires ongoing commitment.

## CONCLUDING THOUGHTS FOR EDUCATORS
## IN THE 21ST CENTURY

For the third time in its history, Montessori education is experiencing a dramatic rise in popularity. The first two iterations of this interest (in the early 1910s and again in the 1960s) were driven primarily by middle-class interest in alternatives to traditional public schooling. The current wave of interest is centered largely in public schools. According to the best available database, there are currently more than 4,000 Montessori schools in the United States.[9] Researchers, too, have started to notice Montessori and have begun to study its contributions. In the years 2000–2005 there have been 32 research studies of Montessori education in the United States.[10]

We close by highlighting three key themes that characterize Montessori's system for elementary children and illuminate the construct of peace as a premise for education: Montessori's vision was at once developmentalist, communitarian, and cosmological. Each of these themes resonates with current discourse in educational theory and practice. Within the intersection of these three themes, we argue, lies the essence of her vision of peace as a premise for education and the most important lessons for contemporary educators.

Cosmic education, like the whole of the Montessori system, begins and ends with a sharp focus on the child as a developing human being. "The child," she proclaimed in 1937, "is also capable of developing and giving us tangible proof of the possibility of a better humanity" (1972, p. 36). Montessori's infinite sensitivity to the processes of human development, honed at the start of her career by her thorough medical and scientific training and elaborated over a lifetime spent largely as a war refugee, inspires us to take seriously her vision of peace as flowing from the child's natural tendencies to learn.

Within the developmentalist frame, education is achieved through fostering those natural tendencies. Development, moreover, is situated within an intentionally created community. For the youngest children, the "prepared environment" fosters key skills necessary for harmonious living: freedom of movement, courtesy, peaceful conflict resolution, and care of the environment itself. And as the child matures, so does the community grow more complex and expansive and the child's responsibility to nurturing community more profound.

In linking world peace with healthy human development, Montessori elaborated a cosmological (Cossentino, 2005) vision of education in which all things are connected—from the order of the universe to organization of classroom space to the structure of the curriculum. Maria Montessori was the first educator of the 20th century to fully elaborate an integrated curriculum, the specifics of which link the moral and social aspects of development with the intellectual. Moreover, in situating peace at the center of her curriculum, Montessori also demonstrated how moral and social development might serve as both the means and end of education. That is, in the Montessori scheme, peace is not made manifest in tolerance, but in respect: respect for the environment as well as respectful relationships. And that respect is acted out in daily interactions both within and beyond the prepared environment. Peace is not achieved through justice, but through deep and active appreciation of the order of the universe and one's place in it. The order of the curriculum—all that emphasis on classification and sequencing—mirrors, even exemplifies, the order of a harmonious universe. Mapping that order allows children to know the logic that holds the universe together, to find it awe inspiring, and to be moved to protect its awesome and fragile beauty.

For 21st-century educators, Montessori's holistic system offers not just an alternative to traditional, transmission approaches to teaching; it provides both a redefined purpose for education, peace, and a redefined means of achieving that purpose. Peace, within the Montessori frame, is achieved through practice. It is a practice that begins within the carefully defined limits of the prepared environment and is embodied in tiny movements—waiting one's turn to use a piece of material, learning to pour from a pitcher with care, moving gracefully around the room so as not to disturb others. As the child matures, so does his or her practice, growing ever more complex and intentional.

# Art, Nature, and Education: Rabindranath Tagore's Holistic Approach to Learning

## Kathleen M. O'Connell

WHEN CONSIDERING individuals whose lives represent the fullest artistic self-expression, it is difficult to find a more productive and humane figure than Rabindranath Tagore. As Asia's first Nobel laureate,[1] his genius helped shape the sensibility of modern Bengal and, more generally, India. Considering that Tagore worked without a computer, or even electricity much of the time, and that he had no secretary until late in his life, his creative output is all the more astonishing.

Tagore composed his first poem at age 8 and by the end of his life had written more than 25 volumes of poetry, 15 plays, 90 short stories, 11 novels, and 13 volumes of essays and had founded and edited numerous journals. He prepared Bengali textbooks, kept up a correspondence comprising thousands of letters, composed more than 2,000 songs (including 2 that would become the national anthems of India and Bangladesh), as well as creating more than 2,000 paintings. Besides his educational and literary work, he was an actor, singer, director-producer, religious commentator, occasional participant in the political arena, cultural ambassador, and initiator of rural development projects. It is also noteworthy that his creative output during the last years of life was not only prolific, but also innovative.

The first section of this chapter focuses on Tagore's philosophy of life and education. It begins with his historical and familial milieu, locating him within the 19th-century period known as the Bengal Renaissance, a particularly significant era in that it represented the first extended contact between

Europe and India. The important role that his family and early childhood experiences had in shaping his educational thought is examined, as well as the way that his poetic sensibility and exposure to rural Bengal affected later priorities in his school at Santiniketan. Three central foci of his educational paradigm are highlighted: direct experience, creative sensibility, and dynamic global interconnectivity.

In the second section I look at the working out of Tagore's educational vision within the three components of his learning center at Santiniketan, which is located about 100 miles from Calcutta on his family's property. These include Santiniketan, a primary school founded in 1901; Visva-Bharati, an all-India, Eastern, and global learning center inaugurated in 1921; and Sriniketan, a rural reconstruction center instituted in 1922. In the third section I examine the envisioned role of the teacher as conceived by Tagore as creative facilitator and moral guide. In the final section I assess Tagore's educational legacy and its relevance for today's world.

## HISTORICAL AND FAMILIAL INFLUENCES

Central to Tagore's life was the development of a creative alternative educational system in Santiniketan (the Abode of Peace) in Bengal, India, to which he dedicated the last 40 years of his life.[2] He indicated in his autobiographical writings, which were mostly written in Bengali, that the evolution of his school at Santiniketan reflects his own personal development. Born in Calcutta, West Bengal, in colonial British India in 1861, Tagore came from a distinguished family whose members were participants in three major revolutions affecting India: religious, cultural, and national. The Tagores were on the forefront of these transformations, and they were instrumental in shaping new forms of Bengali language, literature, music, and art, as well as facilitating socioreligious change and nation building. Tagore's grandfather Dwarkanath was involved in almost every aspect of social reform of his period, supporting hospitals, educational institutions, and the arts and fighting for religious and social reform, as well as for a free press. His father, Devendranath, through his leadership in the religious reform group Brahmo Samaj, was also instrumental in social and religious reform, and he encouraged multicultural exchange in the family mansion. Because of their active roles in these movements as outspoken critics of the status quo, the men were often ostracized, forcing them to cultivate a sense of independence and to create their own standards.[3] Tagore grew up within this atmosphere of critical thought and artistic achievement, and his appraisal of the existing educational system would have been shaped by the high standards that existed within this richly diverse family setting.

Much of the cultural exchange that occurred during this period took place right within the Tagore home, called Jorasanko (the "living university," as he later called it), the sprawling joint family mansion that now houses Rabindra Bharati University, in Calcutta. There, foreign visitors and pundits[4] of great learning would visit his father's drawing room to discuss politics, the scriptures, and sciences while musicians displayed their skills. Tagore's 13 siblings and extended family created a self-contained educational system, and it is not surprising that he found outside schooling greatly lacking by comparison. His immediate family excelled in math, literature, music, theater, and journalism, while his cousins, who shared the family mansion, showed great interest in science and spearheaded a new art movement that became known as the Bengal school of art. As the youngest, Tagore especially benefitted from this richly stimulating environment and was able to develop the many facets of his intellect and creativity in an unregimented manner. His early experiences at Jorasanko greatly affected his later ideas on education and convinced him of the need for a flexible, open-ended educational system that operated at multiple levels, as well as of the desirability of a hospitable community as learning environment.[5]

Tagore's emphasis on individual freedom in education and on the essential role of the arts for developing empathy and sensitivity can be directly linked to these early years. As he wrote,

> Fortunately for me I was brought up in a family where literature, music and art had become instinctive. My brothers and cousins lived in the freedom of ideas, and most of them had natural artistic powers. Nourished in these surroundings, I began to think early and to dream and to put my thoughts into expression. (1917, pp. 139–140)

He also felt an intense connection with the natural environment. Nature was experienced as a vital playmate and companion who had something cupped in her hands and was always asking with a smile, "What do you think I have?" As he discovered, such an early sensitive connection with nature was a state that set children apart from adults and must be nurtured at an early age or it would be lost.

Tagore's poetic perceptions also profoundly defined his approach to education and the outside world. He credits several illuminating experiences from his youth with shaping his life and creative direction; in particular, he spoke of one experience that occurred when he was 18. It began while he was standing on a balcony watching the sun rise, and carried over through the next 4 days. Its impact remained with him all his life; so much so that he was still speaking of it on his 80th birthday. It was a heightened moment, he wrote, as though a mist had lifted and "the invisible screen of the commonplace was removed from all things and all men, and their ultimate significance was intensified in my mind" (1931, pp. 93–94).

The perception of a vital connection between an ever-changing natural world, humanity, and a guiding creative force profoundly influenced Tagore's educational vision. It is worth quoting at length on the epiphany that led him to this worldview.

> The whole scene was one perfect music—one marvelous rhythm. . . . Everyone, even those who bored me, seemed to lose their outer barrier of personality; and I was full of gladness, full of love, for every person and every tiniest thing. . . . That morning was one of the first things which gave me the inner vision, and I have tried to explain it in my poems. I have felt, ever since, that this was my goal: to express the fullness of life, in its beauty, as perfection—if only the veil were withdrawn. (1929, p. 24)

As poet-seer (*kavi*), he felt responsible to a creative force, to which he gave many names over the years: the Great Accomplisher of Creation, Greater Man, Universal Man, the Ever Furtherer, the Exquisite Reveller, the Beguiler, the Great Architect, the Great Rejoicer, and so forth. As the years went on, his vision of a unity underlying creation became expressed educationally in ever-widening terms of global inclusion and cultural interaction.

Another formative experience that set Tagore apart from his peers was his connection with rural Bengal in the 1890s, when his father surprisingly put him in charge of the family's rural properties in East Bengal. This would have been unusual given Tagore's position as the youngest son of the family. At first Tagore's poetic imagination was inspired by the beauty of the countryside, and a series of poems, stories, and letters poured forth. Gradually, though, he became aware of the acute material and cultural poverty that permeated the villages, as well as of the great divide between uneducated rural masses and city elites. These experiences led to the later establishment of a Rural Reconstruction Center at Sriniketan that involved students and teachers in constructive service: literacy training, alternative educational methods, social work, and the promotion of cooperative schemes.

## PHILOSOPHY OF LIFE AND EDUCATION

### Direct Experience

As Tagore matured into one of the world's great artists, he began to critique the existing educational system, something he found woefully inadequate for developing the immense potential of the human personality. Children, he argued, have enormous, unrealized potential and a unique "freshness of the senses" that becomes dulled and is gradually lost if not cultivated in the early years. Education, he argued, must consider all dimensions of the child's personality, not just the verbal or cognitive level. The type of nonlinear, subconscious learning that he envisioned was something vitally connected to all aspects of life, and it contrasted starkly with what he found in the foreign-model schools that he attended and rejected. He likened their negative learning to an educational factory that was "lifeless, colorless, dissociated from the context of the universe, within bare white walls staring like eyeballs of the dead " (Chakravarty, 1966, p. 214). There, the physiological needs of children were stunted and ignored, and they were forced to sit inert, "like dead specimens of some museum," while lessons were pelted "from on high, like hailstones on flowers" (Chakravarty, 1966, p. 214).

Tagore's first major address on education "Siksar Herfer" (Discrepancy in Education), delivered in 1892, constituted one of the first comprehensive critiques of English-medium education in India.[6] In it, he criticized the discrepancies that existed between an English model of education as it existed in England and an English model of education in India. He argued for a creative style of teaching and learning that would encompass the education of the whole child, advocating (1) the need for joyous learning and the experience of mental and physical freedom, (2) a linguistic medium connected to a child's social and cultural environment, (3) accessible well-educated teachers who inspire, (4) a multilevel curriculum to stimulate critical thought and creative imagination, and (5) learning in the holistic world of nature for empathy. Later addresses would reinforce the emphasis upon direct experience in learning and the need to balance cognitive and affective learning:

> We have come to this world to accept it, not merely to know it. We may become powerful by knowledge, but we attain fulness by sympathy. The highest education is that which does not merely give us information but makes our life in harmony with all existence. But we find that this education of sympathy is not only systematically ignored in schools, but it is severely repressed. From our very childhood habits are formed and knowledge is imparted in such a manner that our life is weaned away from nature and our mind and the world are set in opposition from the beginning of our days. Thus the greatest of educations for which we came prepared is neglected, and we are made to lose our world to find a bagful of information instead. We rob the child of his earth to teach him geography, of language to teach him grammar. His hunger is for the Epic, but he is supplied with chronicles of facts and dates. . . . Child-nature protests against such calamity with all its power of suffering, subdued at last into silence by punishment. (1917, pp. 116–117)

For Tagore, creative education starts with a closeness to nature, and one of his central goals was to enable his students to vividly experience the ever-changing patterns of the natural environment. Turning to the indigenous model of the *tapoban*,[7] or "forest school" of ancient India, he set out to develop a small alternative learning center on the family estate in Santiniketan in 1901. In the practical working out of his vision, Santiniketan was an ideal location in that it provided a beautiful natural setting that had associations of physical and mental freedom for Tagore. He had been able to retain his sensitive appreciation of nature, or his "child-mind," as he called it, and to make it the basis for understanding the needs of children.

Through his art and the structure of the curriculum, Tagore tried to convey to the students the subtle resonances that existed between the moods of nature and their own personalities. The school day began with a short period of meditation, and he created seasonal plays and ceremonies to celebrate nature's changes in order to help sensitize the students to its fluidity. "One of the seminal lessons children learn in nature," he writes, "is improvisation without the constant imposition of the ready-made" (1931, p. 178). This gives them the occasion to explore their abilities through "surprises of achievement" and to observe creative patterns in life. The great gift of children, he writes, is that they are able to come directly to the intimacy of this world with the freshness of their senses: "They must accept it naked and simple and must never again lose their power of immediate communication with it" (p. 173).

## Creative Sensibility

Also central to Tagore's educational vision, and linked to a direct experience of nature, was the enhancement of a student's aesthetic sensibility. His goal in starting a school, he stated, was to create a poem "in a medium other than words" (1961, p. 286). Drawing on his home life at Jorasanko, he tried to create an atmosphere at Santiniketan in which the arts would become integral and where there would be a sharpening of the senses. One of the first areas to be emphasized was music. He writes that in his adolescence, a "cascade of musical emotion" gushed forth day after day at Jorasanko. "We felt we would try to test everything," he writes, "and no achievement seemed impossible. We wrote, we sang, we acted, we poured ourselves out on every side" (1917/1962, p. 198). Dance and the visual arts were also built into the daily life of Santiniketan students.

In presenting a model for his teachers, Tagore tried to re-create the same stimulating Jorasanko cultural atmosphere of artists and thinkers to inspire his students. He held up his brother Jyotirindranath as a model educator for how he had treated his pupil—none other than young "Rabi" himself—as an equal and encouraged him emotionally. As he developed his Santiniketan model, Tagore, or Gurudev, as he was affectionately called by his students, provided an inspiring role model, albeit a difficult one to follow. With his multiple talents, he could spontaneously create games, plays, dances, and songs to engage the students.

In an effort to develop self-esteem, Tagore treated the Santiniketan students with great respect. In teaching, he also believed in presenting difficult levels of literature, which the students might not fully grasp, but which would stimulate them. Students were allowed access to the room where he read his new writings to teachers and critics, and they were encouraged to read their own writings aloud in special literary evenings. The writing and publishing of periodicals had always been an important aspect of Jorasanko life, and students at Santiniketan were encouraged to create their own publications and published several illustrated magazines. Children were prompted to follow their ideas in painting and drawing and to draw inspiration from the many visiting artists and writers. Tagore was able to attract such notable artists as Nandalal Bose, Ramkinkar Baij, and Binodbihari Mukherjee to live among the students and mentor them on a daily basis. A highlight of the school year was the Nanda Mela, which celebrated the artistic achievements of faculty and students, permitting them to display and sell their work. This process continues to the present day, when students are fortunate to have resident artists such as K. G. Subramanyan and Jogen Choudhury to mentor and inspire them.

Most of Tagore's dramas were written at Santiniketan, and the students took part in both the performance and production. He was also one of the first to support and bring together different forms of Indian dance. He helped revive folk dances and introduced dance forms from other parts of India, most notably Manipuri, Kathak, and Kathakali. He supported modern dance and was one of the first to recognize the talents of dancer Uday Sankar, who was invited to perform at Santiniketan.

### Dynamic Global Interconnectivity

As Tagore gained international fame and began traveling and establishing links with artists and intellectuals throughout Asia and the West, the educational curriculum at Santiniketan broadened further. His initial educational concern had been to develop an alternate model for primary education. When he established Visva-Bharati as an Indian university, he turned to the development of a national model for higher education.[8] Just as the *tapoban* had served as his prototype for Santiniketan, for Visva-Bharati he referred to the ancient Buddhist monastaries of Nalanda, Taxila, and Vikramshila as Indian models of hospitality, cosmopolitanism, scholarship, and a harmonious relationship with the local community. Visva-Bharati was to operate on three levels: as an Indian university, as an Eastern university, and as a global cultural center.

The motto chosen for Visva-Bharati was *yatra visvam bhavati ekanidam,* or "where the world comes together in a single nest." The constitutional statement, in effect a mission statement, articulates the broad, integrating ideals of the institution and designates Visva-Bharati as an Indian, Eastern, and global cultural center:[9]

- To study the mind of Man in its realisation of different aspects of truth from diverse points of view.
- To bring into more intimate relation with one another, through patient study and research, the different cultures of the East on the basis of their underlying unity.
- To approach the West from the standpoint of such a unity of the life and thought of Asia.
- To seek to realise in a common fellowship of study the meeting of East and West and thus ultimately to strengthen the fundamental conditions of world peace through the free communication of ideas between the two hemispheres.
- With such Ideals in view to provide at Santiniketan a Centre of culture where research into the study of the religion, literature, history, science, and art of Hindu, Buddhist, Jain, Zoroastrian, Islamic, Sikh, Christian and other civilizations may be pursued along with the culture of the West, with that simplicity of externals which is necessary for true spiritual realisation, in amity, good-fellowship and co-operation between the thinkers and scholars of both Eastern and Western countries, free from all antagonisms of race, nationality, creed or caste and in the name of the One Supreme Being who is Shantam, Shivam, Advaitam. (Visva-Bharati Prospectus, 1922, p. i.)

## SANTINIKETAN, VISVA-BHARATI, SRINIKETAN: THE SCHOOL AS MICROCOSM OF THE LIVING WORLD

### Santiniketan

In developing his educational paradigm, Tagore likened the subconscious mind to a tree that absorbs its nutrients from the surrounding atmosphere, and he aimed at creating an open-ended, alternative learning situation that reflected the world. The starting points were the local environment and the natural world. With these in mind, he formulated a curriculum that would revolve organically around nature, with classes held in the open air under the trees, providing for an unstructured appreciation of the plant and animal kingdoms and seasonal change. He also insisted on simplicity in the learning environment, arguing that luxury, too much educational paraphernalia, and excessive concern about methodology actually prevented children from experiencing life directly. He felt that preoccupation with material things coarsened the sensibilities, whereas concern with beauty and order released the mind from inertia, greed, and ineptitude. "The joy of creative writing increases in proportion," he writes, "as we are able to shed the ornate and the superfluous." He argued that the simple ashram procedures provide the opportunity for "revitalizing the principles of cooperation in daily life" (1983, pp. 13–14). For the Santiniketan students, community cooperation extended to caring for their sick peers, as well as helping to fight fires in the neighboring villages.

To illustrate the way in which the externals of education can dominate and overshadow the real purpose of education, Tagore wrote a fable titled "Totakahini," or "The Parrot's Training," featuring a bird that sings all day but never recites scriptures. A brief summary of the allegory provides insight into the simple but penetrating way in which he often presented his educational critique. The story involves a local Raja, who decides that the parrot needs to be educated and summons his pundits, who decree that the bird's ignorance is a result of his living in a nest. A golden cage is built, and the pundits decide that textual materials are needed. Scribes diligently copy from books, and copy from copies, until manuscripts are piled up to an unreachable height. Everyone agrees that great "progress" has been made. Later, the Raja summons his education department to see how things are going. They come to the Great Hall with conch shells, gongs, horns, bugles, trumpets, cymbals, drums, kettledrums, tomtoms, tambourines, flutes, fifes, barrel organs, and bagpipes. The pundits chant mantras, while the goldsmiths, scribes, supervisors, and countless cousins all cheer. The Raja is forced to agree that it all seems "fearfully like a sound principle of Education" (1964, p. 86). Finally, a fault finder asks the Raja if he's actually seen the bird, and the Raja has to admit that he has forgotten entirely about it. Before he has a chance to concentrate on the bird, the pundits distract him with elaborate explanations of the methods they have been using in instructing the bird. By comparison, the bird seems ridiculously unimportant and not worthy of attention. Anyway, its throat has become so choked from the pages of books, it can't complain. Occasionally it flutters its wings in the morning light until a blacksmith forges a chain, and the bird's wings are clipped. At last, the bird dies, and the Raja is informed that its education has been completed.

"Does it hop?" the Raja asks.

"Never!" reply the nephews.

"Does it fly?"

"No."

"Bring me the bird," commands the Raja.

When the bird is finally brought, the Raja pokes its body and discovers that only its inner stuffing of book leaves rustles, as outside the "murmur of the spring breeze amongst the newly budded *asoka* leaves makes the April morning wistful" (1964, p. 88).

Tagore's goals at Santiniketan were for a learning environment that was simple, flexible, and organically related to the child's needs. Children did not sit on chairs, but rather on hand-woven mats beneath the trees, which they were allowed to climb and run around between classes. Nature walks and excursions were a part of the curriculum and students were encouraged to follow the life cycles of insects, birds, and plants. The afternoon schedule included outdoor games and free time in nature; evening functions were also outdoors and astronomy was a part of the evening activities. Class schedules were made flexible to allow for shifts in the weather or giving special attention to natural phenomena.[10]

With one of the world's finest nature poets as their mentor, the Santiniketan children were able to listen to first readings of his work and participate in festivals and plays that he created on–site to celebrate the nuances of nature. Such festivals included the Basant Panchami (Spring Festival) and the Barsha Mangal (Rain Festival), which later included a special tree-planting ceremony, the Brksha Ropana, introduced in July 1928. As part of this ceremony, each child was encouraged to adopt a tree. It was, in Tagore's words, "a ceremony of the replenishing of the treasury of the mother by her spendthrift children" (quoted in Mukherjee, 1962, p. 235). In the villages, he celebrated the harvest cycle with Hala-karshana, a festival celebrating the cultivation of the land, and a harvest ceremony, the Nabanna, which welcomed the new rice crop.

## Visva-Bharati

The meeting-ground of cultures, as Tagore envisioned it at Visva-Bharati, would be a learning center where conflicting interests were minimized, where individuals worked together in a common pursuit of truth and realized "that artists in all parts of the world have created forms of beauty, scientists discovered secrets of the universe, philosophers solved the problems of existence, saints made the truth of the spiritual world organic in their own lives, not merely for some particular race to which they belonged, but for all mankind" (1922, pp. 171–172). At the opening ceremony, he turned over the Santiniketan land, buildings, and library, along with the copyright for his books and interest from the Nobel Prize money, to Visva-Bharati. He spoke of the radical changes taking place in civilization and the need for new forms of education. Visva-Bharati was to be an experiment in which individuals of different civilizations and traditions learned to live together, not on the basis of nationalism, but through a wider relationship of humanity (Sykes, 1947, pp. 84–85).

To encourage mutual growth and understanding, Tagore invited artists and scholars from other parts of India and the world to live together at Santiniketan and on a daily basis to share their cultures with the students of

Visva-Bharati. His goal at Visva-Bharati was nothing less than the establishment of a cultural center in tune with the totality of global life, but he also realized that the only way to start was on a small scale. True to his expectations, stereotypes of various sorts began to break down as the Santiniketan residents lived beside one another over periods of time, forming long-term relationships and sharing their languages and music, dances, and other artistic forms. As an important experiment in human living, Visva-Bharati was highly successful, particularly in the early days when the community was small.

### Sriniketan

There was also the outreach to country and villages, which was represented by Sriniketan activities such as literacy programs, malaria eradication, artisan-revival programs, and health cooperatives. In this way, Tagore worked to reduce the great divide between the educated urban elite and the villagers. Hoping to create a model for the country, he stated, "If we could free even one village from the shackles of helplessness and ignorance, an ideal for the whole of India would be established" (1961, p. 322). With the help of British agronomist Leonard Elmhirst and an able group of volunteers, Tagore set up programs to make the villages surrounding Santiniketan economically independent and culturally vibrant.[11]

Tagore's emphasis on self-reliance and critical thinking was evident from the early days of Santiniketan, when students were required to take care of themselves as much as possible and to assist others. This philosophy characterized the Sriniketan activities as well, and various projects to help the surrounding villages with literacy training, fire control, and health improvements were initiated. As Tagore wrote,

> Children need training in self-reliance and self-help from their early childhood. In our country this aspect of education is sadly neglected. Let the child never tire in his efforts to give play to his creative joy by inventing things with the help of whatever material lies ready at hand. Let him at the same time learn to find delight in voluntarily performing tasks calculated to add to the health, happiness and comfort of the community. . . . We are always ready to suppress any initiative on the part of the children to organize their own immediate environment for themselves. (1983, p. 13)

One of the most innovative of the educational initiatives at Sriniketan was a school called the Home School, or Siksha Satra, meaning "where education is given free." The school began in 1924 with 6 students and had increased to 20 by 1929. The learning framework reflected a more practical adaptation of the Santiniketan ideals: a close connection with the natural environment, independent learning, training of the senses, holistic learning through creative activities, and the development of social responsibility and leadership skills. On the educational side, Tagore urged that mass education in the vernacular be undertaken through *melas*, or "country fairs," that would educate the villagers through folk plays, songs, mythological stories, traveling libraries, and lantern-slide exhibitions. The annual Sriniketan mela, which was instituted in the early 1920s to showcase various aspects of rural education and culture, continues to the present.

## THE TEACHER AS CREATIVE FACILITATOR AND MORAL GUIDE

Throughout his life, Tagore put great emphasis on the importance of the individual, stating that he did not place his faith in any new institution, but in the individuals all over the world "who think clearly, feel nobly, and act rightly, thus becoming the channels of moral truth" (1922, p. 153). In seeking role models for his teachers, Tagore drew upon the forest gurus from the Indian past who, with their family and students, sought to create lives that were in harmony with nature. Along with presenting nature as the prime teacher, Tagore wanted students to live in close association with dedicated teachers of high aspiration who lived a life of "serene sanity." A "guru," as defined by Tagore, was a teacher who devoted his whole mind and spirit to the service of his students, was able to rise above financial considerations, and was able "to put life into his pupils with his own life, light their lamps with his own learning, and make them happy with his affection" (1961, p. 79).

Tagore felt that a teacher's ability to recognize the unique personality of each child and to guide each according to the students' capacities was far more important than facility in a particular teaching method. Teachers were advised not to be preoccupied with method but to allow their instincts to guide them, since each child differed from the next. Thus, "one must learn to know them, to navigate among them as one navigates among reefs. To explore the geography of their minds, a mysterious instinct, sympathetic to life, is the best of all guides" (1917/1962, p. 53).

The teachers whom Tagore sought for Santiniketan were those who were caught up with their subjects and, therefore, taught by transmitting a love of the material. Similarly, he placed ability over teaching qualifications when it came time to choose his instructors. The early Santiniketan teachers were chosen for their skill in a particular discipline, as well as their ability to inspire their young students. Teachers rotated subjects, and they were involved with their own special projects, in which the students were invited to collaborate.

Today, most teachers would be hard put to create a natural *tapoban* setting. Yet even within the crowded urban conditions in which many teachers find themselves, there are lessons to learn from Tagore's example at Santiniketan. One would be the application of environmental relevance, that is, to connect the students to the natural and cultural environment and to study how this relates to the wider world. Tagore knew how influential the teacher as mentor and role model could be, and how much the students gained when a teacher demonstrated a real passion for his or her material. He argued that before one can become an effective teacher, one must develop a personal aesthetic and moral capacity and broaden one's outlook as widely as possible. In teaching, the instructor must always keep in mind that there are many ways to learn and many facets to each student, and that the nonverbal, nonlinear, affective side should be considered, as well as the linear verbal-conceptual side.

## TAGORE'S EDUCATIONAL LEGACY

Tagore's educational efforts were groundbreaking in many respects and must also be seen in the context of a global network of pioneering educators, such as Rousseau, Pestalozzi, Froebel, Montessori, and Dewey, who rebelled against existing systems of rigid, authoritarian education. In a contemporary setting, his philosophy would have resonance with thinkers who advocate organic learning and cultivation of the affective side of the personality. In India, Tagore was one of the first to argue for a humane educational system connected to the environment and aimed at overall development of the personality. Santiniketan became a model for vernacular instruction and the development of Bengali textbooks; it also offered one of the earliest coeducational programs in South Asia. Similarly, the establishment of Visva-Bharati and Sriniketan led to pioneering efforts in many directions, including models for distinctively Indian higher education and mass education, as well as pan-Asian and global cultural exchange.[12]

Tagore's legacy as a pioneer educator is diffuse, living on through a vast circle of influence: artists whose work has affected Indian and foreign art; artists and scholars who went on to found or staff various artistic and academic departments and institutes; schools that have been patterned after the Santiniketan model; former staff members who have gone on to play significant roles in educational policy formation; distinguished graduates (including Indira Gandhi, Satyajit Ray, and Nobel laureate Amartya Sen) who have had a major impact on national and global affairs. Further, the example of Santiniketan and Tagore's articulation of the importance of cultivating one's artistic sensibility has helped to shape curriculums in many schools within India and abroad.[13]

The role of Rabindranath Tagore and Santiniketan in promoting ongoing educational reform must also be mentioned. As Humayun Kabir, a prominent former Indian education minister, observes in his assessment of Tagore's educational work, "Practically every new development in Indian education since the beginning of the century owes something to the work which was initiated at Santiniketan" (1959, p. 52). One can find the influence of Tagore's ideas on vernacular and rural education in such important documents as the 1938 Basic National Education recommendations of the Zakir Hussain Committee, which were drafted by E. W. Aryaratnam, who had earlier been part of the Sriniketan team.

Tagore's life and work have special relevance for our own time. Above all, his insistence on the fullest possible development of the creative personality within a responsible and pluralistic social setting, his resistance to rigid narrowness or dogmatism of any sort, and his advocacy of human freedom and dignity continue to inspire those who strive for harmony in an increasingly divided world. His particular sensitivity to the problems of race, language, cultural differences, economic disparity, and political imbalance speaks to concerns that are with us nearly a century later. From 1912 through the 1930s, his global travels, Nobel Prize fame, and broadened exposure to other educational programs affected both his personal growth and the educational idiom at Santiniketan. Everything he learned became incorporated into his educational vision as he came to view education as a means to mutual understanding as much as to self-understanding. His approach was always open-ended, dynamic, and focused on real-world realities.

Tagore did not live to see India's independence, but he was very much caught up in the issues of national autonomy. As someone well versed in both Indian tradition and Western thought, he was constantly trying to navigate a space for modern India that included the most positive aspects of each, but was not imitative of either. His earlier participation in the Swadeshi movement had influenced his response to Mahatma Gandhi's educational and political goals and means, which he perceived to be narrow, authoritarian, and potentially violent.[14] Thus, at the height of Gandhi's Non-cooperation in 1921, with laws and taxes imposed by Great Britain, Tagore argued for international cooperation and rejected political solutions in favor of social and educational ones. He inaugurated Visva-Bharati and expanded its emphasis on the arts to become an "Indian Center of Culture," broadened its linguistic and cultural links with other parts of Asia to become an "Eastern University," and allied its identity with all humanity in its activities as a "Global Learning Center."

Likewise, Tagore's desire to overcome social and material poverty and to break down the barriers between the urban elites and the uneducated rural population were expressed through the rural reconstruction ventures at Sriniketan. He knew personally the difficulties in trying to overcome innate prejudices and national chauvinism, and he spent his life developing creative ways for individuals to relate harmoniously. Important to this scheme was an emphasis on the aesthetic links between cultures and shared human concerns. His approach avoided stereotypical abstractions and advocated a small-scale approach. As he said, "Unity did not mean uniformity" (1961, p. 247). This places a strong emphasis on human respect and creative ways to bring various individuals into contact with one another in a hospitable and civil environment. Cooperation, mutual understanding, and "education for sympathy" (1917, p. 116) are championed over hostility and confrontation. What becomes important in Tagore's educational vision for educators today are the ways in which cultures and communities have furthered the human race through their creative and constructive visions of a shared humanity.

# Artful Curriculum, Evaluation, and Instruction: Lessons Learned from Rudolf Steiner's Spiritually Based Waldorf Education

## P. Bruce Uhrmacher

AN EMPHASIS ON the arts, the child's changing consciousness, and academics epitomize Waldorf education. But where did this perspective come from and why did it gain popularity? What are the details of its application to education today and the consequences of these principles and practices? In this chapter, I will elucidate the philosophy of education of the founder of Waldorf education, Rudolf Steiner, by discussing how he and those who have promoted the Waldorf approach aspire to create a better world through a distinctive fusion of traditional and nontraditional ways of educating. In particular, I highlight two core ideas in the Waldorf philosophy: the role of stories and storytelling, and the art of evaluation.[1] As we explore these ideas, Steiner's alternative views will be proposed as a path to refresh, revitalize, and reconceptualize our educational imagination. Were our world moving easily toward peace, justice, global prosperity, and environmental sensitivity, we might not bother to look beyond present-day philosophies of education. But given the many troubling trends in the modern world, alternative ideas such as those at the foundation of Waldorf education may offer new opportunities.

## THE GENESIS OF STEINER'S WORLDVIEW

Rudolf Steiner was born in 1861 to Austrian parents in the small town of Kraljevec, Austria (now in Croatia). His father worked for the railroad and before Rudolf was 8 the family had moved several times. Steiner's school experiences were mixed—some stimulating and some quite dull. At the start, when he reached school age he was taught by an "old man for whom teaching was a burdensome business," says Steiner. "However, it was also a burdensome business for me to be taught by him" (1928/1977, p. 21). After an incident in which Steiner was wrongly accused of messing up the school room with ink, his father decided to educate Rudolf himself: "Henceforth I sat by the hour next to him in his office and had to write and read while he attended to his duties" (p. 22). At age 11, he had a history teacher "who appeared to lecture to us when he taught, but he was, in fact, reading from a book" (p. 43). The young boy decided, "I could just as well read what was in the book. From the teacher's 'lecture' I got nothing. I took in nothing by listening to him read. So I separated the sections of Kant's . . . book [*Critique of Pure Reason*] and fastened them inside the history book which I had in front of me during the lesson, and now I read Kant while from the rostrum history was being 'taught'" (p. 43). In addition to philosophy, geometry caught the young Steiner's attention.

Although academically precocious, as a result of his working-class origins and his father's desire that he become an engineer, Steiner attended the *Realschule*, or trade school, instead of the *Gymnasium*, which provided an academic curriculum. Later, from 1879 to 1883, he was enrolled in the Vienna Polytechnic, a technical college, instead of a university. Nevertheless, Steiner taught himself the more academic curriculum that he missed. Feeling the loss of having to study the classics from German translations, Steiner taught himself both Greek and Latin, which were part of a Gymnasium education. Next, at the polytechnic in Vienna, Steiner tutored a Gymnasium student, and eventually taught himself the subjects he would have studied had he attended a Gymnasium. By attending a school for working-class students and teaching himself the academic curriculum, Steiner attained an understanding of two worlds—the academic and the vocational—which later helped him fashion the Waldorf school. And indeed, Waldorf schools emphasize both hand and mind. Foreign languages are taught, as are woodworking and handcrafts.

Complementary to Steiner's synthesis of academic and vocational education was the undercurrent of his spiritual experience. When Steiner was quite young an apparition of a woman appeared to him and asked him for assistance. Although taken aback, Steiner was certain of what he saw but not sure how to help. The following day he learned that the woman who had come to him, one of his cousins, had committed suicide. This experience, and others like it, pointed to what he would later refer to as an "undeniable truth," leading him to write, "That the spiritual world is a reality was as certain to me as the reality of the physical. But I needed some kind of justification for this assumption" (1928/1977, p. 29).

Steiner sought justifications for his beliefs in philosophy and science, but in his view, these fields were moving toward existential and materialist orientations, that is, a godless and skeptical approach toward anything that does not have a material basis. For the most part, Steiner had to examine his spiritual experiences on his own. As he put it:

> And it was always the same in regard to my experiences of the spiritual world. No one was interested to hear about them. At most, from this or that quarter people would bring forward something spiritualistic. Then it was I who did not wish to listen. . . . But then it happened. (1928/1977, p. 60)

On his trips by train to Vienna during his college years, Steiner frequently traveled with an herbalist, "a simple man of the people" (1928/1977, p. 60), with whom he was able to speak about his spiritual experiences: "When with him, one could enter deeply into nature's secrets. On his back he carried the bundle of healing herbs; in his heart he carried the results of what he had won from nature's spirituality while gathering them" (p. 61). From this friendship, Steiner indicates he was able to attain glimpses into a spiritual world unbounded by organized religion.

Thus, Steiner's interest in mystical knowledge began with the apparition when he was a young boy, developed in 1879 as he came to know the herbalist, and came into focus in 1888 when he encountered theosophy. Appealing to the intelligentsia throughout Europe, theosophy combined a study of world religions, ancient mysteries, philosophy, science, and psychic investigation. In 1912, when theosophists declared the 14-year-old Krishnamurti (1895–1986) their new Christ, Steiner broke with the group. A year later, in 1913, the Anthroposophical Society, based on the writings and lectures of Steiner himself, was formed in Berlin.

## Anthroposophy

Much like theosophy, anthroposophy provides an intellectual rationale and meditative practices for spiritual investigation. Unlike theosophy, which sought greater spiritual grounding in Eastern religious practices, anthroposophy was decidedly anchored in Western practices—particularly Christianity. For Steiner, what he refers to as the "Christ event" represents an evolutionary advancement in human consciousness. In other words, an acceptance of Christ within was understood by Steiner as the key to opening up one's powers of perception to be able to perceive directly the spiritual world (see McDermott, 1984, pp. 212–226).

The word *anthroposophy* is derived from *anthropos* (man) and *sophia* (wisdom). It may be thought of as a spiritual path of self-development. Steiner perceives three key elements in it. First, intertwined with the visible world is a spiritual one. Steiner was arguing not only that a spiritual world exists, but that the spiritual world interpenetrates the sensory world. All attempts to deny the existence of the spiritual world or to solve problems on a solely material level were doomed to fail. Second, human beings have the potential to perceive and enter into the spiritual world. According to Steiner, within us are latent organs of perception that can penetrate the spiritual world. Third, when spiritual investigators achieve the intuitive stage of apprehension they consciously enter into an objective spirit, whose findings can, to some degree, be articulated and tested. As a result of his spiritual research, Steiner offered comprehensive, complex, and spiritually based views of a wide variety of practical topics. These included biodynamic farming, medicine, architecture, and beekeeping. Steiner believed that anyone could achieve the same results if they used the same meditative techniques.

## Steiner's Conception of the Human Being

Steiner was well aware of the direction in which modern science was headed in its analysis of the human being, but taking his lead from his own inner visions and from Western mystical traditions, he used an analysis and a language very different from modern science. For instance, Steiner talked about the human being in terms of four aspects: the physical, etheric, astral, and ego bodies. Like the mineral world, the human being has a physical body, material and corpselike until it becomes enlivened with an etheric (energy) body. Humans—like the plant world—have an etheric body that forms and preserves the physical body. It animates our physical selves. Next, like animals, humans have an astral body, our world of emotions. But whereas animals only have physical, etheric, and astral bodies, humans—unlike everything from the mineral, plant, and animal worlds—have an ego, the sense of an individual "I". Developmentally speaking, these forces grow at different stages. Said Steiner: "It is on these four members of the human being that the educator works. . . . It must not be imagined that they develop uniformly in the human being, so that at any given point in his life . . . they are all equally far developed" (1909/1965, p. 12).

The terms *astral*, *ego*, and *etheric bodies* sound strange in discourse outside religious studies; but it should be pointed out that throughout the course of history, the human being has been conceived of in various ways by various cultures. Aristotle, for example, believed in a hierarchy of souls (Hergenhahn, 1986, p. 39); yoga speaks of seven bodies, as does ancient Indian medicine (the seven chakras) (Berman, 1989, p. 140). Steiner points out that his observations of the various bodies were also discerned by Saint Augustine (Steiner, 1986). Indeed, the notion of bodies as composed solely of mind and matter is a recent scientific account.

## Three Stages of Child Development

Not unlike that of well-known child psychologist Jean Piaget (1896–1980), Steiner developed a theory of human development. Steiner and Piaget both noted three distinct stages of cognitive growth in which children gain logical awareness as they grow older. Further, both believed that pushing children toward such awareness too early was harmful (see Ginsberg, 1982). Steiner, however, brings two other observations to bear. First, he takes into account his view that individuals are reincarnated beings. Thus, in addition to the issues of heredity and environment is the added dimension of a reincarnated soul. This explains why he believed that cosmic purposes should enter into the analysis of the gifted child, or the wayward child. Second, Steiner elaborates on a holistic development of the human being. He does not focus on cognitive growth alone but approaches each stage of a child's growth with concern for emotional and volitional development as well.

At birth, Steiner suggests, the infant consists largely of an undifferentiated, still-developing physical body. Gradually, an etheric (life or energy) body works down from the head as an awakening force. The reason, therefore, that Waldorf educators do not teach children to read or memorize facts before the age of 7 is their belief that the etheric body is part of the physical body and still working to develop it. When one teaches children intellectual material too early, they believe one could be causing harm to the child. During this period, children learn almost everything through imitation (Steiner, 1909/1965). The second stage occurs around the age of 7 when children lose their baby teeth. According to Steiner, the second set of teeth pushing out the first set visibly represents the etheric body breaking out of its "etheric envelope." Steiner characterized the second stage as the time of feeling, a period that lasts until the age of 14 and that requires teaching through vivid images and rhythm. Steiner argued that "everything that one brings to a child at this age must be given in the form of fairy tales, legends, and stories in which everything is endowed with feeling" (Steiner, 1988b). Finally, the third stage, from puberty to age 21, is marked by the release of the astral body, the body of consciousness. As the vehicle of "pain and pleasure, of impulse, craving, passion, and the like" (1909/1965, p. 12) the astral body, freed from the physical body, creates yet another mind-and-body relationship. *Thinking* and *judgment* are the two catchwords for this phase of development. At this stage Waldorf educators resort to abstract thinking more freely.

From this brief sketch, one can begin to understand how Waldorf educators approach the teaching of varied concepts. Let us take moral education as a quick example. Waldorf educators stress the importance of having good role models around young children since they learn primarily through imitation. As students grow older, they learn moral lessons through stories and their feelings about these stories. Later, Waldorf educators might approach moral issues from a critical standpoint that encourages discussion and dialogue. Obviously, the Waldorf perspective on teaching something like moral education is more complicated than this overview, but the point worth noting is how Waldorf educators incorporate concepts of child development into curricular ideas.

## THE BIRTH OF WALDORF EDUCATION

On April 23, 1919, Rudolf Steiner was invited by industrialist Emil Molt to lecture to the workers of the Waldorf-Astoria cigarette factory in Stuttgart, Germany. Molt was a progressive manager who endeavored to keep his employees productive and satisfied during difficult times. He offered, for example, adult education classes on literature, history, and geography. Molt was also a theosophist who had heard Steiner lecture and invited him to speak to his workers at a factory whose name would, in time, become associated with the schools that developed out of Steiner's philosophy.

Sitting on benches, chairs, and large bags of tobacco, the men and women who labored in the factory heard the philosopher talk about his newly published book, *The Threefold Commonwealth*, in which he elaborated on decentralizing and internationalizing what he conceived as the three spheres of social life—the spiritual-cultural, legal-political, and economic. Armistice had recently been agreed, ending World War I (1914–1918), and the assembled laborers, worn out from war, were worried about the failing economy. Threatened by social upheaval, they perhaps yearned to hear something hopeful about their lives in postwar Germany.

Steiner's speech was about constitutional states limiting themselves to the enactment and enforcement of laws to protect their citizens and allowing economic and cultural affairs to transcend national boundaries. Initially his talk failed to rouse much enthusiasm in the workers (Oberman, 1997), but one of his points did connect with his audience:

> All of you, as you sit here, from the sixteen-year-old girl apprentice to the workers in their sixties, suffer from the fact that your real personality has been buried because from a certain moment there was only the hard school of life for you, but no longer any real education. (quoted in Carlgren, 1981, p. 15)

According to Ida Oberman, a historian of Waldorf education, Steiner captivated his audience with a vision of comprehensive human growth:

> In his later memoirs the factory owner Molt referred to this day as Waldorf's birthday. And indeed, the factory floor was the cradle and Steiner's tobacco speech marked the birth of "Waldorf" education. (1997, p. 2)

Several days after the speech, Steiner met with Molt and two others to discuss the formation of a school. It was agreed that the school should be open to all children regardless of religious, social, or economic background, and it should offer a 12-year curriculum (Barnes, 1980, p. 2). The Waldorf School opened in Stuttgart in the fall of 1919 with 253 children. By Steiner's death in 1925, enrollment had reached 800 (Oberman, 1997, p. 5).

Steiner lived to see the opening of four Waldorf schools: two in Germany and one each in the Netherlands and Great Britain. The first Waldorf school in the United States opened in 1928 in New York City through the efforts of Irene Brown, who had heard Steiner lecture in Oxford. There were four American Waldorf schools by 1947. Today, there are about 150 Waldorf schools in North America. Excluded from this number are some Waldorf charter schools and programs operating in public schools. There are also about 870 Waldorf schools in 60 countries worldwide.

## SUSTAINING WALDORF EDUCATION

Generally, Waldorf schools are founded through parent initiatives. That is, a group of parents decide to start a school for their children and often the school begins as a preschool and expands. Although the first Waldorf school was for working-class youth, most Waldorf schools today are independent and, therefore, cater to affluent people—though each school usually reserves some money to help families of need. It should be noted that one of the reasons that Waldorf education is "independent" is its spiritual orientation grounded in a generally Christian perspective. Christian festivals are celebrated and some Christian psalms are read in class, but courses in religion are not part of the Waldorf curriculum.

While anthroposophy is not taught in Waldorf schools, it is the spiritual basis for most Waldorf educators. The Anthroposophical Society is housed in Dornach, Switzerland, in a magnificent structure designed by Steiner called the Goetheanum. The society is composed of numerous "sections" for different areas of study: medicine, mathematics, astronomy, and pedagogy, among others. While the pedagogic section does not issue directives, generally, at least one teacher at a Waldorf school is a member of this section.

The Association of Waldorf Schools of North America (AWSNA), formed in 1979, assists growing schools by providing guidance, suggestions, and a support network. AWSNA also ensures that its members "are committed to work out of the spiritual impulse of anthroposophy" (Uhrmacher 1991b, p. 68). New Waldorf initiatives (often a preschool or kindergarten class) in which parents may not know too much about the undergirding of Waldorf education are referred to as "federated schools" and may request introductory assistance from AWSNA. Sponsored schools are those that have classes up to third grade and are under the guidance of a sponsorship committee, often individuals from a nearby Waldorf school. Finally, full-member schools may take part in delegates' meetings, where common concerns are discussed.

Each individual Waldorf school is run by a board of directors (or trustees), a "college of teachers," and an administrative committee. The real power in the school is held by the college of teachers, those individuals (mostly but not exclusively teachers) who have made a "special commitment to the care and growth of the school" (Uhrmacher, 1991b, p. 75). These dedicated anthroposophists meet for 4 to 5 hours weekly to discuss, among other matters, academic standards, teacher evaluation, dress code, discipline, and hiring and firing of teachers. There are also weekly faculty meetings for all teachers. The administrative committee, made up of either paid staff or teachers who teach part time, implements the policies made by the college of teachers. The board of directors, consisting of parents, is responsible for handling financial and legal issues. Perhaps most significant about this arrangement is the fact that teachers are at the center of the school—not paid administrators, board members, or even parents.

Waldorf education has its own teacher-training institutions. The two most prominent in the United States are Sunbridge College in Spring Valley, New York, and the Rudolf Steiner College in Sacramento, California. Teacher training is usually a 2-year program, but in order to meet the demand for new teachers, both colleges offer extension programs where prospective teachers can attain a certificate by working at a school and attending the college over several summers. Since the demand for Waldorf teachers far exceeds the number of graduates each year, Waldorf schools often hire non-Waldorf-trained teachers.

What takes place in a Waldorf school or classroom will vary somewhat, but by and large one might expect the following attributes: From first through eighth grade, students learn reading, writing, arithmetic, history, and geography (among other subjects), largely through artistic activities that include drawing, painting, clay modeling, poetry, and drama. For example, children might draw a lion after hearing the popular story of the mouse and the lion. In addition, all students have the opportunity to learn two foreign languages, singing, recorders and string instruments, eurythmy, form drawing, handwork, and woodworking.[2] While many of these subjects are taught by specialized teachers, to enhance the stability of the curriculum, the same classroom teacher often remains with the same group of students from first through eighth grade.

One constant across grade levels is the Main Lesson, a 2-hour block of time set aside each morning, in which a particular subject is taught over 3 to 4 weeks. Sometimes the subject is discipline based (e.g., arithmetic) and sometimes it is thematic ("Man and Animal"). Through the use of this extended block of time, Waldorf educators try to avoid the fragmentation of curriculum plaguing many schools. Indeed, Steiner's innovative approach to curricula is one of the hallmarks of a Waldorf education.

Steiner provided "indications" for Waldorf educators and their curricula. He did not want to create a rigid structure for either. Over time, however, Steiner's indications, which can be found in books such as *Practical Advice to Teachers*, have achieved great status, and many Waldorf teachers aspire to emulate his advice. Other Waldorf practices, such as the use of artistic warm-ups (e.g., flute playing) to wake up a class or to settle the children down, seems to have emerged from Waldorf teacher-training programs. Therefore, while teachers are free to conduct classes in ways they see fit, limited only to following a spirit of anthroposophy, one finds that Waldorf educators tend to run classes in a similar style.

One additional point about the Waldorf organization is noteworthy. Through the efforts of enterprising individuals at the teacher-training institutions, Waldorf education has gained entrance into two new arenas. There are today Waldorf-inspired practices in public schools. Although it remains controversial both inside and outside Waldorf communities, because of the spiritual impulse behind Waldorf education, there are classrooms and charter schools using the methods Steiner espoused in public education around the country (see McDermott, Byers, Dillard, Easton, Henry, & Uhrmacher, 1996).[3] Second, the Waldorf teacher-training programs also provide ideas and resources for home schoolers, a growing population in the United States.

## THE WALDORF EXPERIENCE: MISS ROGERS'S FOURTH-GRADE CLASSROOM

As Waldorf schooling is different from most methods of traditional education, it is useful to examine how it operates in the classroom. To illuminate Steiner's philosophy of education, I turn in this section to the classroom of a Waldorf teacher, Miss Rogers, in Sunnyville, California.[4] Below we examine several aspects of Miss Rogers's fourth-grade classroom. What we will see here is typical of what we might find in other classrooms. First, we have a teacher who began at the school as a parent. Kathy Rogers graduated from the Rudolf Steiner College in 1984. Prior to taking the teacher-training program, Miss Rogers took part in the founding of the Sunnyville Waldorf School, which her daughter attended from kindergarten to eighth grade.

Miss Rogers aims to provide students with the potential to gain "power over their own souls." She will accomplish her aim by offering stories, pictures, rituals, and ceremonies punctuated with symbolic meaning. Second, as we will see in the example below, Miss Rogers and other Waldorf educators employ novel forms of evaluation.

Miss Rogers begins her school day at 8:30 A.M. and stands just inside her classroom door, greeting the students with a pleasant "Good morning" while shaking each student's hand. Students and teacher talk briefly during this period. Then Miss Rogers plays her flute while students hang up their jackets and proceed to their desks. When students settle in their seats, Miss Rogers says, "Good morning, fourth grade," and the students in turn reply, "Good morning, Miss Rogers." Next, without much prompting, students stand beside their desks and recite a variety of verses (poems and psalms). At about 9:15 Miss Rogers begins her Main Lesson. Currently, students are studying a unit called "Man and Animal."[5] In a letter introducing the topic to the students' parents, Miss Rogers wrote:

Dear Fourth-Grade Parents:

... Today we began one of the most significant blocks in the curriculum, that block called Man & Animal. It is the first "science" block, and is brought to them at that time when their consciousness is again beginning to focus on things in the world in a new way. ... We begin with a look at MAN and try to awaken in the children a feeling that Man represents a synthesis, a bringing together of the three kingdoms of nature. (in Uhrmacher, 1991b, p. 177)

As mentioned earlier, Steiner did not write curricula, but through his lectures to educators he gave numerous indications of the types of ideas and content that could be offered. In regard to this particular unit of the Main Lesson, Steiner provided two major ideas. First, he noted, "The aim is not so much that the pupils should accumulate a great deal of knowledge, but that we prepare the ground for them to acquire the right feeling for the world" (1986, pp. 177–178). Second, he emphasized the importance of students' receiving a fundamental understanding of their place in the world of nature:

The child grows with all the kingdoms of the earth. He no longer merely stands on the dead ground of the earth, but he stands on the living ground, for he feels the earth as something living. He gradually comes to think of himself standing on the earth as though he were standing on some great living creature, like a whale. This is the right feeling. (1988a, p. 65)

Thus "Man and Animal," which will last approximately four weeks, teaches students, among other things, to perceive their relationship to the animal kingdom. The hope is that by encouraging students to feel connected to animals a moral responsibility will follow, that is, they will care about and care for them.

Over the course of the next 2 weeks in which I observed the class, the Main Lesson consisted of the following:

1. As preparation for a story, teacher and students recite a verse of poetry or a psalm. Then Miss Rogers helps a student light a candle, which is used to create a quiet mood.
2. Students recapitulate the previous day's story or lesson ("Who remembers yesterday's story?"). After students tell part of the story, she might ask, "Then what happened?"
3. Miss Rogers tells the students an imaginative or a factual story (lasting from 5 to 15 minutes); she tells the story without use of a text. Waldorf teachers have numerous Waldorf resources from which to choose a story.
4. Miss Rogers presents the day's academic content, or begins the creative activity (e.g., sculpting); after telling a story, she might present some academic content (e.g., about wolves or penguins or another animal). In the "Man and Animal" unit, she relates the content to humans. She then has students do something with the content. For example, she had students sculpt the human body out of clay. She would ask students if the animal they had talked about was more headlike, trunklike, or limblike.
5. Students write and draw in their Main Lesson books. What they write and draw is teacher directed. Both are to relate to the previously told story. Miss Rogers offers tips on how to mix colors, though she may let students choose their own visual content. She often has a paragraph on the blackboard that students are to copy. For example:

Man has been created three in one. We are head, trunk, and limbs. With our head we want to take the whole world into ourselves. . . . All that we take in through our head is digested in our trunk, where it becomes something now. It becomes what I am! With my limbs I am able to give back to the world all I have become by "eating" it, but now in a new form.

## Interpreting the Main Lesson

When I asked Miss Rogers about the purpose of stories in the main lesson, she replied:

One way of thinking about it is to divide it into thinking, feeling, and willing. The thinking aspect is the content, what I say. But you also want to get those feelings engaged; so often

> the stories will do that for you. And then the will activity is when they do something with the content. That can be a play or writing.[6]

While Miss Rogers relays some facts about animals and humans, she is not overly concerned about having students memorize these details. More important for her is having students gain a deeper understanding of the interrelationships among humans and animals. Miss Rogers's overall approach is influenced by Steiner and by the Russian naturalist Peter Kropotkin (1842–1921), who wrote *Mutual Aid* to demonstrate cooperative activities in animal and human communities. According to Miss Rogers, "There are theories that mankind or animal life evolved more out of mutual aid than out of cutthroat dog eat dog thing. . . . that is the picture we try to give the children."[7] Cognitively, Miss Rogers aims to give a "picture" or "image" of person-animal relationships, but she does not force her message. She offers it to her class and allows students to receive what they will.

Affectively, Miss Rogers tries to convey the feeling that humans are morphologically similar to animals. If she is successful, her use of stories will structure the kinds of feelings students have for animals, so that when they get older, the students will continue to feel a connection to the animal world. If students feel a kinship toward animals, then these feelings will orient them toward acting responsibly. Miss Rogers tries to achieve this aim through imaginative stories about anthropomorphized animals in particular. One story, for example, was about a red hen that keeps calling the crocodile that is about to eat her "brother." The crocodile is puzzled by this statement and ultimately refrains from eating the red hen.

### The Role of Stories and Storytelling

Steiner urged his teachers to teach through stories, and he demanded that they tell the stories from memory rather than read the children books. Indeed, we saw in Miss Rogers's classroom that she did just that. It is useful to interpret these practices from the point of view of modern educational ideas. Today, some educators point out that stories serve transformative, transfigurative, and moral functions. According to the educational scholar Philip Jackson, "The hope is that the message will not simply be heard and understood but will be taken to heart" (1995, p. 9). In this way, stories transform us. In addition, Jackson points out that stories help us recognize who we are. He refers to this aspect as a transfigurative function. Stated differently, by "identifying ourselves with characters in texts (and perhaps with more than just the characters, perhaps with the constellation of meanings embodied in the text as a whole) we somehow become ourselves" (McEwan

& Egan, 1995, p. 12). Miss Rogers would concur with these important functions of stories.

There is also, according to education professor Carol Witherell, a moral dimension to stories:

> A good story engages and enlarges the moral imagination, illuminating possibilities for human thought, feeling and action in ways that can bridge the gulf between different times, places, cultures, and beliefs. (Witherell, 1995, p. 40)

Though Steiner and Miss Rogers would not use this terminology to talk about stories, both would agree with all that has been said. Moreover, Steiner noted that good storytelling moves us. In numerous lectures he asked what children were to make of teachers who relied too much on textbooks. Responding to this, Steiner noted, "Even if your effort is far inferior to published stories . . . it will work more directly upon the child because the process of your creating will communicate itself to him" (Steiner, 1981, p. 70). Through storytelling, the teacher reveals that the embodied information and all that goes with it are part of the teacher.

Waldorf educators seek to conserve the ancient arts of creating and telling stories, which have been central to every culture on the planet. Today, with movies, television, and the Internet, educators may choose to find stories through technology and have them told by professional actors. But when we make such choices, we must ask, What is being lost with the discontinuation of face-to-face communication? Waldorf education stands in modern societies as a reminder that such communication is essential to who we are as human beings and that stories serve an educational function.

## Evaluation in Waldorf Education

From the opening of the first school, Waldorf educators have delayed the giving of letter grades until the middle or high school years. In Sunnyville, California, Waldorf teachers begin letter grading in eighth grade. Before this grade level, they use various strategies to assess students. Here I discuss two of the most important: poetic writing and drawing. Both are used to help students reflect on who they are as human beings.

At least once a year, Miss Rogers draws a picture and writes a verse about each student. In addition to drawing a picture of a lion, here is what she said about Zachary in the second grade:

> Strongest are not walls of stone
> or slowly-molded bone,
> Steadfast is the lion's part,
> A brave, willing, helpful heart.

And in the third grade she wrote,

> He walks so tall and straight with grace
> He has a smiling handsome face.
> A heart that strives to do the good,
> Come pinches or hits or what meanness would. (both verses in Uhrmacher,
>     1991b, p. 188)

The point here is not to assess Miss Rogers's poetic abilities, but to note that in this second poem, she captures positive aspects of Zachary (he is kind and helpful and handsome) and places these next to aspects that she would like from him (to stand straight, smile more, be lionlike). The poem is a type of assessment, but it does not limit Zachary to a one-dimensional being. Rather, it captures him, albeit in a simplified way, poetically and meaningfully.

What should one make of these evaluative representations? Like all systems of evaluation, they have their strengths and weaknesses. Whereas traditional grading schemes act as a sorting mechanism to track students in classes, disciplines, and even careers, Waldorf rejects this in favor of other advantages. Two disadvantages are that drawing and writing poetry are time consuming and demand a great deal of creativity from teachers. However, there are significant advantages to this system: First, the Waldorf style of assessment, especially in the student's younger years, does not allow administrative purposes to intrude on the teacher-student relationship, a danger Nel Noddings warns of when she argues that traditional grading schemes, such as numbers or letters, impinge on this relationship:

> Here is a demand that both know to be an intrusion. The teacher does not grade to inform the student. She has far better, more personal ways to do this. She grades to inform others about the student's progress. (1984, pp. 193–194)

A second advantage is that the Waldorf type of evaluation actually provides valuable educational information. Such information is not limited to the cognitive alone, nor is it meant as some kind of final assessment. Miss Rogers is not saying that Zachary is failing because he is not lionlike. Rather, she uses the picture and poem as a means to encourage Zachary toward developing certain characteristics. Thus, the assessment is formative (process oriented) rather than summative, and it provides information in ways letter grades simply cannot match.

Third, it is clear that when Miss Rogers creates poems and verses for students, she is giving them personal gifts. This exchange between teacher and student is intimate and thought provoking and reflects a caring attitude that a mere letter grade cannot convey.[8] Additionally, the Waldorf style of assessment encourages teachers to see each child holistically. Poems require that the poets be observant about their students and that they think about them from various points of view. A good poem often gets at tensions, contradictions, paradoxes, and essences. Moreover, having children see their teacher write poems and draw pictures is a good way to encourage students to draw and write as well.

For all these reasons, educators ought to consider artistic forms of evaluation. While this is seemingly a difficult task, consider how long teachers spend creating grading rubrics and agonizing over letter grades. Admittedly, artistic forms of evaluation will not suit every teacher, but why not allow those who have an interest and predisposition toward these approaches the opportunity to try it out? Why not see what such artistic forms may yield?

## THE IMPORTANCE OF STEINER'S IDEAS
## AND WALDORF EDUCATION

In conclusion, Waldorf education continues to thrive worldwide. Undoubtedly some readers of this essay may feel quickly drawn to Steiner's ideas, while others may feel dismay that anyone would take him seriously. Indeed, Steiner and Waldorf education have their critics. Anthroposophy itself has been referred to as a "hodgepodge of 19th century romanticism, Christianity, Eastern mysticism and various perplexing notions" (McGrath, 1977, p. 100), and some regard it as "a synthetic mixture, a surface barbarization of the Gospel by means of Indic, Gnostic, and mystery elements" (Aulthaus, 1962, p. 19). Adherents to anthroposophy, however, suggest that its credibility should be tested by its results, and indeed even the two critics mentioned above (McGrath and Aulthaus) admit that the results are impressive. Anthroposophy has produced organic and holistic approaches to medicine, agriculture, architecture, and education, all of which continued to flourish worldwide long after Steiner's death in 1925.

Critics of Waldorf education argue that it needs to do much more to make its curriculum multicultural (McDermott et al., 1996). Moreover, there are critiques of Waldorf pedagogy—it is too rigid and lacking in flexibility; it is too teacher directed and lacking in student dialogue and decision making; and there is too much rote memorization. To its credit, AWSNA has taken action to address the concerns it recognizes as valid (e.g., multicultural education) and has engaged in dialogue with critics who argue against the Waldorf perspective (e.g., Waldorf educators do not believe that schools should be student led).[9] All school systems have their faults and shadows and Waldorf education is no exception. But as Waldorf schools work to fix their problems, let's not overlook their strengths. While many school systems today fear giving teachers too much power and rely on national testing to determine what kind of curriculum should be offered to students, Waldorf schools provide a successful example of teacher-led schools. While many schools look to narrowing curriculum and pedagogy through state standards and state testing and, thus, risk losing the meaning and purpose of education, Waldorf educators emphasize an artistic approach that engages students in mind and body. Teaching through stories and storytelling, for example, is a pedagogical device worthy of emulation. In fact, mainstream educators have recently come to recognize the importance of stories (see McEwan & Egan, 1995). Also, using an artistic approach to evaluate students has great merit and, in my view, ought to be the topic of further research. Innovative and wonderfully creative, this idea seems to be just one of many examples of how Steiner's philosophy as it is practiced in Waldorf schools might inform mainstream education.

While many schools debate their purpose and mission, Waldorf educators have always been clear. In the words of Rudolf Steiner:

> Often today, people's education lags far behind the talents and tendencies that destiny implanted in them. We must keep pace with those forces to the extent that the human beings in our care can attain all that their destinies will allow— the fullest clarity of thought, the most loving deepening of feeling, and the greatest possible energy and capacity of will. This can be done only through an art of education and teaching. (1997, p. 34)

# Caring for Others as a Path to Teaching and Learning: Albert Schweitzer's Reverence for Life

## A. G. Rud

> Let your life speak.
> —George Fox, in 1652

NOBEL PEACE LAUREATE (1952) Albert Schweitzer helps us think intelligently and imaginatively about the values and purposes of education in our time. Known and revered primarily for more than a half century of humanitarian work at the hospital he established in Lambaréné, Gabon, in West Africa, Schweitzer's decision to dedicate his life to medical service in Equatorial Africa came after years of study and reflection in other disciplines. As a young man, Schweitzer was a noted biblical scholar, minister, organist, and author of a number of philosophical and theological works before choosing to study medicine in 1905 at the age of 30. In ways we are just beginning to understand, all this eventually filtered into his life's goal of serving others.

To argue for Schweitzer's legacy for current educational practice, I will focus on three particular areas: education for service, education for environmental awareness, and education for hospitality and community. His work in Africa and his writings provide rich seams of thought to mine for a philosophy of education that can both inspire and empower the educational process in our schools. Schweitzer believed that teachers should "not only pass on knowledge," but also transmit "the deep realization that the heart must always play its part as well as reason" (Free, 1982, p. 59). Schweitzer's educational legacy has been the subject of three brief articles in the United States (Abrell, 1974, 1978, 1981), and a sustained theoretical examination supports his claim that "the school will be the way" while lending credence to the fact that schools around the world have been named in his honor. First, from his answer to the question, "What should we humans educate ourselves to be and to do?" Schweitzer's philosophy of life and his actions show us that education should teach us how to serve others and our world, rather than be mere consumers. Second, through an interpretation of his principle "Reverence for Life," Schweitzer offers an understanding of our environment as more than home and neighborhood, as nature itself, an organic, living source of all that has value. Finally, I will explore how education in learning the art of hospitality helps us to form meaningful, respectful, fulfilling communities of learning.

### SCHWEITZER'S MORAL EDUCATION

Schweitzer made an early commitment not to harm living things and to live in accordance with the demands of a conscience and a sense of duty toward others. He was sensitive to the suffering of downtrodden humans and hapless animals, a fact made clear by well-known incidents from his childhood. He was haunted for weeks by the sight of a limping horse being beaten with a stick as it was dragged to the slaughterhouse. While still attending nursery school, he was given the task of restraining his dog, Phylax, from attacking the postman. Schweitzer recalled the delight he felt at wielding a switch like a lion tamer to drive his barking and snarling dog into a corner of the yard. Later he reproached himself for this behavior, knowing he could have restrained the dog by merely holding his collar and stroking him (Schweitzer, 1925/1997, p. 39). One of the most famous incidents of his aversion to needless suffering centers on his decision not to kill a bird, portrayed vividly in the Academy Award–winning documentary on Schweitzer (Hill & Anderson, 1957). He recounts this story later in life:

> We approached a leafless tree in which birds, apparently unafraid of us, were singing sweetly in the morning air. Crouching like an Indian hunter, my friend put a pebble in his slingshot and took aim. Obeying his look of command, I did the same with terrible pangs of conscience and vowing to myself to miss. At that very moment the church bells began to ring out into the sunshine, mingling their chimes with the song of the birds. It was the warning bell, half an hour before the main bell ringing. For me, it was a voice from Heaven. I put the slingshot aside, shooed the birds away so that they were safe from my friend, and ran home. Ever since then, when the bells of Passiontide ring out into the

sunshine and the naked trees, I remember, deeply moved and grateful, how on that day they rang into my heart the commandment "Thou shalt not kill."

From that day on I have dared to free myself from the fear of men, and when my innermost conviction was at stake, I have considered the opinions of others less important than before. I began to overcome my fear of being laughed at by my classmates. The way in which the commandment not to kill and torture worked on me is the great experience of my childhood and youth. Next to it, all others pale. (Schweitzer, 1925/1997, pp. 38–39)

This defining moment of Schweitzer's childhood, and other experiences recalled in his *Memoirs*, became a de facto moral education. What he observed helped to educate him toward what philosophers the world over call "the Good," that which funds human life with compassion, decency, justice, and grace. Schweitzer's reflections upon his experiences drove home the lesson.

Schweitzer, the son of a Lutheran pastor, was considered a "hopeless dunce in school until he saw the point of study" (Brabazon, 2005, p. 13). He questioned the works of the great philosophers, and contemporary ones such as Marx, Freud, and Nietzsche, for the basis of ethics that he would not find, to his satisfaction, until later, in Africa. He loved playing the organ, wrote a seminal work on Bach, and would later earn money for his African hospital by giving concerts in Europe. He focused on the life of Jesus of Nazareth, finding fault in previous scholarship, and wrote a study of the "historical Jesus." Even though he was a successful scholar and musician, he decided in his early 20s that he would occupy himself with scholarship and music only until the age of 30, after which he would devote himself to a life of service.

Schweitzer's motivation for service, while informed by such youthful experiences, evolved in early adulthood with the help of a soul mate. Information and insight into Schweitzer's life mission comes in recently translated and published letters (R. S. Miller & Woytt, 2003) exchanged between 1905 and 1912 with Hélène Bresslau, whom he married in 1913 (see Brabazon, 2000, pp. 139–163). These letters are a portal into his private thoughts as he and his future wife develop their relationship and decide upon the focus of their lives' work (R. S. Miller, personal communication, March 12, 2005). His early letters to her are short, while her first letter to him is longer and is remarkable in tone. She reveals her longing for advice: "To be sure, I do not yet know my way—it is much easier for a man whose profession gives him direction—will you help me to find mine?" (3: p. 4).[1] Schweitzer, in writing back to her, is also unsure of present circumstances, while knowing that a direction for both will come forth: "You are not the cause of my restlessness, neither am I; it is the movement of the needle of the compass until it finds the pole. We will find it." (4: p. 5).

Schweitzer found that his life as a musician, pastor, and professor did not provide outlets for what was churning within him. Reflecting upon

Friedrich Nietzsche's *Beyond Good and Evil* in a letter to Hélène, Schweitzer found that philosopher entirely too inward and focused on egotistic needs. Nietzsche did not come out of his cage, but tore himself to pieces in the end (23: p. 24) because he could not focus his energies outward toward action. For Schweitzer, the primacy of action over inwardly focused, self-destructive, mere thought is capsulated in this dictum, "I believe because I act" (24: pp. 24–25). This is Schweitzer's answer to Descartes's famous dictum, *cogito ergo sum*—I think, therefore I am:

> Descartes started on this basis. But he built an artificial structure by presuming a person knows nothing and doubts all, whether outside himself or within. And in order to end doubt, he fell back on the fact of consciousness: I think. Surely, however, that is the stupidest primary assumption in all philosophy! Who can establish the fact that he thinks, except in relation to thinking something? And what that something is, is the important matter. (quoted in Brabazon, 2005, p. 153)

As Schweitzer later reflected when he and Hélène were about to go to Lambaréné, what appealed to him about being a doctor there was that he could just act, and he assured his sponsor, the Paris Missionary Society, whose leaders were concerned about his unorthodox religious writings, that he would not preach. In fact, he planned on being "dumb as a carp" (1933/1998a, p. 115). However, several months after arriving in Africa, Schweitzer was invited to take part in the preaching by the missionaries there. To his great delight, he found they shared a "piety of obedience to Jesus," and a practical approach to simple Christian activity, quite free from the dogma and misgivings of the Missionary Society's committee in Paris.

The Schweitzer-Bresslau letters reveal Schweitzer's developing motivation to work as a missionary doctor in Africa and to leave behind the life he had as a respectable, bourgeois pastor and intellectual. Schweitzer, with Hélène's nurturing help, embarks on what we might call a "moral narrative," where his beliefs and actions are deliberately reconstructed through his writings and behavior to state his moral purpose to the world. Mark Johnson (1993) discusses learning morality as an outcome of construing or conceiving one's life as a story or narrative. This perspective captures Schweitzer's own development and deeds. As Schweitzer's view of the world evolves, he takes a holistic approach to morality as he integrates past experiences, such as the incident of the bird and slingshot, into his narrative by reflecting upon their importance to his moral development. Schweitzer also shows moral imagination and empathy while also doing something effective within the world, as he constructs and runs a hospital in Equatorial Africa and raises funds for this work himself by frequent concerts and lectures in Europe and elsewhere. At the same time he embeds himself in a "different" culture, thus acting as an implicit critique of the more hedonistic and materialistic aspects of Western society.[2]

Schweitzer goes beyond what James Rest, following moral philosopher Lawrence Kohlberg, describes as "conventional moral thinking (the morality of maintaining social norms because they are the way we do things)" and also beyond what Rest terms "postconventional thinking (the morality that rules, roles, laws, and institutions must serve some shareable ideal of cooperation)" (Rest, Narvaez, Bebeau, & Thoma, 1999, p. 2).[3] Through his life of action, Schweitzer becomes what the philosopher Ann Hartle (2003) calls Montaigne: a "great-souled man without pride." The comparison is apt. Hartle sees Montaigne as building upon the Aristotelian term *megalopsuchia*, sometimes translated as "magnanimity" or "great-souledness."[4] Aristotle had said in *The Art of Rhetoric* that "magnanimity is the virtue that disposes us to do good to others on a large scale" (1.9; quote from Aristotle 1992). For Hartle, Montaigne develops a sense of Christian magnanimity, blending classical great-souledness with Christian humility. This same humility is evident in Schweitzer. It can be seen in his decision to abandon a comfortable life and study medicine in his 30s, in his conviction to go work in Africa, and in his magnanimity toward helping others on a sustained and large scale.

Schweitzer's resolve did not fail him, though he had doubts and setbacks. He and his wife were prisoners of war during World War I. When they returned to Africa years later in 1924, the hospital was dilapidated and untended and had to be rebuilt. As he was determined to be at his best and to live according to his principles, so too can such a principled life serve to call others, including educators, to not only be at their best, but also to reflect and scrutinize life choices. He encouraged others to "find their own Lambaréné" in their lives and communities, where they could construct and enact their own moral narratives.

Schweitzer's life itself is a moral narrative from which we all may learn what it means to be an educated person. Narrative has unity and a sense of unity is sorely needed in order to build identity. Teachers, teacher educators, school leaders, and others should focus on teaching and modeling ways for children to see their lives as a narrative unity so that young people might develop the skills of reflecting deeply and effectively upon the many choices and dilemmas that life presents. Early experiences such as Schweitzer's observations about animals grounded his later moral reflections and helped him to understand morality in a holistic way. Such a unified vision of one's life is what educators can support, to offset the many ways that one's being is wrenched apart into the discrete roles of consumer, market-driven producer, spectator, and so forth. Building on Schweitzer's construction of such a moral narrative is his educational legacy. I will now explore three themes: education for service, education for environmental awareness, and education for hospitality and community.

## EDUCATION FOR SERVICE

For Schweitzer, service was a calling toward a very simple task, where a "human being is always a human being, always someone who has a right to the assistance and sacrifice of his fellow men" (Brabazon, 2005, p. 76). Service for Schweitzer is selfless and constant, and looking toward the needs of the other, whether that is a human being or another living thing. It is an emptying of the ego and a facing outward toward others. Schweitzer saw how egoistic needs could be destructive, such as in Nietzsche's philosophy or in the colonialism that rapaciously took resources from Africa. He went to Africa to atone for these acts. Schweitzer reached out to what he called the "Fellowship of those who bear the Mark of Pain" (Schweitzer, 1930/ 1998b, p. 128), realizing that what makes us human is our vulnerability and sensitivity to the suffering of others. This condition calls us to join others to try to make a better world. Service for Schweitzer thus is an ontological exercise, where we bring about a new reality through our selfless actions.

Reflection on Schweitzer's resolve to serve humanity leads us to ask why educators invest in and devote themselves to prompting knowledge and self-awareness in others. We who teach work for and hope for change for the better; as William Ayers puts it, the fundamental message of all teachers to students is that you can change your life (2004, p. 34). And, too, teachers may respond to the "call to teach." David Hansen (1995) likens this idea of a pedagogical vocation to "a mirror into which all prospective and practicing teachers might look . . . that invites teachers to self-scrutiny and self-reflection" (p. 139). In Hansen's view, this mirror is not merely reflective, but beckoning, in that it "calls [teachers] to be at their best when in the presence of their students. It urges them to act, at a minimum, as if their work were a vocation, regardless of whether they in fact view it as such" (p. 139).

When Schweitzer decided to leave his successes in scholarship and music at age 30 and enter medical school, in October 1905, he too was called to act in service. Schweitzer was deeply concerned by what he saw as a decaying European culture. In a sermon just before his 30th birthday in January 1905, he contrasted what he saw as the selfless work of missionaries to a European colonialist culture that "speaks so piously of human dignity and human rights and then disregards this dignity and these rights of countless millions and treads them underfoot, only because they live overseas or because their skins are of different color or because they cannot help themselves" (quoted in Brabazon, 2005, pp. 76–77). Schweitzer's contemporary Oswald Spengler, author of *The Decline of the West*, was read widely for his historical dissection of the supposed ills of European culture, as were the more lyrical writings of Friedrich Nietzsche. Schweitzer parted company with both these thinkers, making committed *action* his means of cultural and spiritual regeneration. He wrote:

But was I to teach [in a seminary] that which I did believe? If I did so, would this not bring pain to those who had taught me? Faced with these two questions, I decided that I would do neither. I decided that I would leave the seminary. Instead of trying to get acceptance for my ideas, involving painful controversy, I decided I would make my life my argument. I would advocate the things I believed in terms of the life I lived and what I did. Instead of vocalizing my belief in the existence of God within each of us, I would attempt to have my life and work say what I believed. (Schweitzer, quoted in Cousins, 1985, p. 125)

For Schweitzer, it was a turn toward action and to others, a turn away from the scholarly life per se, that defined his view of service. It was not just the acquisition and consumption of knowledge, but rather the formation of a passionate commitment toward the specific path and goal of service to benefit others based on a selfless duty in regard to other human beings, indeed to all living things. Schweitzer was determined to find a thought that would ground and animate all thinking and action, especially his own. He struggled to be not merely part of an end-of-century pessimism, where he "felt like someone who has to replace a rotten boat that is no longer seaworthy with a new and better one, but does not know how to proceed" (1933/ 1998a, p. 154). Schweitzer sought a bedrock principle upon which to affirm civilization and to make it whole from the inside out, rather than presuming that society should be manipulated through the application of tools from science and technology.

As Schweitzer established his new hospital in Lambaréné in the spring of 1913, his mind was engaged in an active quest for this grounding principle. In September 1915, while on a journey up the Ogooué River, he found it:

Lost in thought I sat on the deck of the barge, struggling to find the elementary and universal concept of the ethical that I had not discovered in any philosophy. I covered sheet after sheet with disconnected sentences merely to concentrate on the problem. Two days passed. Late on the third day, at the very moment when, at sunset, we were making our way through a herd of hippopotamuses, there flashed upon my mind, unforeseen and unsought, the phrase "reverence for life." The iron door had yielded. The path in the thicket had become visible. Now I had found my way to the principle in which affirmation of the world and ethics are joined together. (1933/1998a, p. 155)

Reverence for Life is the principle on which Schweitzer would base his entire thought and action in Africa. He achieved this, like Descartes did with his *cogito*, by seeking what was elemental and foundational. Unlike Descartes's *cogito*, however, Schweitzer's principle of Reverence for Life moves one *outward* to a connection with a larger whole that is nature and other living beings. He recognizes existence is "unfathomably mysterious." Yet there is reciprocity with other living things in granting the same kind of feeling toward oneself that one feels toward another. This is what Schweitzer means when he says that "[man] experiences that other life in his own" (1933/1998a, p. 157). Reverence for Life extends to nature, so that *all* living creatures and organisms share this inherent right for "reverence" for the very quality of possessing life. By observing Reverence for Life, Schweitzer wanted to help individuals "think more deeply and more independently" (1933/1998a, p. 223). He believed that purpose and motive must be found by each individual, beyond the consumerist culture that threatens the development of such independent thinking and being:

> The spirit of the age never lets him find himself. Over and over again, convictions are forced upon him just as he is exposed, in big cities, to glaring neon signs of companies that are rich enough to install them and enjoin him at every step to give preference to one or another shoe polish or soup mix. (1933/1998a, p. 225)

This "spirit of the age" forces individuals into a kind of herd, so that they are not thinking for themselves but want others to do this for them, that "in spite of his great technological achievements and material possession, he [the individual] is an altogether stunted being, because he makes no use of his capacity for thinking" (1933/1998a, pp. 225–226). Schweitzer valued freedom of thought above a slavish and fundamentalist application of even his grounding principle to all situations.

> From the natives I buy a young fish eagle, which they have caught on a sandbank, in order to rescue it from their cruel hands. But now I must decide whether I shall let it starve, or whether I shall kill a certain number of small fish every day in order to keep it alive. I decide upon the latter course. But every day find it rather hard to sacrifice—upon my own responsibility—one life for another. (Schweitzer, quoted in Free, 1982, p. 18)

## EDUCATION FOR ENVIRONMENTAL AWARENESS

Education for environmental awareness is grounded on the realization that human beings are part of the world and not in dominion over it. This false or deluded sense of dominion has led to exploitation of nonrenewable natural resources at the expense of sustained living. Such dominion is ultimately a lack of respect for one's surroundings. The source of this lack of respect is ontological; it is seeing human beings as apart from, rather than part of, the natural environment. Schweitzer's principle of Reverence for Life helps to overcome this cleavage between humans and the world. At times he expounded this view in a way many would find extreme:

You are walking along a path in the woods. The sunshine makes lovely patterns through the trees. The birds are singing, and thousands of insects buzz happily in the air. But as you walk along the path, you are involuntarily the cause of death. Here you trod on an ant and tortured it; there you squashed a beetle; and over there your unknowing step left a worm writhing in agony. Into the glorious melody of life you weave a discordant strain of suffering and death. You are guilty, though it is no fault of your own. And, despite all your good intentions, you are conscious of a terrible inability to help as you would like to. Then comes the voice of the tempter: Why torture yourself? It is no good. Give up, stop caring. Be unconcerned and unfeeling like everybody else. (Brabazon, 2005, pp. 147–148)

This example highlights Schweitzer's argument that as long as humans believe that they have a natural right to superiority and dominion over the rest of the natural world, a true ethic of Reverence for Life cannot be achieved. One of the lessons from taking Reverence for Life seriously is environmental awareness.

Such awareness has been a curricular aim, albeit on the fringe of practice, for more than 30 years. Well-known texts at the beginning of the current environmental movement, such as Rachel Carson's *Silent Spring* (dedicated to Schweitzer) and Aldo Leopold's *A Sand County Almanac* alerted us to the fragility of the planet and our place in it. The stresses on the biosphere, caused by increased industrialization coupled with rapid population increases and continued use of fossil fuels, have not been met with a proactive public policy. By connecting Schweitzer's Reverence for Life principle to John Dewey's thoughts about nature, we can see how education for environmental awareness can be strengthened.

In Chapter 1 of *Experience and Nature*, John Dewey discusses what he calls "*the* philosophic fallacy" regarding nature (LW1, p. 34). The primary, or ordinary, experience one has with nature shows us its mutability, and even, as Dewey states, what Santayana calls its "exuberance." The fallacy of philosophers is to try to convert nature into something quite other: permanent, unchanging, eternal, a thing rather than a process. This fallacy is taken even further when nature becomes merely a commodity, such as the timber on the Ogooué River in Schweitzer's time, or the oil in Alaska today.

Dewey argued against dualism in its many guises—mind and body, individual and society, content and form. Yet he recognizes that our "intricate relation" with nature involves not only a recognition of instability, change, volatility, and exuberance, but also that these qualities spawn our yearning for permanence, and thus lead to philosophical inquiry. We see impermanence, and strive for a kind of understanding, creating art and culture. The fallacy is in the fixation of thought and of nature as split, and not recognizing the dynamism and dialectic of this process. A typical human wish is to control and eliminate change, to fix a process to an essence. Dewey shows how only a provisional fixity can be achieved in cultural, especially artistic, production. The works of art, of culture, are simply structures by which to view a changing reality. And in any case, these objects themselves, subject to endless interpretation, are never fixed in an absolute sense.

Schweitzer wanted to meet Dewey during the former's only trip to the United States, in 1949, to give the Goethe address in Aspen, Colorado. There is, however, no firm evidence that they were able to arrange a meeting. And yet we know that Dewey and Schweitzer read each other's work, and we can surmise that they would have had in common this argument against such dualisms. Schweitzer's daily challenges with the volatility, impermanence, and certainly the exuberance of a lush tropical Africa illustrate Dewey's concept of "a changing reality." Within that dynamic world of nature, Reverence for Life grounded Schweitzer's entire philosophy and his daily work. Once, an antelope fawn was brought to Schweitzer after some local hunters had unsuccessfully tried to trap its mother. Schweitzer named it Léonie and nursed it on a bottle. Léonie and another antelope, Théodore, would then accompany him on strolls to the river and lick the salty sweat off his arm. For Schweitzer, "reverence" was physical as well as spiritual. He also had a down-to-earth sense of reverence for others with whom he might disagree, an attitude that allowed him to be patient and compassionate in trying circumstances:

> I still hear the Doctor's words when faced with someone difficult. He would always say in Alsatian, "Weisch, mir mien ne ewe vertraje," which means, "You know how it is, we have to put up with this." His point was to tolerate and accept the other person. (Munz, 2005)

Thus, Schweitzer's philosophy of Reverence for Life touched all aspects of his life and was extended to all living beings.

The English word *reverence* does not amply or aptly translate the German word *ehrfurcht*, which connotes awe and majesty (*Ehre*, "honor"; *Furcht*, "fear") such as experienced in contemplating a waterfall or in the awful presence of a destructive tornado or flood. Furthermore, the German word further connotes a sense of being humble in the face of all living things *and* a sense of responsibility to them. Schweitzer transformed his philosophical idea of Reverence for Life into action at his hospital at Lambaréné, as well as in the work of countless others who remember his legacy. By meeting nature mostly on its own terms, as Schweitzer did each day in his African hospital, one may be prevented from making nature into what some of us hope it can be, but cannot unless we wish to destroy it—namely, a lifeless, manipulated commodity.

The pedagogical implications for viewing nature in the related ways of Dewey and Schweitzer are important. In *The Play of Ideas*, Dewey spoke about the common educational practice of "reduplication" (LW4, pp. 112–113). Reduplication occurs when one applies without attention some principle or bit of information, merely mimicking what has already been created. Dewey said this could be no more than a pale copy, like a photograph. The practice of reduplication in many of our schools today supports what Dewey calls "*the* philosophic fallacy," and by extension, the unthinking, unaware, and even fearful manipulation of nature. In a quest for certainty enacted every day in schools, the common practice of "teaching to the test," or learning atomized factual information about a topic with no connection to an imaginative or useful application, is this same reduplication. A child's mouthing or scribbling platitudes about his or her country or flag pales in importance to that same child's learning how to resolve conflict by discussing these differences among others in a respectful, democratic arena. Recognizing nature in its ordinariness, as well as with an awe-filled reverence coupled with a sense of responsibility, as Dewey points to and Schweitzer exemplifies, should be one of the ends of an environmentally aware practice in education. We would do well to teach our students, and show them by example, that we are stewards of our environment with a moral duty to live in harmony with, and preserve, our natural world, rather than exploiting and destroying it. Schweitzer's Reverence for Life can be our model for this endeavor.

## EDUCATION FOR HOSPITALITY AND COMMUNITY

Schweitzer's work can teach us about the importance of hospitality and community in teaching and learning. We live now in a culture of accountability and bottom-line results. School leaders and teachers are under increasing pressure to improve students' test scores and meet mandated standards. At the same time, we do not want to "leave children behind."[5] Schweitzer's work points to deeper and more generative meanings that can be an antidote to the deadening within educational practice that occurs too often with the emphasis upon external mandated standards and accountability. His hospital in Lambaréné, designed and operated to emphasize *hospitality* and *community* to its patients and their families, can provide an example for an invitational practice of learning within education.

Hospitality is something beyond the "hospitality industry" or what Henri Nouwen calls a "soft sweet kindness, tea parties, bland conversations, and a general atmosphere of coziness" (Nouwen, cited in Rud, 1995, p. 119). Hospitality is, rather, the activity of receiving another person, listening to that person, and being open to what that person has to say. Here there is often a reversal of roles accompanied by a humbling experience: "In teaching, when you listen to the student, the student becomes the teacher" (Rud, 1995, p. 121). Such listening to others becomes part of the pedagogy of hospitality. Max van Manen calls this *tact* in teaching (Rud, 1995, p. 122), where you are present in mind, body, and soul for the student. This is in contrast to a detached and instrumentalist view of teaching where the student is a receptacle to be filled with knowledge, or a chunk of raw material to be worked on in making a finished "product." At the hospital in Lambaréné, Schweitzer did not try to change native customs, but adapted Western medical practices so that they would work alongside more traditional modes of African healing. He listened well to learn the needs of his patients and their families, and tried to provide for their comfort in healing.

Schweitzer was savagely criticized late in life for the backwardness of his hospital. To many outside observers, it lacked cleanliness and modern equipment. But for Schweitzer, it was a "Garden of Eden" (1933/1998a, p. 211), operating more like a healing or "clinical" community (Montague, 1965, p. 49). Today's hospitals, with their emphasis on regulation, cutting-edge medical science, and the intellectual understanding of disease and illness, simply do not match the holistic and hospitable environment that Schweitzer enacted at Lambaréné. He accommodated extended families when they came to the hospital; he knew the value of having family and others there to support the healing. He thus built trust in the give-and-take between the hospital staff and patients.

Schweitzer purposely allowed the hospital on the banks of the Ogooué River to develop as an African village because he saw that the *communal* aspects of African life, such as allowing patients and their accompanying families to cook their own meals, were a healing resource alongside traditional Western medicine. Having the extended families of patients present and engaged in work around the hospital, such as tending gardens, also was shrewd management of resources, in that many more patients could be served. Thus the practical purposes of affirming the members of that native culture that include healing and cost benefits were joined to a moral purpose (namely, affirming connection between members of that culture and preserving life).

Allowing the entire family, and their animals, to accompany the sick person appalled some visitors. Schweitzer's medical practice has been criticized as not only unhygienic and backward, but also patronizing and colonialist. W.E.B. Du Bois faults Schweitzer for not realizing "what modern exploitation means, of what imperial colonialism has done to the world" but goes on to say that "he deserves every tribute that we can give him for trying to do his mite, his little pitiful mite, which in a sense was but a passing gesture, but perhaps in the long run will light that fire in Africa which will cleanse that continent and the world" (1945, p. 126). While Schweitzer's attitude toward African societies and culture is controversial, and beyond the scope of this chapter, it should be mentioned that he was well aware of the destructive and intrusive aspects of European culture in Africa, from the psychological to the material:

> The cheap enamelled [*sic*] ware has driven out the solid, home-made wooden bucket, and round every negro [*sic*] village there are heaps of such things rusting in the grass. (1930/1998b, p. 95)

Schweitzer's Reverence for Life led him to criticize exploitation and violence, whether he witnessed it done to a helpless horse on the streets of Günsbach or to wild animals along the banks of the Ogooué River in Lambaréné. Schweitzer clearly had respect for the community-spirited Africans he treated, so much so that he learned from them how to shape an effective health-care facility that has served the people of Gabon for nearly a century (1913–  ).[6]

While Schweitzer may not have fully comprehended the impact of colonial practices, his work reveals ethical commitment more than ethnocentric blindness, as Du Bois notes. He understood the harm embedded in colonialism, witnessing firsthand the effects of alcohol and infectious diseases on native populations. Yet Schweitzer was a man of his times, thinking that Europeans had a natural authority over natives. Nevertheless, his example shows how each person can build narrative structure into their moral lives whereby they can increasingly move beyond cultural prejudices and "take in more and more of the human tapestry into which we are all woven, despite countless differences" (D. T. Hansen, personal communication, March 15, 2006). Schweitzer's later writings about the danger of nuclear weapons show that he was not driven by ideology but built on this ethical commitment that he developed through continuous reflection upon his work throughout his life. This reflection was linked to practical concerns in service of others, a concern that had evolved to encompass the global community. While Schweitzer expressed grave concern about global conflict in his Nobel Peace Prize lecture, he used the funds from the prize to build, near his hospital, a facility for lepers, called Village Lumière (Village of Light).

Many hospitals and schools sit apart from the communities they serve. This separateness is hardened by procedures aimed at a standardization of practice, whether it is for the treatment of disease or the learning of mathematics, that can be replicated anywhere. Schweitzer's hospital grew out of an organic relationship with the people it served, as well as the particular characteristics of its setting in Gabon. It is similar to a variety of innovative social practices in education, from settlement homes in the late 19th and early 20th centuries, such as Jane Addams's Hull House in Chicago, to current efforts to incorporate cultural practices in schooling and make schools more caring and homelike. Jane Roland Martin's "schoolhome" does not envision school as "a special kind of production site" where standards must be met and quality control exerted, nor does it "picture young children as raw material, teachers as workers who process their students before sending them on to the next station on the assembly line, or curriculum as the machinery that over the span of twelve or so years forges America's young into marketable products" (Martin, 1992, p. 41). Rather, she sees the model as Maria Montessori's Casa dei Bambini, where one is comfortable and secure, "at home" in a place that supports learning (p. 12). In such institutions, hospitality is thus not a byproduct of centrally mandated arrangements, but is part of the culture, just as it was and is at the Albert Schweitzer Hospital. Just as such core beliefs and practices animate healing, so do they animate learning. Schweitzer recognized that he had to be open to the native culture in which he built his hospital and practiced medicine in order to be effective in his work.

## CONCLUSION

There is a story told about a young schoolboy in France in the 1950s who was asked to name the person who represented the best hope for the world, and the boy replied that it was an old man who was working as a doctor in Africa. While the line of influence from Schweitzer to our current educational practices may not be as direct, it can be just as powerful. Schweitzer urged educators to "instill in your students an awareness that they are on this earth to help and serve others" (Free, 1982, p. 59). Teachers sometimes despair of reaching every student and making a difference. School leaders feel constricted by conflicting mandates of accountability and finding ways to enable every child to succeed and not be left behind. Teacher educators wonder if what they discuss in our colleges and universities will make a mark on teacher candidates, and be transformed into their own reflective practices. Schweitzer realized that such work may be modest at times, but it certainly is no less important than heroic deeds:

> Of all the will toward the ideal in mankind only a small part can manifest itself in public action. All the rest of this force must be content with small and obscure deeds. The sum of these, however, is a thousand times stronger than the acts of those who receive wide public recognition. The latter, compared to the former, are like the foam on the waves of a deep ocean. (1933/1998a, p. 90)

The rich example of Schweitzer's life and work serves, much as Hansen's (1995) idea of vocation as a mirror, to call us to reflect on our own motivations to teach and learn. And, too, Schweitzer's philosophy of Reverence for Life shows us ways to teach others about nature in its ordinariness and majesty, so that we can live and abide in its midst in a better and more accommodating way. His once-modest hospital in Lambaréné—inauspiciously begun in a chicken coop in 1913—is now a significant health-care center managed by an international consortium of Europeans, Americans, and Gabonese, with a new research laboratory and success in reducing the impact of malaria in the region. But most important, the hospital has maintained the "Schweitzer spirit" for nearly a century with an attitude of service, a respect for nature, and a welcoming spirit to those who come to be healed. Just imagine the consequences of a similar spirit taking hold in American classrooms. "Truth has no special time of its own. Its hour is now" Schweitzer said. As we listen to his truth, we hear a full life of commitment speaking to the present and the future. Emboldened by this example, we might even envision an educational philosophy based on the simple humanity of Reverence for Life.

# Notes

## Introduction

1. The definitive edition of Dewey's Collected Works was published by the Center for Dewey Studies at Southern Illinois University, Carbondale, between 1967 and 1991. The 37 volumes are divided into Early Works (EW) written between 1882 and 1898, Middle Works (MW) written between 1899 and1924, and Later Works (LW) written between 1925 and 1953. The notations employed throughout this volume indicate both the era and the volume number, as is customary when citing the work of John Dewey.

## Chapter 2

1. Freire's approach to human nature, his idea that we have an "ontological need" for freedom and that to be creative is to express our "true" nature, has been challenged by many contemporary philosophers. These critics argue that what are often seen as "fixed" or "stable" features of human nature are really not fixed at all but the result of socialization patterns that vary with historical and cultural circumstances. For further discussion of this issues, see Rorty, 1989, pp. 189–198.

2. Freire's commitment to a "liberatory" politics has led some commentators to claim that his idea of I-thou dialogue in the classroom is not as open-ended and tolerant as it seems. They claim that Freire's own political agenda influences the sort of problem-posing discussion he wants teachers to engage in with their students. For discussion of the potential conflict between Freire's desire to let students name their world and his desire to have them be transformed in class solidarity with the poor, see Boston, 1972; Walker, 1981.

3. Although Freire and many liberation theologians synthesize Christian and Marxist utopian visions, others find irreconcilable tensions between the Christian New Millennium and a Marxian classless society. In particular, commentators who place the Marxian vision in the tradition of faith in the inevitable perfectibility of human beings see it as incompatible with Christianity's emphasis on original sin, discipline of the body, and the need for perpetual moral regeneration. For more on tensions between Christian and Marxian visions, see Lasch, 1991.

## Chapter 3

1. I do not intend the word *Negro* to be derogatory or defamatory. I use this term both to remain consistent with Du Bois's own language and, more important, to remind the reader of Du Bois's overarching project of enumerating the unique spirit of the Negro world race. As such, *Negro* should always connote for the reader, according to Du Bois, a race of people with an essential moral message for the world.

2. Herbert Aptheker published Du Bois's manuscript in 1973, appending three more of Du Bois's essays on educational thinking, and called it *The Education of Black People: Ten Critiques, 1906–1960.*

3. For example, see Alridge, 1999; Gordon, 1999; McSwine, 1999; Provenzo, 2002; and Rabaka, 2003.

4. To my knowledge, Zamir's *Dark Voices* (1995) offers the only systematic reading of *Souls.* For the purposes of this chapter, I attend mostly to the educational philosophy therein. Unless otherwise noted, all page references in this chapter are from *Souls.*

5. Ironically, this was the day before the historic Civil Rights March in Washington, DC.

6. Du Bois details his African and White European ancestry in his other major work, *Darkwater: Voices from Within the Veil* (1920/1996).

7. Du Bois was also influenced by Fisk's renowned Jubilee Singers, whose notion of bringing Negro music to the world to improve human culture writ large constitutes a persistent theme in *Souls.*

8. For more on Du Bois's reworking of previously published essays and new materials into the chapters of *Souls*, see Appiah, 2005; Rutledge, 2001; and Zamir, 1995.

9. In an essay titled "The Conservation of Races," from 1897, Du Bois wrote that "other race groups are striving, each in its own way, to develop for civilization its particular ideal, which shall help to guide the world nearer that perfection of human life for which we all long" (1986, p. 819). Du Bois extended his reflections in *The Gift of Black Folk: The Negroes in the Making of America* (1924/1970), first published in 1924. As David Levering Lewis reminds us, *The Gift* was commissioned by the Knights of Columbus (along with other texts such as *The Germans in the Making of America* and *The Jews in the Making of America*) "to blunt the runaway momentum of Anglo-Saxon racism and religious bigotry" (2000, p. 95).

10. For more on the etymology of "book-learning" see, Brann, 1979, p. 16.

11. "Of the Coming of John" actually features two childhood playmates named John, one White and the other Black, who leave home for the sake of education and return to disastrous fates. Du Bois raises the question, Which of these two in fact meets with the worse end?

12. The power of music had been with Du Bois since his days at Fisk University. There, he both witnessed and experienced the extraordinary power of the Negro spirituals to move people to tears.

13. For further details about the history of Tuskegee and Washington's role in leading it, see http://www.tuskegee.edu/Global/story.asp?S=1070392&nav=menu200_2\

14. An often-overlooked disagreement between Du Bois and Washington that has rich historical significance is in their work on designing the social studies curriculum for public schooling. Johnson (2000) reminds us that when Du Bois would not accept the pseudoscientific racial hierarchy, he was removed from the project. Washington remained. One wonders how a social studies curriculum shaped by critical race theories would have changed American perceptions.

15. Du Bois's essay "The Field and Function of the Negro College," from 1933, emphasizes the necessity of education to create democratic culture. "The Function of the Negro State University," from 1941, and "The Future and Function of the Private Negro College," from 1946, appear in Du Bois, 1973.

16. To read Fisk's full mission statement, visit the school's home page: http://www.fisk.edu

17. For further details, see their shared Web site: http://www.webdubois scholars.org/academy.html

## Chapter 4

1. The Manchurian Incident (September 1931) is generally considered the defining moment in the turn to militaristic nationalism in Japan.

2. In 1891, the Ministry of Education issued a directive that schools with total enrollment of 70 or fewer students should be organized into one-room schools. At the same time, the Hokkaido Normal School began conducting research into the best methods and practices for this type of education at its attached elementary school. This is where Makiguchi taught for 4 years.

3. Similarly denoted citations refer to the volume and page of Makiguchi, 1983–1985. Where appropriate, reference is also made to *Education for Creative Living: Ideas and Proposals of Tsunesaburo Makiguchi*, a condensed English rendering of Makiguchi's pedagogical writings translated by A. Birnbaum and edited by D. M. Bethel, or to *A Geography of Human Life*, also edited by D. M. Bethel.

4. Among the signers of a letter of support for Makiguchi's theories were League of Nations undersecretary general Inazo Niitobe and Tsuyoshi Inukai, who became prime minister in 1931. Inukai's assassination in 1932 marked another turning point in the silencing of liberal voices in Japan's descent into fascism and is often seen as the point when the stature of liberal educators and politicians diminished considerably.

5. Makiguchi was not fully satisfied with the term *happiness* and writes that he struggled for more than a decade to find a more adequate word to express the goal of life and learning but that, in the end, he could not (1983–1988, vol. 5, p. 120).

6. See Gardner's conception of multiple intelligences (1983) and Renzulli's notion of tapping the qualities of giftedness in all students (Renzulli & Reis, 1985).

7. Nichiren Buddhism clarifies that "Buddha" should not be understood as an external God, savior, or force, but as a potentiality inherent in every individual.

## Chapter 5

1. Not all the residents were women, but they were in the majority and shaped the fortunes of Hull House and were in turn most closely identified with

it. Prominent among them were Julia Lathrop, Alice Hamilton, Florence Kelley, Grace and Edith Abbott, and Sophinisba Breckinridge.

2. Pragmatism is an American philosophical movement begun in the late 19th century by Charles Sanders Peirce and William James in Cambridge, Massachusetts, that was further elaborated by John Dewey, George Herbert Mead, and Jane Addams, among many others in Chicago, and by W.E.B. Du Bois, who spanned both groups. Responding to the Darwinian evolutionary challenge to static categories, it begins with experience, understood as the ongoing transaction of organism and environment, and seeks to intentionally transform situations for the better. For pragmatists, knowledge is instrumental, a tool for organizing experience satisfactorily, and values are social, naturalistic, pluralistic, developmental, and experimental. See Dewey, MW10, pp. 3–48; and Addams, 1935/2004.

3. See Addams, 1912/1981; and Lagemann, 1985, pp. 1–42.

4. For the role that perplexities play in Addams's analyses, see Seigfried, 2002, pp. xxii–xxxi.

5. Dewey, LW8, p. 196. Dewey participated in Hull House activities and was a close friend of Addams. Their mutual influence can be seen in Seigfried, 1999, pp. 207–230.

6. Addams, 1907, 10. See also Addams, 1912/2002d.

7. Louise W. Knight connects Addams's emphasis on cooperation with the 1840s movement of social Christianity (2005, pp. 173–174). For how Addams's theory of cooperation worked in practice, see pp. 277–279, 287–290, 392–393. See also Seigfried, "Educational Experiments in Cooperation" in Seigfried, 1996, pp. 90–108, 197, where I assert that "the constant coupling of cooperation with experimentation, also found throughout Jane Addams's writings about Hull House, is a distinctive feature of pragmatist feminism."

8. On Addams's nondogmatic approach, see Seigfried, in press.

9. Addams's groundbreaking book *The Long Road of Women's Memory* (1916/2002b), which explores the dynamic and transformative character of memory, is developed to a great extent through her power to achieve striking insights through engaging socially marginalized persons in conversation.

10. See Seigfried, 2003, pp. 31–48.

11. See Seigfried 2002, pp. xxii–xxxi.

## Chapter 6

1. The members of the Eight-Nation Alliance Expeditionary Force were the United Kingdom, the United States, Japan, Russia, France, Italy, the Austro-Hungarian Empire, and Germany.

2. John King Fairbank (1907–1991), Harvard Sinologist, is regarded as the originator of modern Chinese studies in the United States.

3. The Four Books refers to the Great Learning (Da Xue), the Doctrine of the Mean (Zhong Yong), the Analects of Confucius (Lun Yu) and the Mencius (Meng Zi). The Five Classics refers to the Book of Songs (Shi Jing), The Spring and Autumn Annals (Chun Qiu), the Book of History (Shang Shu), the Book of Rites (Li Ji), and the Book of Change (Zhou Yi).

4. Nanjing was spelled Nanking prior to 1979, since the Pinyin system of writing Chinese with letters instead of characters—called romanization—was instituted in 1979 after the Cultural Revolution (1966–1976). In this chapter, we adopt the current names for Chinese cities.

5. Generally, a Chinese person has two names. At home, parents often call their children by nickname, or *xiaoming* (little name). When children grow up and go to school, their registered names on the students list are called *xueming*, or *damin* ("student name" or "big name"). The latter is the "official" name. So here Tao means that the two names indicate the same person.

6. The Treaty of Versailles, signed in 1919 at the Paris Peace Conference in the Palace of Versailles, formally ended World War I.

7. After the Opium Wars, China was forced to adopt an "open-door policy." The foreign powers thus acquired regions where their citizens could settle down. During the second half of the 19th century, Russia had the Liaodong peninsula, the Germans grabbed Shandong, the British took Weihaiwei and Kowloon and the New Territories, north of Hong Kong. The British exerted exclusive rights to the Yangtze, while the French grabbed Kwanchow Bay. The plots of land granted to foreigners in these regions were called *concessions*.

8. These experiments were aimed at restoring Tao's educational ideas, such as "life is education." The districts include villages in Shanxi, Sichuang, and Jiangsu Provinces.

## Chapter 7

1. Montessori (1948/1973a) mapped four "planes of development": birth to 6, 6 to 12, 12 to 18, and 18 to 24. See *From Childhood to Adolescence* for a more elaborated description of her theory of development.

2. Several biographies of Montessori are available. E. M. Standing (1984/1957), one of Montessori's devoted followers, published one in 1957. Montessori, having read large portions of the manuscript, wrote to Standing to express her approval of his "enthusiastic impressions," though she did offer "some minor corrections of 'historical' detail." In 1976 Rita Kramer published the definitive scholarly biography of Montessori. More recently, Gerald Gutek (2004), drawing upon Kramer and Montessori's writings, offers a succinct biography and analysis. All three sources inform our discussion of Montessori's life.

3. The Italian unification movement, or Risorgimento, was a series of military and diplomatic events that unfolded in the 19th century as several small independent states (e.g., Sardinia, Lombardy, the Papal States, the Kingdom of the Two Sicilies, Tuscany, Parma, and Modena) were unified to form a republic. The year 1870 is considered the conclusion of this movement because in October 1870, after Napolean III withdrew his troops from Rome during the Franco-Prussian War (1870–1871), the Papal States were left unprotected. The Italian army entered Rome, and Rome voted for union with Italy (http://www.arcaini.com/ITALY/ItalyHistory/ItalianUnification/htm).

4. Montessori was buried in Amsterdam, but a tablet placed at her parents' gravesite in Rome explains that Montessori "rests far from own beloved country,

far from her dear ones buried here, at her wish a testimony to universality of the work which made her a citizen of the world."

5. The Geneva lecture was delivered to the International Office of Education in 1932, the Brussels address was given before the European Congress for Peace in 1936, and the Copenhagen lectures were given over several days at the Sixth International Montessori Congress in 1937.

6. For a more extended discussion and synthesis of Montessori's vision of the prepared environment, see Whitcomb, 2000.

7. For a fuller discussion of the construct of "work" as it is enacted in Montessori classrooms, see Cossentino, 2006.

8. For a fuller discussion of the triad of preparation, observation, and invitation constituting the Montessori practitioner's expertise, see Cossentino, 2005.

9. For a comprehensive directory of Montessori schools, see http://www.montessoriconnections.com/. Our analysis of this database shows that there are 251 public and 122 charter Montessori schools in the United States.

10. See, for example, April Jones, *Montessori Education in America: An Analysis of Research Conducted from 2000–2005*, unpublished masters project, the College of William and Mary, 2005. The following scholars have published monographs or empirical studies in the past two years: Lillard (2005), Rathunde & Csikszentmihalyi (2005a; 2005b).

## Chapter 8

1. Tagore was awarded the Nobel Prize in Literature in 1913 for his book of poems *Gitanjali* (Tagore, 1912), a volume originally written in Bengali and translated into English by himself. It should be noted that most of Tagore's writings were in Bengali, though he often lectured and wrote essays in English. While he was in England in 1912, his work had been appreciated by such poets as William Butler Yeats, who wrote a preface to *Gitanjali*. The initial proposal to the Swedish Academy came from Thomas Sturge Moore, a fellow of the (British) Royal Society. The citation for Tagore's award noted "his profoundly sensitive, fresh and beautiful verse, by which, with consummate skill, he has made his poetic thought, expressed in his own English words, a part of the literature of the West" (www.nobelprize.org/literature/laureates/1913).

2. Material for this chapter has been drawn from my study of Tagore's educational work, *Rabindranath Tagore: The Poet as Educator* (O'Connell, 2002), where a fuller treatment of the history and educational aspects of Santiniketan in relation to Tagore's own life can be found.

3. As Tagore writes: "We were ostracized because of our heterodox opinions about religion and, therefore, we enjoyed the freedom of the outcaste. We had to build our own world with our own thoughts and energy of mind. . . . I was born in a family which had to live its own life, which led me from my young days to seek guidance for my own self expression in my own inner standard of judgment" (Tagore, 1928/1988, pp. 4–5).

4. In traditional India, a *pundit* would be described as "a learned Hindu; one versed in Sanskrit and in the philosophy, religion, and jurisprudence of India" (*Oxford English Dictionary*, 2nd ed. [Claredon Press: Oxford, 1989]).

5. As Tagore noted, "There is a private corner for me in my house with a little table, which has its special fittings of pen and ink-stand and paper, and here I can best do my writing and other work. There is no reason to run down, or run away from this corner of mine, because in it I cannot invite and provide seats for all my friends and guests. It may be that this corner is too narrow, or too close, or too untidy, so that my doctor may object, my friends remonstrate, my enemies sneer. . . . My point is that if all the rooms in my house be likewise solely for my own special convenience, if there be no reception room for my friends or accommodation for my guests, then indeed I may be blamed. Then with bowed head I must confess that in my house no great meeting of friends can ever take place" (Tagore, 1961, pp. 228–229).

6. Macaulay's Minute on Indian Education (1835), had advocated that government education in India be English in content and medium. This had resulted in a foreign curriculum and many teachers, whose English was minimal, teaching in a language they did not understand. Tagore effectively argued that such education was inappropriate and actually harmful to Bengali children.

7. The *tapoban* communities, he writes, in "The Teacher," were groups "living in the heart of nature, not ascetics fiercely in love with a lingering suicide, but men of serene sanity who sought to realize the spiritual meaning of their lives" (1931, p. 168).

8. *Visva* means "world," "universe," "all," "every," "entire," or "whole." Bharati means India, culture, and learning, as symbolized by the goddess Saraswati, who presides over eloquence and narrative. This could be translated, according to a play on words to represent the different levels of exchange as "the Culture of the World"; "All Indian"; "All Culture"; or, as we might say today, "All Discourses."

9. The school's constitution was drawn up by Prasanta Mahalanobis, professor of physics at Presidency College and a pioneer of statistical research in India, and Tagore's son, Rathindranath. Both were named Karma-Sachivas (secretaries) of Visva-Bharati, overseeing its development.

10. This was built right into the Patha-Bhavan syllabus, which states, "When in the rainy season sudden storms of rain come, the pupils delight in going out with their teachers into the midst of the heaviest deluge and getting thoroughly wet" ("Patha-Bhavana, Santiniketan," 1938, p. 5).

11. For a discussion of the successes and problems of Sriniketan, see Das Gupta, 1979, 354–378.

12. For further assessment and description of these models, see Mukherjee, 1962, pp. 185–243.

13. Such schools would include Dartington Hall in England; the Rabindranath Tagore Foundation School in Hungary; and in India, Patha Bhavan in Santiniketan, north of Kolkata (formerly Calcutta), the Tagore Academy of Bharatnatyam in Coimbatore, and the Kerala Kalamandalam Center school in Cheruthuruthy.

14. The relationship between Gandhi and Tagore is a fascinating one. They had great respect for each other and carried on a lengthy correspondence over many years. When Gandhi left South Africa in 1915, the students from his Phoenix School were relocated to Santiniketan, and after Tagore's death in 1941, it was Gandhi who secured the funds to sustain Visva-Bharati. However, they differed greatly in their temperament and outlook, and there were several occasions when they resorted to public debate over such issues as nationalism, birth control, technology, and childhood education. For an excellent article describing these differences, see

Sibnarayan Ray, "Tagore-Gandhi Controversy," in *Gandhi, India, and the World* (Philadelphia: Temple University Press, 1970), pp. 119–141.

## Chapter 9

1. In earlier writings, I have examined many aspects of Waldorf education, which first emerged in 1919, including the importance of imagination (Uhrmacher, 1991a), the use of focal activities (1993b), the uses of image, rhythm, story, and movement (1993a), and the emphasis on preparing an aesthetic environment (2004). I have also suggested criteria to be considered in attempts to borrow ideas from Waldorf education (1997).

2. Eurythmy is an artistic activity in which students make movements to letters, words, or music. Form drawing is an exercise in which students draw geometric forms. Handwork usually entails sewing and knitting.

3. Some Waldorf educators fear losing the spiritual grounding of Waldorf principles; some outsiders to Waldorf education fear having anthroposophy anywhere near public education.

4. Pseudonyms are used for the location of this Waldorf school and for the teacher's name (the use of *Miss* is discussed in note 5). The descriptions and interview material are from data collected for Uhrmacher, 1991a. Some interview material has been extracted from the researcher's original notes and is not to be found in the dissertation.

5. A feminist critique of the language used in Waldorf education would take issue with its male-oriented language and rightly fear that a patriarchal worldview is being taught. In regard to the feminist critique, I find no evidence that Waldorf education is sexist. Steiner himself was an advocate for women's rights. In addition, women involved in the anthroposophical movement have been reflective on women's issues from their spiritual perspective (see Matthews, Schaefer, & Staley, 1986). In addition, Waldorf education since 1919 has always offered the same curriculum to all students. All students take woodworking as well as sewing. The use of *Man* in "Man and Animal" and the preference for *Miss* over *Ms.* seem to be organizational preferences or idiosyncrasies (depending upon your point of view) rather than symbolic of a patriarchal organizational perspective.

6. Unpublished interview material collected for Uhrmacher, 1991a.

7. Unpublished interview material collected for Uhrmacher, 1991a.

8. Teachers who are bound to letter grading might also be caring and use the grades to provoke students' attitudes. The mark of a letter grade, however, in my opinion, cannot compete with a picture or poem in terms of the quality of the representation.

9. A great deal of discussion on the pros and cons of Waldorf education takes place on the Internet. For criticism, see www.waldorfcritics.org; for defense of Waldorf philosophy and practices, see www.waldorfanswers.org.

## Chapter 10

1. I refer to the letters in Miller and Woyt by letter number and page number, such that 1: p. 1 is letter 1 on page 1.

2. His critique is not only implicit, but also explicit, as he discusses the real harm that Europeans brought to Africa as a result of their need for raw materials such as mahogany wood. See Schweitzer's "Lumbermen and Raftsmen in the Primeval Forest" (Schweitzer, 1998b).

3. I am indebted to John Pomery for these insights.

4. I thank John Kirby for the discussion of Aristotle.

5. The No Child Left Behind Act (http://www.ed.gov/nclb/) was signed into law by President George W. Bush on January 8, 2002.

6. The original hospital was established in 1913 and rebuilt in 1924. In 1927, Schweitzer moved to a larger site 3 kilometers north and created a new facility. Finally, in 1981, a modern hospital was built up the hill from the 1927 hospital, which has now become part of a "Zone Historique" that includes numerous renovated buildings and a museum.

# References

Abrell, R. (1974). Albert Schweitzer: Educator for a season. *Contemporary Education 46*(1): 28–33.

———. (1978, Spring). The school will be the way. *Humane Education* 2:10–11.

———. (1981). The educational thought of Albert Schweitzer. *The Clearing House 54*(7): 93–296.

Addams, J. (1907). *Newer ideals of peace*. New York: Macmillan.

———. (1930). *The second 20 years at Hull-House*. New York: Macmillan.

———. (1981). *Twenty years at Hull-House*. New York: Penguin Books. (Original work published 1912)

———. (1982). A function of the social settlement. In *The social thought of Jane Addams*, ed. C. Lasch, 183–199. New York: Irvington. (Original work published 1899)

———. (2002a). *Democracy and social ethics*. Urbana: University of Illinois Press. (Original work published 1902)

———. (2002b). *The long road of women's memory*. Urbana: University of Illinois Press. (Original work published 1916)

———. (2002c). The objective value of a social settlement. In *The Jane Addams reader*, ed. J. B. Elshtain, 29–45. New York: Basic Books. (Original work published 1893)

———. (2002d). *Peace and bread in time of war*. Urbana: University of Illinois Press. (Original work published 1916)

———. (2004). *My friend, Julia Lathrop*. Urbana: University of Illinois Press. (Original work published 1935)

Alridge, D. P. (1999). Conceptualizing a Du Boisian philosophy of education: Towards a model for African-American education. *Educational Theory 49*(3): 359–379.

Anderson, R. F. (2006). Poetically dwelling with the veil: The intellectual, moral, and aesthetic dimension of W. E. B. Du Bois's educational philosophy. In *Philosophy of Education 2005*. Urbana, IL: Philosophy of Education Society.

Appiah, K. A. (2005, Spring). The problem of the 21st century: Du Bois and cosmopolitanism. *Columbia College contemporary civilization coursewide lecture*. http://www.college.columbia.edu/core/lectures/spring205/index.php.

Appiah, K. A., & Gates, H. L. (1999). *Africana*. New York: Perseus Book Groups.

Aristotle. (1992). *The art of rhetoric*. New York: Penguin.

Aulthaus, P. (1962). Evangelical faith and anthroposophy. *The Lutheran Quarterly 14*(1): 3–20.

Ayers, W. (2004). *Teaching toward freedom: Moral commitment and ethical action in the classroom.* Boston: Beacon Press.

Barnes, H. (1980). An introduction to Waldorf education. *Teachers College Record* 81:323–336.

Berman, M. (1989). *Coming to our senses: Body and spirit in the hidden history of the West.* New York: Bantam Books.

Berryman, P. (1987). *Liberation theology.* Philadelphia: Temple University Press.

Bethel, D. M. (1973). *Makiguchi the value creator.* New York: Weatherhill, Inc.

——, ed. (1989). *Education for creative living: Ideas and proposals of Tsunesaburo Makiguchi,* trans. A. Birnbaum. Ames, Iowa: State University Press.

——, ed. (2002). *A geography of human life.* San Francisco: Caddo Gap Press. (Original work published 1903)

Blount, J. M. (2002). Ella Flagg Young and the Chicago schools. In *Founding mothers and others: Women educational leaders during the Progressive Era,* ed. A. R. Sadovnik and S. F. Semel, 163–176. New York: Palgrave Macmillan.

Boostrom, R. (2005). *Thinking: The foundation of critical and creative learning in the classroom.* New York: Teachers College Press.

Boston, B. O. (1972). Paulo Freire: Notes of a loving critic. In *Paulo Freire: A revolutionary dilemma for the adult educator,* ed. S. M. Grabowski, 83–92. Syracuse: Syracuse University Publications in Continuing Education.

Brabazon, J. (2000). *Albert Schweitzer: A biography.* 2nd ed. Syracuse: Syracuse University Press.

——, ed. (2005). *Albert Schweitzer: Essential writings.* Maryknoll, NY: Orbis Books.

Brann, E. T. H. (1979). *Paradoxes of education in a republic.* Chicago: University of Chicago Press.

Carlgren, F. (1981). *Education towards freedom.* 3d ed. Trans. J. Rudel & S. Rudel. East Grinstead, England: Lanthorn Press.

Carson, R. (1962). *Silent spring.* Boston: Houghton Mifflin.

Chakravarty, A., ed. (1966). *A Tagore reader.* Boston: Beacon Press.

Cohen, S. (1969). Maria Montessori: Priestess or pedagogue? *Teachers College Record* 71(2): 313–326.

Commager, H. D. (1950). *The American mind.* New Haven: Yale University Press.

Cone, J. H. (1986). *A Black theology of liberation.* Maryknoll, NY: Orbis Books.

Cossentino, J. (2005). Ritualizing expertise: A non-Montessorian look at the Montessori method. *American Journal of Education* 111(2): 211–244.

——. (2006). Big work: Goodness, vocation, and engagement in the Montessori method. *Curriculum Inquiry* 36(1), 63–92.

Cousins, N. (1985). *Albert Schweitzer's mission: Healing and peace.* New York: W. W. Norton.

Cuban, L. (1992). Curriculum stability and change. In *Handbook of research on curriculum,* ed. P. Jackson. Washington, DC: American Educational Research Association.

Dai, B. (1982). *Tao Xingzhi de shengping jiqi xueshuo* [Tao Xingzhi's life and philosophy]. Beijing: Renmin Jiaoyu Chubanshe.

Das Gupta, U. (1979). Rabindranath Tagore on rural reconstruction. *The Indian Historical Review,* 4(2): 354–378.

de Melo Silva, V. (2000). Makiguchi project in action: Enhancing education for peace. In *Ideas and influence of Tsunesaburo Makiguchi: Special issue of the Journal of Oriental Studies, 10*. Tokyo: The Institute of Oriental Philosophy. Available: http://www.iop.or.jp/0010s/start0010s.htm

Dewey, J. (1972). My pedagogic creed. In *The early works of John Dewey, 1882–1898*. Vol. 5, ed. J. A. Boydston, 84–95. Carbondale: Southern Illinois University Press. (Original work published 1897)

———. (1976). *The school and society*. In *The middle works of John Dewey, 1899–1924*. Vol. 1, ed. J. A. Boydston, 1–112. Carbondale: Southern Illinois University Press. (Original work published 1900)

———. (1976). The school as social center. In *The middle works of John Dewey, 1899–1924*. Vol. 2, ed. J. A. Boydston, 80–93. Carbondale: Southern Illinois University Press. (Original work published 1902).

———. (1977). The relation of theory to practice in education. In *The middle works of John Dewey, 1899–1924*. Vol. 3, *Essays on the new empiricism, 1903–1906*, ed. J. A. Boydston, 249–272. Carbondale: Southern Illinois University Press. (Original work published 1904)

———. (1980). The need for a recovery of philosophy. In *The middle works of John Dewey, 1899–1924*. Vol. 10, ed. J. A. Boydston, 1–48. Carbondale: Southern Illinois University Press. (Original work published 1917)

———. (1981). *Experience and nature*. In *The later works of John Dewey, 1925–1953*. Vol. 1, ed. J. A. Boydston, 1–328. Carbondale: Southern Illinois University Press. (Original work published 1925)

———. (1984). The play of ideas. In *The later works of John Dewey, 1925–1953*. Vol. 4, ed. J. A. Boydston, 112–135. Carbondale: Southern Illinois University Press. (Original work published 1925)

———. (1984). *The public and its problems*. In *The later works of John Dewey, 1925–1927*. Vol. 2, ed. J. A. Boydston, 235–372. Carbondale: Southern Illinois University Press. (Original work published 1927)

———. (1985). *Democracy and education*. In *The middle works of John Dewey, 1899–1924*. Vol. 9, ed. J. A. Boydston, 3–370. Carbondale: Southern Illinois University Press. (Original work published 1916)

———. (1987). *Art as experience*. In *The later works of John Dewey, 1925–1953*. Vol 10, ed. J. A. Boydston, 1–340. Carbondale: Southern Illinois University Press. (Original work published 1934)

———. (1988). Experience and education. In *The later works of John Dewey, 1925–1953*. Vol. 13, ed. J. A. Boydston, 1–88. Carbondale: Southern Illinois University Press. (Original work published 1938)

———. (1988). The case for Bertrand Russell. In *The later works of John Dewey, 1925–1953*. Vol. 14, ed. J. A. Boydston, 231–234. Carbondale: Southern Illinois University Press. (Original work published 1940)

———. (1989). How we think. In *The later works of John Dewey, 1925–1953*. Vol. 8, *Essays and How We Think*, ed. J. A. Boydston, 105–352. Carbondale: Southern Illinois University Press. (Original work published 1910)

Du Bois, W.E.B. (1945). The black man and Albert Schweitzer. In *The Albert Schweitzer jubilee book*, ed. A. A. Roback, 121–127. Cambridge, MA: Sci-Art Publishers.

———. (1970). *The gift of black folk: The negroes in the making of America*. New York: Washington Square Press. (Original work published 1945)

———. (1973). *The education of Black people: Ten critiques, 1906–1960,* ed. H. Aptheker. Amherst: University of Massachusetts Press.

———. (1986). Dusk of dawn. In *Writings,* ed. N. Huggins, 549–793. New York: Library of America. (Original work published 1940)

———. (1994). *The souls of black folk.* Toronto, Ontario: Dover Publications. (Original work published 1903)

———. (1996). Darkwater: Voices from within the veil. In *The Oxford W. E. B. Du Bois reader,* ed. E. Sundquist, 481–622. New York: Oxford University Press. (Original work published 1920)

Duffy, M., & Duffy, D. (2002). *Children of the universe.* Cincinnati: Parent Child Press.

Egan, K. (2002). *Getting it wrong from the beginning: Our progressivist inheritance from Herbert Spencer, John Dewey, and Jean Piaget.* New Haven: Yale University Press.

Follett, M. P. (1924). *Creative experience.* New York: Longman Green and Co.

Free, A. C., ed. (1982). *Animals, nature, and Albert Schweitzer.* http://www.awionline.org/schweitzer/as-idx.htm (accessed January 15, 2006).

Freire, P. (1972a). Conscientizing as a way of liberating. In *Paulo Freire,* 3–10. Washington, DC: U.S. Catholic Conference.

———. (1972b). Letter to a young theology student. In *Paulo Freire,* 11–12. Washington, DC: U.S. Catholic Conference.

———. (1978). *Pedagogy in process: The letters to Guinea-Bissau,* trans. C. St. John Hunter. New York: Continuum.

———. (1987). *The politics of education: Culture, power, and liberation,* trans D. Macedo. Westport, CT: Bergin and Garvey.

———. (1996). *Education for critical consciousness,* trans. M. Bergman Ramos. New York: Continuum. (Original work published 1969)

———. (1999). *Pedagogy of hope,* trans. R. R. Barr. New York: Continuum. (Original work published 1992)

———. (2000). *Pedagogy of the heart,* trans. D. Macedo and A. Oliveira. New York: Continuum. (Original work published 1997)

———. (2003). *Pedagogy of the oppressed,* trans. M. Bergman Ramos. New York: Continuum. (Original work published 1970)

Gardner, H. (1983). *Frames of mind: The theory of multiple intelligences.* New York: Basic Books.

Garrison, J. (1997). *Dewey and eros: Wisdom and desire in the art of teaching.* New York: Teachers College Press.

Ginsberg, I. (1982). Jean Piaget and Rudolf Steiner: Stages of child development and implications for pedagogy. *Teachers College Record* 84:327–337.

Gluck, C. (1985). *Japan's modern myths: Ideology in the late Meiji period.* Princeton: Princeton University Press.

Gordon, L. R. (1999). African-American philosophy: Theory, politics, and pedagogy. In *Philosophy of Education Yearbook 1998.* Urbana, IL: Philosophy of Education Society.

Gross, C. H. (1970). *Soka Gakkai and education.* East Lansing: Institute for International Studies, Michigan State University Press.

Gutek, G. L., ed. (2004). *The Montessori method: The origins of an educational innovation, including an abridged and annotated edition of Maria Montessori's The Montessori method.* Lanham, MD: Rowman & Littlefield.

Gutierrez, G. (1973). *A theology of liberation.* Maryknoll, NY: Orbis Books.

Hansen, D. T. (1995). *The call to teach.* New York: Teachers College Press.

Hartle, A. (2003). *Michel de Montaigne: Accidental philosopher.* New York: Cambridge University Press.

Hergenhahn, B. R. (1986). *An introduction to the history of psychology.* Belmont, CA: Wadsworth.

Hill, J. C. (Producer and Director), & Anderson, E. (Producer). (1957). *Albert Schweitzer* [Motion Picture]. Los Angeles: Louis de Rouchemont Associates.

hooks, b. (1994). *Teaching to transgress: Education as the practice of freedom.* New York: Routledge.

Ikeda, D. (1968). *The human revolution,* Vol. 1. Tokyo: Seikyo Press.

———. (2001). *Soka education: A Buddhist vision for teachers, students, and parents.* Santa Monica, CA: Middleway Press.

———. (2006). *To the youthful pioneers of soka: Lectures, essays, and poems on value-creating education.* Tokyo: Soka University Student Union.

Ikeda, S. (1969). *Tsunesaburo Makiguchi.* Tokyo: Nihon Sonoshobo.

Jackson, P. (1995). Narrative landscapes and the moral imagination: Taking the story to heart. In *Narrative in teaching, learning, and research,* ed. H. McEwan and K. Egan, 3–23. New York: Teachers College Press.

"Jane Addams." (2004). In *The Blackwell guide to American philosophy,* ed. A. T. Marsoobian and J. Ryder. Malden, MA: Blackwell.

Japanese Special Higher Police. (1943a, July). Soka Kyoiku Gakkai honbu kankeisha no chianijiho ihan jiken kenkyo [The arrest of persons related with Soka Kyoiku Gakkai headquarters for the charge of violating the peace preservation law]. *Tokko geppo* [Monthly report of the Special Higher Police].

———. (1943b, August). Soka Kyoiku Gakkai kaicho Makiguchi Tsunesaburo ni taisuru jinmon chosho basui [Excerpt from interrogation record of Soka Kyoiku Gakkai president Tsunesaburo Makiguchi]. *Tokko geppo* [Monthly report of the Special Higher Police].

*Jiaoyuchao* [Educational tide]. (1919–1921). Hanzhou, Zhejiang Province.

Joffee, M. (2004). Public charter school renewal application: Part 1 (Retrospective analysis). Document on file at the Renaissance Charter School, Jackson Heights, NY.

———. (2006). *The value creation school: A case study of collaborative leadership in a K–12 focus school.* Unpublished doctoral dissertation. New York: Teachers College, Columbia University.

Johnson, D. (2000). W. E. B. Du Bois: Thomas Jesse Jones and the struggle for social education, 1900–1930. *Journal of Negro History* 85(3): 71–95.

Johnson, M. (1993). *Moral imagination: Implications of cognitive science for ethics.* Chicago: University of Chicago Press.

Kabir, H. (1959). *Education in new India.* London: Allen & Unwin.

Kadamus, J. A. (2005, May 11). Renewal of charter school charters: Memo of deputy commissioner of the New York State Department of Education. http://www.regents.nysed.gov/2005Meetings/May2005/0505emscvesida7.htm (accessed February 2, 2006).

Knight, L. W. (2005). *Citizen: Jane Addams and the struggle for democracy.* Chicago: University of Chicago Press.

Kramer, R. (1976). *Maria Montessori: A biography.* New York: Putnam.

Kumagai, K. (1978). *Makiguchi Tsunesaburo.* Tokyo: Daisan Bunmeisha.

———. (2000). Value-creating pedagogy and Japanese education in the modern era. In *Ideas and influence of Tsunesaburo Makiguchi: Special issue of the Journal of Oriental Studies, 10.* Tokyo: The Institute of Oriental Philosophy. Available: http://www.iop.or.jp/0010s/kumagai.pdf.

Lagemann, E. C. (1985). Introduction. In *Jane Addams on education,* ed. E. C. Lagemann, 1–42. New York: Teachers College Press.

———. (1996). Experimenting with education: John Dewey and Ella Flagg Young at the University of Chicago. *American Journal of Education, 104*(3), 171–185.

Lasch, C. (1991). *The true and only heaven: Progress and its critics.* New York: W. W. Norton.

Latta, M. (2002). Seeking fragility's presence: The power of aesthetic play in teaching and learning. In *Philosophy of Education 2002,* ed. S. Fletcher, 225–233. Urbana, IL: Philosophy of Education Society.

Leopold, A. (1949). *A sand county almanac.* New York: Oxford University Press.

Lewis, D. L. (2000). *W. E. B. Du Bois: The fight for equality and the American century, 1919–1963.* Toronto, Ontario, Canada: Fitzhenry & Whiteside.

Lillard, A. S. (2005). *Montessori: The science behind the genius.* New York: Oxford University Press.

Macaulay, J. B. (1835). Minute on education. Available: http://www.mssu.edu/projectsouthasia/history/primarydocs/education/Macaulay001.htm

Makiguchi project in Panama. (2001, Fall). *SGI Quarterly.* Available: www.sgi.org/english/Features/quarterly/0110/world8.htm (accessed February 2, 2006).

Makiguchi, T. (1983–1988). *Makiguchi Tsunesaburo zenshu* [Collected works of Tsunesaburo Makiguchi]. Vols. 1–10. Tokyo: Daisan Bunmeisha.

Mao Dun. (1984). Women you Zeren shi Tamen Yongyan Busi [We have the responsibility to make them live forever]. In *Jinian Tao Xingzhi* [In memory of Tao Xingzhi]. Hunan: Hunan Jiaoyu Chubanshe. (Original document dated 1946)

Marrazzi, M. (2001, January). Springtime of peace. *SGI Quarterly.* www.sgi.org/english/Features/quarterly/0101/casestudy.htm (accessed February 2, 2006).

Martin, J. (2002). *The education of John Dewey.* New York: Columbia University Press.

Martin, J. R. (1992). *Schoolhome: Rethinking schools for changing families.* Cambridge, MA: Harvard University Press.

Marx, K. (1978). Theses on Feuerbach. In *The Marx-Engels reader,* 2nd ed., ed. R. C. Tucker, 143–145. New York: Norton. (Original work published 1888)

Matsuoka, M. (2005). *Nichiren Bukkyo no shakai shisoteki tenkai* [Nichiren Buddhist social thought in modern Japan]. Tokyo: University of Tokyo Press.

Matthews, M., Schaefer, S., & Staley, B. (1986). *Ariadne's awakening: Taking up the threads of consciousness.* Gloucestershire, U. K.: Hawthorne Press.

McDermott, R., Byers, P., Dillard, C., Easton, F., Henry, M., & Uhrmacher, P. B. (1996). The urban Waldorf school. *Urban Education Review, 28*(2): 119–140.

McDermott, R. A., ed. (1984). *The essential Steiner*. San Francisco: Harper & Row.

McEwan, H., & Egan, K., eds. (1995). *Narrative in teaching, learning, and research*. New York: Teachers College Press.

McGrath, N. (1977, September 25). Learning with the heart. *New York Times Magazine*, 100, 107.

McSwine, B. L. (1999). The educational philosophy of W. E. B. Du Bois. In *Philosophy of Education Yearbook 1998*. Urbana, IL: Philosophy of Education Society.

Metraux, D. (1994). *The Soka Gakkai revolution*. Lewiston, NY: University Press of America.

Miller, G. D. (2002). *Peace, value, and wisdom: The educational philosophy of Daisaku Ikeda*. Amsterdam: Rodopi.

Miller, R. S., & Woytt, G., eds. (2003). *The Albert Schweitzer–Hélène Bresslau letters, 1902–1912*, trans. A. B. Lemke. Syracuse, NY: Syracuse University Press.

Miyata, K. (1997). Makiguchi Tsunesaburo wa Kanto wo koeta ka (Did Tsunesaburo Makiguchi go beyond Kant?) Tokyo: Daisan Bunmeisha.

———. (2000). Tsunesaburo Makiguchi's theory of the state. In *Ideas and Influence of Tsunesaburo Makiguchi: Special Issue of the Journal of Oriental Studies, 10*, Tokyo: The Institute of Oriental Philosophy. Available: http://www.iop.or.jp/0010s/start0010s.htm.

Montague, J. F. (1965). *The why of Albert Schweitzer*. New York: Hawthorn Books.

Montessori, M. (1912). *The Montessori method*, trans. Anne E. George. New York: Frederick A. Stokes. (Original work published 1909 in Italian as *Il Metodo della Pedagogia Scientifica applicato all'educazione infantile nelle Case dei Bambini*.)

———. (1917). *Advanced Montessori method*. London: William Heinemann.

———. (1966). *The secret of childhood*. New York: Fides. (Original work published 1936)

———. (1967a). *The discovery of the child*. New York: Ballantine Books. (Original work published 1962)

———. (1967b). *To educate the human potential*. Adyar, India: Kalakshetra.

———. (1972). *Education and peace*. Chicago: Henry Regenery Company.

———. (1973a). *From childhood to adolescence*. New York: Schocken Books. (Original work published 1948)

———. (1973b). *The Montessori elementary material*. New York: Schocken Books.

———. (1994). *The absorbent mind*. Oxford, England: ABC-Clio, Ltd. (Original work published 1949)

Mukherjee, H. B. (1962). *Education for fulness: A study of the educational thought and experiment of Rabindranath Tagore*. Bombay: Asia.

Munz, W. (2005, November). *Reverence for life at Lambaréné in Albert Schweitzer's last years*, trans. P. Marxsen. Paper presented at "The Ethics of Reverence for Life Colloquium," Marc Bloc University, Strasbourg, France.

Noddings, N. (1984). *Caring: A feminine approach to ethics and moral education*. Berkeley: University of California Press.

Oakeshott, M. (1989). *The voice of liberal learning: Michael Oakeshott on education*, ed. T. Fuller. New Haven: Yale University Press.

Oberman, I. (1997). The mystery of Waldorf: A turn-of-the-century German experiment on today's American soil. Paper presented at the annual meeting of the American Education Research Association, Chicago.

O'Connell, K. M. (2002). *Rabindranath Tagore: The poet as educator*. Calcutta: Visva-Bharati.

Outlaw, L. T., Jr. (2000). W. E. B. Du Bois on the study of social problems. *Annals* 568(1): 281–297.

Pagan, I. T. (2001). *Makiguchian pedagogy in the middle school science classroom*. Unpublished doctoral dissertation, New York, Teachers College.

Patha-Bhavana, Santinikettan. (1938, August). *Visva-Bharati Bulletin*, No. 4, 1–11.

Plato. (2004). *Gorgias*, trans. W. Hamilton & C. Emlyn-Jones. London: Penguin Books.

Provenzo, E. F., Jr. (2002). *Du Bois on education*. Lanham, MD: AltaMira Press.

Rabaka, R. (2003). W. E. B. Du Bois's evolving Africana philosophy of education. *Journal of Black Studies* 33(4): 399–449.

Rathunde, K., & Csikszentmihalyi, M. (2005a). Middle school students' motivation and quality of experience: A comparison of Montessori and traditional school environments. *American Journal of Education* 111(3): 341–371.

———. (2005b). The social context of middle school: Teachers, friends, and activities in Montessori and traditional school environments. *The Elementary School Journal* 106:59–79.

Renzulli, J. S., & Reis, S. M. (1985). *The schoolwide enrichment model*. Mansfield Center, CT: Creative Learning Press.

Rest, J., Narvaez, D., Bebeau, M. J., & Thoma, S. J. (1999). *Postconventional moral thinking: A neo-Kohlbergian approach*. Mahwah, NJ: Lawrence Erlbaum Associates.

Rockefeller, S. C. (1991). *John Dewey: Religious faith and democratic humanism*. New York: Columbia University Press.

Rorty, R. (1989). *Contingency, irony, and solidarity*. Cambridge U. K.: Cambridge University Press.

Rud, A. (1995). Learning in comfort: Developing an ethos of hospitality in education. In *The educational conversation: Closing the gap*, ed. J. Garrison & A. Rud, 119–128. Albany: State University of New York Press.

Rutledge, R. R. (2001). Metaphors of mediation: Race and nation in Black Atlantic literature. Doctoral dissertation, Washington University. UMI Dissertation Services.

Ryan, A. (1995). *John Dewey and the high tide of American liberalism*. New York: W. W. Norton.

Saito, S. (1981). *Wakaki Tsunesaburo Makiguchi* [The youthful Makiguchi Tsunesaburo]. Tokyo: Daisan Bunmei Sha.

———. (1989). *Nihonteki shizenkan no henkakatei* [The transition of Japanese views on nature]. Tokyo: Denki University Press.

Santoro Gomez, D. (2005). *The space for good teaching*. Unpublished doctoral dissertation, Teachers College, Columbia University, New York.

Sato, H. (2000). Nichiren thought in modern Japan: Two perspectives. In *Ideas and influence of Tsunesaburo Makiguchi: Special issue of the Journal of Oriental Studies, 10*. Tokyo: The Institute of Oriental Philosophy. Available: http://www.iop.or.jp/0010s/start0010s.htm.

Schwab, J. J. (1978). The "impossible" role of the teacher in progressive education.

In *Joseph J. Schwab: Science, curriculum, and liberal education*, ed. I. Westbury and N. J. Wilkof, 167–183. Chicago: University of Chicago Press.

Schweitzer, A. (1997). *Memoirs of childhood and youth*, trans. K. Bergel & A. R. Bergel. Syracuse, NY: Syracuse University Press. (Original work published 1925)

———. (1998a). *Out of my life and thought*, trans. A. B. Lemke. Baltimore: Johns Hopkins University Press. (Original work published 1933)

———. (1998b). *The primeval forest: Including* On the Edge of the Primeval Forest *and* More from the Primeval Forest. Baltimore: Johns Hopkins University Press. (Original work published 1931)

Seager, R. H. (2006). *Encountering the Dharma: Daisaku Ikeda, Soka Gakkai, and the globalization of Buddhism*. Berkeley: University of California Press.

Semel, S. F., & Sadovnik, A. R., eds. (1999). *Schools of tomorrow, schools of today: What happened to progressive education*. New York: Peter Lang.

Seigfried, C. H. (1996). *Pragmatism and feminism: Reweaving the social fabric*. Chicago: University of Chicago Press.

———. (1999). Socializing democracy: Jane Addams and John Dewey. *Philosophy of the Social Sciences*, 29(2): 207–230.

———. (2002). Introduction. In *Democracy and social ethics*, by J. Addams. Urbana: University of Illinois Press

———. (2003). The dilemma of democracy: Diversity of interests and common experiences. In *Renascent pragmatism: Studies in law and social science*, ed. A. Morales, 31–48. Brookfield, VT: Asgate.

———. (in press). The courage of one's convictions or the conviction of one's courage? Jane Addams's principled compromises. In *Women's experiences shaping theory*, ed. W. Chmielewski, M. Fischer, & C. Nackenoff. Urbana: University of Illinois Press.

Sharma, N. (1998). *Value creators in education: Japanese educator Makiguchi and Mahatma Gandhi and their relevance for the Indian education*. New Delhi: Regency.

Shor, I., & Freire, P. (1987). *A pedagogy for liberation: Dialogues on transforming education*. Westport, CT: Bergin & Garvey.

Soka Gakkai Educators Division, eds. (2000). *Kyoiku no mezasu beki michi* [The path forward for education]. Tokyo: Otori Shoin.

Standing, E. M. (1984). *Maria Montessori: Her life and work*. New York: New American Library. (Original work published 1957)

Steiner, R. (1965). *The education of the child in the light of anthroposophy*. Spring Valley, NY: Anthroposophic Press. (Original work published 1909)

———. (1977). *Rudolf Steiner: An autobiography*, trans. R. Stebbing. Blauvelt, NY: Rudolf Steiner.

———. (1981). *The renewal of education*, trans. R. Everett. E. Sussex, U.K.: Kolisko Archive. Lectures given April 20–May 11, 1920, Basel, Switzerland.

———. (1986). *Soul economy and Waldorf education*, trans. R. Everett. Spring Valley, NY: Anthroposophic Press. Lectures given December 23, 1921–January 7, 1922, Dornach, Switzerland.

———. (1988a). *The child's changing consciousness and Waldorf education*, trans. & ed. R. Everett. Hudson, NY: Anthroposophic Press. Lectures given April 15–22, 1923, Dornach, Switzerland.

————. (1988b). *The kingdom of childhood.* 2nd ed. London: Rudolf Steiner Press. Lectures given August 12–20, 1924, Holland.

————. (1997). *The roots of education.* Hudson, NY: Anthroposophic Press. Lectures given April 13–17, 1924, Bern, Switzerland.

Sykes, M. (1947). *Rabindranath Tagore.* Madras: Longmans, Green.

Tagore, R. (1912). *Gitanjali.* London: Chiswick Press.

————. (1917). *Personality.* London: Macmillan.

————. (1922). *Creative unity.* London: Macmillan.

————. (1929). *Letters to a friend.* London: George Allen & Unwin.

————. (1931). *The religion of man.* Boston: Beacon Press.

————. (1961). *Towards universal man.* New York: Asia. (Posthumous collection)

————. (1962). *Reminiscences.* Madras: Macmillan. (Original work published 1917)

————. (1964). Totakahini. In *Boundless sky*, ed. S. R. Das. Calcutta: Visva-Bharati.

————. (1983). *Introduction to Tagore.* Calcutta: Visva-Bharati. (Posthumous collection)

————. (1988). *Lectures and addresses*, ed. A. Xoares. Madras: Macmillan. (Original work published 1928)

Tanner, L. N. (1997). *Dewey's laboratory school: Lessons for today.* New York: Teachers College Press.

Tao Xingzhi. (1983–1985). *Tao Xingzhi Quanji* [Collected works of Tao Xingzhi] (6 vols.), ed. Institute of Educational Science, Huazhong Normal University. Hunan: Hunan Jiaoyu Chubanshe.

————. (1991). *Tao Xingzhi Quanji* [Collected works of Tao Xingzhi] (13 vols.), ed. Association of Tao Xingzhi Study. Sichuang: Sichuang Jiaoyu Chubanshe.

Tao Xingzhi & Zhu Jingnong (1923). *Pingmin qianzike* [Thousand character text], Vol. 1. Shanghai: Commercial Press.

Taylor, P. V. (1993). *The texts of Paulo Freire.* Buckingham, U.K.: Open University Press.

Tsunesaburo Makiguchi: The value creator. (1996, January). *SGI Quarterly.* Available: www.sgi.org/english/archives/quarterly/9601/feature.html (accessed February 5, 1996).

Uhrmacher, P. B. (1991a). Visions and versions of life in classrooms. *The Journal of Curriculum Theorizing* 9(1): 107–116.

————. (1991b). Waldorf schools marching quietly unheard. Unpublished doctoral dissertation, Stanford University.

————. (1993a). Coming to know the world through Waldorf education. *The Journal of Curriculum and Supervision* 9(1): 87–104.

————. (1993b). Making contact: An exploration of focused attention between teacher and students. *Curriculum Inquiry* 23(4): 433–444.

————. (1997). Evaluating change: Strategies for borrowing from alternative education. *Theory into Practice* 36(2): 71–78.

————. (2004). An environment for developing souls: The ideas of Rudolf Steiner. In *Pedagogy of Place: Seeing space as cultural education*, ed. D. Callejo Perez, S. Fain & J. Slater, 97–120. New York: Peter Lang.

Van Manen, M. (1991). *The tact of teaching: The meaning of pedagogical thoughtfulness.* New York: State University of New York Press.

*Visva-Bharati Prospectus.* (1922). Allahabad, India: Indian Press.

Walker, J. (1981). The end of dialogue: Paulo Freire on politics and education. In *Literacy and revolution: The pedagogy of Paulo Freire*, ed. R. Mackie, 120–150. New York: Continuum.

Walker, V. S. (1996). *Their highest potential: An African-American school community in the segregated South.* Chapel Hill, NC: Chapel Hill.

Weaver, R. M. (1948). *Ideas have consequences.* Chicago: University of Chicago Press.

Westbrook, R. B. (1991). *John Dewey and American democracy.* Ithaca: Cornell University Press.

Whitcomb, J. A. (2000, April). Montessori's vision of the prepared environment. Paper presented at the annual meeting of the American Educational Research Association, New Orleans.

Witherell, C., with H. T. Tran & J. Othus (1995). Narrative landscapes and the moral imagination: Taking the story to heart. In *Narrative in teaching, learning, and research,* ed. H. McEwan & K. Egan, 39–49. New York: Teachers College Press.

Zamir, S. (1995). *Dark voices: W. E. B. Du Bois and American thought, 1888–1903.* Chicago: University of Chicago Press.

Zhang, K., & Tang, W. (1992). *Pingfan de shensheng: Tao Xingzhi* [Tao Xingzhi, A Confucius after Confucius]. Hubei: Jiaoyu Chubanshe.

Zhou, H., ed. (1991). *Tao Xingzhi yanjiu zai haiwai* [Study on Tao Xingzhi in overseas China]. Beijing: Renmin Jiaoyu Chubanshe.

Zhang Baogui, ed. (2001). *Duwei yu Zhongguo* [John Dewey and China]. Hebei: Hebei Renmin Chubanshe.

# About the Boston Research Center

THIS WORK was developed in association with the Boston Research Center for the 21st Century (BRC), an international peace institute that envisions a worldwide network of global citizens developing cultures of peace through dialogue and understanding. The center was founded in 1993 by Daisaku Ikeda, a peace activist and the president of Soka Gakkai International (SGI), one of the most dynamic and diverse Buddhist organizations in the world.

BRC programs include public forums, scholarly seminars, and peacemaking circles that are diverse and intergenerational. Through these programs, scholars and activists are able to forge unexpected connections, refresh their sense of purpose, and learn from one another in a spirit of camaraderie. The BRC also works to encourage the peaceful aspirations of young people through multiauthor books for university courses in ethics, peace studies, education, and comparative religion. BRC books have been adopted by professors in more than 165 American colleges and universities for use in more than 400 courses to date. Order information can be found on the Center's Web site (www.brc21.org).

Address: 396 Harvard Street, Cambridge, MA 02138
Tel: 617-491-1090
Fax: 617-491-1169
E-mail: center@brc21.org
Web site: www.brc21.org

Project Manager: Patti M. Marxsen
Developmental Editing: Helen Marie Casey and James McCrea

# About the Editor and the Contributors

**David T. Hansen** is Professor and Director of the program in Philosophy and Education at Teachers College, Columbia University, New York. He has taught at several levels, including high school, and received his undergraduate and doctoral degrees from the University of Chicago. Before taking up his present position, he served as director for 10 years of a secondary teacher education program at the University of Illinois at Chicago. Hansen has been particularly interested in the moral dimensions of teaching and teacher education. That interest is part of a larger project to reimagine the humanistic roots of education in an era that all too often reduces education to a mere means to an end. Hansen has written widely on this theme, including in *The Call to Teach* (1995) and *Exploring the Moral Heart of Teaching: Toward a Teacher's Creed* (2001) and in a review chapter in the *Handbook of Research on Teaching*, published in 2001 by the American Educational Research Association, titled "Teaching as a Moral Activity." He lives in New York City with his wife, Elaine V. Fuchs, who is a molecular biologist at Rockefeller University. In their spare time they enjoy friends, opera and other classical music, walks in Central Park, and traveling abroad.

**Rodino F. Anderson** studied the liberal arts at St. John's College, Annapolis, Maryland, with emphasis on the aesthetics of music. At his 1999 graduation he received the Walter. S. Baird Prize for a music composition. After teaching mathematics, science, and philosophy at Tampa Catholic High School, Tampa, Florida (1999–2001), Rodino matriculated in the PhD program in Philosophy and Education at Teachers College, Columbia University. Awarded both a college fellowship and a competitive Diversity Fellowship (2002–2003), he has worked on collaboratively creating a unique foundations course for the program centered on American Philosophies of Education. He has been appointed as visiting professor (2006–2007) at Bowdoin College.

**Jacqueline Cossentino** is Assistant Professor in the Department of Educational Policy and Leadership at the University of Maryland, College Park. She is also the head of the Williamsburg Montessori School (Virginia), which serves as the primary site of her current research on Montessori practice and culture. Her work on Montessori concentrates on the intersections of educational purpose and action and has appeared in the *American Journal of Education, Curriculum Inquiry, Montessori Life,* and the forthcoming *Inside Montessori: Unexpected Lessons for Educational Reform.*

**Stephen M. Fishman** teaches philosophy at the University of North Carolina, Charlotte. Since attending his first Writing Across the Curriculum workshop in 1983, he has been studying student writing and learning in his classes. He is an alumnus of Camp Rising Sun, Rhinebeck, New York, an international scholarship camp founded in 1930 to promote world peace. With his coauthor Lucille McCarthy, Fishman has conducted a number of theory/practice studies of the classroom. Reports of these have appeared as articles in *College English, Research in the Teaching of English, Written Communication,* and *College Composition and Communication.* In addition, Fishman and McCarthy have coauthored three books, *John Dewey and the Challenge of Classroom Practice* (Teachers College Press, 1998), *Unplayed Tapes: A Personal History of Collaborative Teacher Research* (Teachers College Press, 2000), and *Whose Goals? Whose Aspirations? Learning to Teach Underprepared Writers Across the Curriculum* (Utah State University Press, 2002).

**Andrew Gebert** studied poetry in workshops led by Carol Berge in Woodstock, New York (1971–1973). He has worked as a professional translator of Japanese since 1982. Most recently, his translation of Daisaku Ikeda's poems *Fighting for Peace* was released by Dunhill in 2004. He received his original language training at Columbia University (1976–1978), his BA from Empire State College, State University of New York (1999), and his MA in the intellectual history of Japan from Waseda University, Tokyo (2005) and is presently pursuing a PhD at Waseda University.

**Monte Joffee** is a co-founder of the Renaissance Charter School in New York City and has been its principal since 1993. He is an adjunct instructor at the College of Saint Rose, where he has helped initiate its new innovative supervision certification program designed specifically to prepare educators to serve as founders and leaders for charter and small schools. Joffee is a doctoral student at Teachers College, Columbia University, and his dissertation is an ethnographic case study of the stages of development of a new focus school and its collaborative leadership model. His academic interests include the development of new schools, alternative models of education that promote humanism as well as rigorous academic standards, and systemic change in urban school systems. He is also the vice director of the SGI-USA Educators Division, a nationwide group of approximately 1,000 Buddhist educators in the pre-K–12 private and public sectors.

**Lucille McCarthy** teaches composition and literature at the University of Maryland, Baltimore County. She is the coauthor of *Thinking and Writing in College* with Barbara Walvoord (1990) and *The Psychiatry of Handicapped Children and Adolescents* with Joan Gerring (1988). With her coauthor Stephen Fishman, McCarthy has conducted a number of theory/practice studies of the classroom. Reports of these have appeared as articles in *College English, Research in the Teaching of English, Written Communication*, and *College Composition and Communication*. In addition, Fishman and McCarthy have coauthored three books, *John Dewey and the Challenge of Classroom Practice* (Teachers College Press, 1998), *Unplayed Tapes: A Personal History of Collaborative Teacher Research* (Teachers College Press, 2000), and *Whose Goals? Whose Aspirations? Learning to Teach Underprepared Writers Across the Curriculum* (Utah State University Press, 2002).

**Kathleen M. O'Connell** teaches courses on Rabindranath Tagore and Satyajit Ray at New College, University of Toronto, Toronto, Canada. She completed an MA in Comparative Literature at Jadavpur University, India, and a PhD in South Asian Studies at the University of Toronto. She has spent extended periods of research at Tagore's Santiniketan. Her research interests include Rabindranath Tagore, Satyajit Ray, and Bengali literature and cultural history. Publications include *Rabindranath Tagore: The Poet as Educator* (Visva-Bharati, 2002) and *Bravo Professor Shonku*, a translation (Bengali to English) of stories by Satyajit Ray (Rupa, 1985).

**A. G. Rud** teaches courses in the cultural foundations of education at Purdue University. He received his BA in religion from Dartmouth College, and his MA and PhD in philosophy from Northwestern University. Rud is the editor of *Education and Culture*, the journal of the John Dewey Society, and is completing a book on Albert Schweitzer's legacy for education.

**Charlene Haddock Seigfried** is Professor of Philosophy and American Studies at Purdue University. Her areas of specialization include American philosophy, pragmatism, and feminist theory, with a particular focus on social and political philosophy, pragmatist metaphysics, theory of knowledge, and value theory. Her recent book publications include *Feminist Pragmatism and Feminism: Reweaving the Social Fabric* (University of Chicago Press, 1996) and *William James's Radical Reconstruction of Philosophy* (State University of

New York Press, 1990). She served as editor for *Interpretations of John Dewey*, part of the Re-Reading the Canon series published by Pennsylvania State University Press (2002).

**Wang Weijia** was born in Wuhan and educated at Central China Normal University. She is currently working in the Institute of Chinese Modern History and the East-West Cultural Exchange Research Center of Central China Normal University. Her research field is Christian higher education in modern China and the history of Christianity in China.

**P. Bruce Uhrmacher** is Associate Professor of Education and Director of Curriculum and Instruction in the College of Education at the University of Denver. He is the coeditor of *Intricate Palette: Working the Ideas of Elliot Eisner* and the recipient of the University of Denver Distinguished Award, 2004. Uhrmacher's research interests include alternative education, aesthetic education, arts-based research, and Waldorf education. He is the book review editor for the *International Journal of Leadership in Education* and faculty advisor for the Aesthetic Education Institute of Colorado, cosponsored by the College of Education and Young Audiences.

**Jennifer A. Whitcomb** is the Assistant Dean for Teacher Education at the University of Colorado at Boulder and is a coeditor of the *Journal of Teacher Education*. Her research interests focus on the intersection between and within the practice and structure of teacher education and teacher learning.

**Zhang Kaiyuan** was born in July 1926 in Wuxing Country, Zhejiang Province, China. He attended the University of Nanking and subsequently taught at Central China Normal University (CCNU). He is a founder and director of the Research Institute of the Revolution of 1911, the Research Institute of Modern Chinese History (formerly the Research Institute of History at the CCNU), and the Center for the Study of Chinese Christian Colleges. Zhang was the president of the CCNU from 1983 to 1990. He is known internationally for his research on the Revolution of 1911 and the Miner Searle Bates Papers. His publications, which include *From Yale to Tokyo* and *Eyewitness to Massacre*, have been reviewed in more than 100 countries.

# Index